23416

ISSUES IN CONTEMPORARY ECONOMICS
Volume 5: The Greek Economy: Economic Policy for the 1990s

This is IEA conference volume no. 102

ISSUES IN CONTEMPORARY ECONOMICS

Congress Editor: Amartya Sen

IEA conference volume series

Series Standing Order

If you would like to receive future titles in this series as they are published, you can make use of our standing order facility. To place a standing order please contact your bookseller or, in case of difficulty, write to us at the address below with your name and address and the name of the series. Please state with which title you wish to begin your standing order. (If you live outside the United Kingdom we may not have the rights for your area, in which case we will forward your order to the publisher concerned.)

Customer Services Department, Macmillan Distribution Ltd,
Houndmills, Basingstoke, Hampshire, RG21 2XS, England.

Issues in Contemporary Economics

**Proceedings of the Ninth World Congress of the
International Economic Association, Athens, Greece**

Congress Editor: Amartya Sen

**Volume 5
THE GREEK ECONOMY: ECONOMIC POLICY FOR THE 1990s**

Edited by
Thanos S. Skouras

M in association with the
INTERNATIONAL ECONOMIC
ASSOCIATION

First published 1992

UNESCO Subvention 1990–91/DG/7.6.2/SUB.16(SHS)

Published by
THE MACMILLAN PRESS LTD
Houndmills, Basingstoke, Hampshire RG21 2XS
and London
Companies and representatives
throughout the world

ISBN 0–333–53726–2

A catalogue record for this book is
available from the British Library

Printed in Hong Kong

Contents

BK Titles

Preface

Amartya Sen   NA

'Reading maketh a full man,' according to Francis Bacon, and 'conference a ready man'. Those who missed the Ninth World Congress of the International Economic Association, held at Athens during August–September 1989, may no longer have the chance of being 'ready' (for whatever), but these proceedings offer them an opportunity of reading the papers presented there, and thus achieving 'fullness' (presumably, a solid, if somewhat obscure, virtue). Less immodestly, we at the International Economic Association are happy to be able to make a selection of the many interesting and productive papers presented at the Ninth World Congress available in book form (in five volumes).

Each of the previous World Congresses of the International Economic Association had one 'unifying' theme (the last one had the theme 'The Balance between Industry and Agriculture in Economic Development'.[1] The Ninth Congress had no such unique theme. Instead papers were invited and contributions sought in a number of different theme areas, covering different parts of the discipline of economics. The purpose of choosing a plurality of themes was to make it possible for economists all over the world to participate in this World Congress despite wide variations in their specialisation. To some extent this had been implicitly permitted in previous conferences too by their taking a rather liberal view of the allegedly unifying theme – and by practising what I can only describe as 'diversity in unity'.

The Ninth Congress went a good deal further in making the conference open to economists of different interests and expertise. Since these conferences are three-yearly phenomena, it seems unreasonable to make economists of particular specialisation wait many multiples of three years for their turn to come up. We were rewarded in the Ninth Congress by the attendance of economists of widely different fields and practice. As the variety of papers in these volumes indicates, the range of economic issues covered was quite remarkable.

The programme consisted of twenty-two sections – fifteen sections for presentation of invited and contributed papers and seven sections for panel discussion. The conference was planned by a Programme Committee, which I was privileged to chair. Each member of the committee took particular responsibility for inviting and selecting papers for one session.

Paper Sections

1. *General Microeconomics* (Takashi Negishi)
2. *General Microeconomics* (Jean-Paul Fitoussi)
3. *Welfare and Social Choice* (Kenneth Arrow)
4. *Econometrics* (Marc Nerlove)
5. *Centrally Planned Economies* (Béla Csikós-Nagy)
6. *Economic History* (Marcello de Cecco)
7. *International Economics* (Elhanan Helpman)
8. *Economic Development* (Victor Urquidi)
9. *Labour Economics* (Richard Layard)
10. *Public Economics* (Lawrence Summers)
11. *Industrial Economics* (Jean Gabszewicz)
12. *Agricultural Economics* (Glenn Johnson)
13. *Food and Nutrition* (Amartya Sen)
14. *Theory of Policy* (Heraklis Polemarchakis)
15. *Economics of Integration* (George Kottis)

Panel Sections

P.1. *Women's and Men's Roles in the Economy of the Future* (Barbara Bergmann)
P.2. *The Greek Economy Today* (Thanos S. Skouras)
P.3. *Game Theory and Economics* (Partha Dasgupta)
P.4. *Rational Expectations after the Event* (Frank Hahn)
P.5. *Neo-Marxian Perspectives on Production Relations and Property Rights* (Stephen Marglin)
P.6. *What Remains of Development Economics?* (Louis Lefeber)
P.7. *Social Justice and Quality of Life* (Zdzislaw Sadowski)

The Programme Committee refereed the papers proposed for presentation, and the final programme was drawn up on that basis. I take this opportunity of thanking the members of the Programme Committee for their immense help in making the Ninth World Congress a success. Not only did they select, severally or jointly, the invited paper writers and assess the contributed papers, but they were also responsible for the selection and appropriate revision of the invited papers for inclusion in these proceedings.

Neither the discussants' comments, nor any reports of the general deliberation in the sessions, are being published. Instead, the paper writers were encouraged to take note of the comments and suggestions made in the sessions, with appropriate acknowledgement.

There were also five invited plenary lectures (in addition to the presidential address), and we were lucky enough to have as plenary speakers: Abel G. Aganbegyan ('Economic Restructuring of the USSR and International Economic Relations'); A. B. Atkinson ('Basic Income Schemes and the Lessons from Public Economics'); Zsuzsa Ferge ('Mechanisms of Social Integration: the Role of the Market'); Frank Hahn ('History and Economic Theory'); and Mahar Mangahas ('Monitoring the Economic and Social Weather in the Philippines').

The proceedings of the congress are being published in five volumes, edited respectively by: Kenneth J. Arrow (vol. 1: *Markets and Welfare*); Marc Nerlove (vol. 2: *Macroeconomics and Econometrics*); Partha Dasgupta (vol. 3: *Policy and Development*); Nancy Folbre, Barbara Bergmann, Bina Agarwal and Maria Floro (vol. 4: *Women's Work in the World Economy*); Thanos S. Skouras (vol. 5: *The Greek Economy: Economic Policy for the 1990s*).

Each editor has his or her own 'Introduction' to the respective volume, and so I need not go into substantive contents of the volumes in this general Preface. I take this chance of thanking the volume editors for their tremendous help in producing these proceedings.

One of the new things in the Ninth Congress was a very active working session – spread over two full days – on 'women's and men's roles in the economy of the future', organised by Barbara Bergmann. This is the first time the International Economic Association has had a special session on gender issues in economics, and the idea met with a remarkably active and positive response. There were so many contributions in this field that a special volume is being devoted to the papers presented at this session (volume 4).

There was also a full day meeting on the Greek economy. This too had many participants, with presentation of different interpretations and approaches, and the papers from this session are published in this volume.

I should like to put on record our great debt to our Greek hosts. We are most grateful for the co-operation of the respective Greek governments and the Bank of Greece, and for the superb work done by the Local Organising Committee, under the leadership of Maria Constantopoulos (the others in the committee were Panayotis Korliras, George Kottis and Thanos S. Skouras). The Local Advisory Board was chaired by George Kottis. I would also like to thank Patricia Hillebrandt, Rita Maurice and Maureen Hadfield for looking after the editorial arrangements for these proceedings. Without their efficient help, my task as general editor of these volumes would have been impossibly hard. I am also most grateful to Michael Kaser, the Editor, and Jean-Paul Fitoussi, the Secretary General of the International Economic Association for their constant help in organising the congress and in the publication of these proceedings. I would also like to acknowledge my debt to Kenneth Arrow, the preceding President of the IEA, whose wise counsel I have had to seek on many occasions.

Note

1. The proceedings of that conference were published in five volumes (*The Balance between Industry and Agriculture in Economic Development*, London: Macmillan, 1988), edited respectively by Kenneth J. Arrow (the last President of the IEA), Jeffrey G. Williamson and V. R. Panchamukhi, Sukhamoy Chakravarty, Irma Adelman and Sylvia Lane, and Nurul Islam.

The International Economic Association

A non-profit organisation with purely scientific aims, the International Economic Association (IEA) was founded in 1950. It is in fact a federation of national economic associations and presently includes fifty-eight such professional organisations from all parts of the world. Its basic purpose is the development of economics as an intellectual discipline. Its approach recognises a diversity of problems, systems and values in the world and also takes note of methodological diversities.

The IEA has, since its creation, tried to fulfil that purpose by promoting mutual understanding of economists from the West and the East, as well as from the North and the South, through the organisation of scientific meetings and common research programmes, and by means of publications on problems of current importance. During its forty years of existence, it has organised eighty-six round-table conferences for specialists on topics ranging from fundamental theories to methods and tools of analysis and major problems of the present-day world. Nine triennial World Congresses have also been held, which have regularly attracted the participation of a great many economists from all over the world.

The Association is governed by a Council, composed of representatives of all member associations, and by a fifteen-member Executive Committee which is elected by the Council. The present Executive Committee (1989–92) is composed as follows:

President	:	Professor Anthony B. Atkinson, UK
Vice-President	:	Professor Luo Yuanzheng, China
Treasurer	:	Professor Alexandre Lamfalussy, Belgium
Past President	:	Professor Amartya Sen, India
Other Members	:	Professor Abel Aganbegyan, USSR
		Professor Kenneth J. Arrow, USA
		Professor Edmar Lisboa Bacha, Brazil
		Professor B. R. Brahmananda, India
		Professor Wolfgang Heinrichs, GDR
		Professor Edmond Malinvaud, France
		Professor Takashi Negishi, Japan
		Professor Don Patinkin, Israel

xi

		Professor Agnar Sandmo, Norway
		Professor Erich Streissler, Austria
		Professor Stefano Zamagni, Italy
Advisers	:	Professor Mohammed Germouni, Morocco
		Professor Oleg T. Bogomolov, USSR
Secretary-General	:	Professor Jean-Paul Fitoussi, France
General Editor	:	Mr Michael Kaser, UK
Adviser to General		
Editor	:	Professor Sir Austin Robinson, UK
Conference Editor	:	Dr Patricia M. Hillebrandt, UK

The Association has also been fortunate in having secured the following outstanding economists to serve as President:

Gottfried Haberler (1950–3), Howard S. Ellis (1953–6), Erik Lindahl (1956–9), E. A. G. Robinson (1959–62), G. Ugo Papi (1962–5), Paul A. Samuelson (1965–8), Erik Lundberg (1968–71), Fritz Machlup (1971–4), Edmond Malinvaud (1974–7), Shigeto Tsuru (1977–80), Victor L. Urquidi (1980–3), Kenneth J. Arrow (1983–6), Amartya Sen (1986–9).

The activities of the Association are mainly funded from the subscriptions of members and grants from a number of organisations, including continuing support from UNESCO.

Acknowledgements

The hosts for the Ninth World Congress of the International Economic Association were the Hellenic Economic Association and the Athens School of Economics and Business. We are grateful to them for the organisation of the Congress, for a stimulating social programme with generous hospitality and for the welcome given to economists from all over the world. The task was daunting but the execution ensured a successful Congress. The International Economic Association wishes to express its thanks on behalf of all participants.

The Congress would not have been possible without the financial help from the Greek Government and the Bank of Greece. The International Economic Association and the Greek host organisations express their appreciation for this support.

The members of the IEA Programme Committee and the Local Organising Committee and Advisory Board are listed overleaf. Our special thanks go to Professor Maria Constantopoulos, the Managing Chairman of the Local Organising Committee, who gave unstintingly of her time and energy to make the Congress a success.

This volume is published by the International Economic Association under the auspices of ISSC and with the financial assistance of UNESCO.

The IEA Programme Committee

Kenneth J. Arrow
Barbara Bergmann
Marcello de Cecco
Béla Csikós-Nagy
Partha Dasgupta
Jean-Paul Fitoussi
J. J. Gabszewicz
Frank Hahn
Elhanan Helpman
Glenn L. Johnson
George Kottis
Richard Layard
Louis Lefeber
Stephen Marglin
Takashi Negishi
Marc Nerlove
Heraklis Polemarchakis
Amartya Sen
Lawrence Summers
Thanos S. Skouras
Victor L. Urquidi

Local Organising Committee

Panayotis Korliras (Chairman)
Maria Constantopoulos (Managing Chairman)
George Kottis
Thanos S. Skouras

Local Advisory Board
George Kottis (Chairman)
Angelos Angelopoulos
Dimitris Chalikias
Nickolas Consolas
Constantine Drakatos
George Drakos
Rossetos Fakiolas
Argyris Fatouros
Constantine Kyriazis
Maria Negreponti-Delivanis
George Oekonomou
Stylianos Panagopoulos
Alexandros Yanniotis
Xenophon Zolotas

List of Contributors

Professor George C. Bitros, Athens University of Economics and Business, Greece

Professor Maria Constantopoulos, Athens University of Economics and Business, Greece

Professor George D. Demopoulos, Athens University of Economics and Business, Greece

Professor George E. Drakos, University of Piraeus, Greece

Professor Theodore A. Georgakopoulos, Athens University of Economics and Business, Greece

Professor George Hadjimatheou, City of London Polytechnic, UK

Professor Joseph Hassid, University of Piraeus, Greece

Professor Matthew J. Lambrinides, Pantion University, Greece

Professor Lucas Papademos, Bank of Greece and University of Athens, Greece

Professor Theophanis B. Pakos, Pantion University, Greece

Professor E. Pournarakis, Athens University of Economics and Business, Greece

Professor Stylianos A. Sarantides, University of Piraeus, Greece

Professor Alexander H. Sarris, University of Athens, Greece

Professor Thanos S. Skouras, Athens University of Economics and Business, Greece

Professor Loukas Tsoukalis, University of Athens, Greece

Professor John Tzoannos, Athens University of Economics and Business, Greece

Professor Nikos Vernardakis, University of Patras, Greece

Professor Evangelos A. Voloudakis, Deree College, Athens, Greece

Abbreviations and Acronyms

CD	Certificate of deposit
CP	Consumer prices
DCE	Domestic credit expansion
EC	European Community
ECU	European currency unit
EMS	European Monetary System
EMU	Economic and Monetary Union
ERM	Exchange rate mechanism
ESM	European single market
GDP	Gross domestic product
GNI	Gross national income
GNP	Gross national product
GRT	Gross registered tonnes
IMF	International Monetary Fund
IMP	Integrated Mediterranean Programmes
ITT	Information technology and telecommunications
LDC	Less developed country
NIC	Newly industrialising country
NOW	Negotiable orders of withdrawal
OECD	Organisation for Economic Co-operation and Development
PASOK	Pan-Hellenic Socialist Movement
PSBR	Public sector borrowing requirement
R&D	Research and development
RP	Repurchase agreement
SA	Société anonyme
SEA	Single European Act
SME	Small and medium-sized establishments/enterprises
VAT	Value added tax
WSP	Wholesale prices

Introduction

Thanos S. Skouras

The decade of the 1980s was one in which economic policy in Greece was marked by the ascendancy to power, for the first time ever, of a socialist government. The way in which the socialist party (PASOK) rose to power in 1981 considerably limited its economic policy options. The most prominent element in its electoral campaign was its twin opposition to NATO and the EC. This hostility towards the West, coupled with an ideological attitude that was antithetical to business and profit making and that was openly expressed through the state-controlled mass media, immediately narrowed the socialist government's economic policy options. The business climate and the prospects for private investment were, not surprisingly, rather depressed. As if this were not enough, and in fulfilment of popular electoral expectations, wages were raised by nearly 50 per cent within a few months of the new government's coming to power. Under these circumstances, it was natural that the new government's ambitious hopes for economic growth were concentrated on the public sector. The vigorous expansion of the public sector seemed to be the only way to achieve such growth.

But if the above explains the setting off on the trail of an ever-expanding public expenditure that characterised the socialist government's eight years of rule, it does not account for its direction. It certainly was not inevitable, despite the accumulated social demands and the evident underdevelopment of welfare services, that public expenditure should ignore the clear need for investment in infrastructure. The advantages of this type of public expenditure are not difficult to see.[1] Investment in infrastructure increases productivity and improves the profitability of the private sector by both boosting demand and reducing costs. Furthermore it does not permanently reduce the private sector's supply of labour by swelling the ranks of civil servants. As a consequence it allows for a reduction in public expenditure, if and when circumstances change, unlike the inelastic obligations created by the hiring of public employees. Finally this truly Keynesian method of demand regulation and government intervention would have filled a real need in the Greek economy as investment in infrastructure, in real terms, had been declining since the early 1970s. Why then was this direction of public expenditure growth not chosen?

It is not easy to answer this question on economic grounds. An answer may possibly be found in the realms of ideology and political practice – in the mistrust of the socialist government towards private firms, mainly contractors, who would have gained most directly from such public expenditure, and also in the government's preference for a type of public expenditure that created personal political obligations and thus most efficiently led to the expansion of the party clientele. In any case it is a not unwarranted conjecture that the socialist government's single most decisive error in economic policy was the relative neglect of investment in productive infrastructure and emphasis on unproductive consumption expenditure. It is this choice, more than any other, that made the large budget deficits, the increasing government debt, the strong inflationary tendencies and the worsening macroeconomic imbalances practically inevitable and difficult to reverse.

If taking the wrong direction in public expenditure expansion was the initial decisive error with the most extensive repercussions that PASOK made in its first term in office, it certainly was not the only error in economic policy.[2] During its second term of office, after a notable recovery in profits and improvement in the business and investment climate following the adoption in the autumn of 1985 of a stabilisation policy, a crucial error was committed in prematurely abandoning that stabilisation policy at the end of 1987. The reason again was political, induced by the desire to expand the room for manoeuvre in order to be able to call an early election, at an opportune time before the expiry of the government's term of office in June 1989. This, at least, is the only explanation that can make some sense of the abrupt policy turn. As it happened the serious illness of the prime minister, and the corruption scandals that attended his recovery, prevented the calling of an early election. But the economic policy followed during this period, aimed at success in the polls, was seriously flawed. Instead of taking the necessary but unpopular corrective measures, the budget deficit was allowed to grow and the worsening macroeconomic imbalances were ignored. One of the worst distortions during this period was the serious loss of competitiveness by Greek industry caused by the, politically, less costly policy of using the exchange rate as a means to contain inflation.

The election stalemate of June 1989 has meant that political considerations of electoral success would continue to take precedence in the formulation of economic policy, at least until a stable government emerged. It is at this juncture and against this background that the papers in this volume were presented to the 9th World Congress of the IEA.

Having been asked to organise the session on the Greek economy, I felt that, if a real contribution were to be made, it was important to turn our attention to the future and, as far as possible, map out the contours of economic policy for the coming decade. The intention was to ascertain the extent of agreement regarding appropriate economic policy within the Greek academic profession. For this reason I invited a number of established academic colleagues drawn from the main university institutions and covering a wide spectrum of political affiliations and opinions to participate in the session on the Greek economy.[3]

The guidelines in the invitation letter were as follows:

There are two common questions which, in their respective concerns, all introductory comments should address. These are (i) what is the immediate policy that ought to be pursued in view of 1992? and (ii) what is the desirable and likely target by the turn of the century? In other words, there should be an outline of the practical steps or path to be taken in the short to medium term, as well as a realistic vision of what the particular area of concern will look like around the year 2000. This is, of course, closely related to the development of the Greek economy as well as to the modernisation of the relevant institutions that one can reasonably expect in the future. It is hoped that an answer to these two questions in the various areas of economic policy-making will provide a clear view of the possibilities and the limits with respect to the formulation of policy in the next decade. It will certainly reveal how the community of Greek academic economists views the boundaries of feasible policies and likely outcome in the 1990s.

One question on which there was wide agreement was the desirability of eliminating the budget deficits, which were generally considered to be a prime cause of the macroeconomic imbalances in the Greek economy. T. Georgakopoulos points out that, despite its very rapid growth in the 1980s, the highly centralised expenditure of the Greek state is today, as a percentage of gross national product (GNP), about the same as the EC average. He nevertheless believes that, given the public sector's relative inefficiency and the financial difficulties that the present levels of spending give rise to, it should be reduced and that public enterprises should, in many cases, be transferred to the private sector. This would not only increase efficiency but would also contribute to the urgently needed reduction in budget deficits and public debt. To this latter end, government expenditure should be restrained, especially in general administration and defence, and revenues should be increased through a reform of income taxation, which would reduce evasion and abolish all exemptions, while taxing income from all sources at relatively low and moderately graduated rates (not exceeding 25–30 per cent).

Though not for a moment disputing the desirability, G. Drakos doubts the feasibility, from the political point of view, of substantially cutting public expenditure in the short run. He pins his hopes on institutional reform and advocates three broad lines of action to be adopted immediately: (i) privatise state-owned firms that operate in non-monopolistic markets; (ii) apply the benefit approach to taxation wherever possible so that the direct beneficiaries of state expenditure on services bear the cost of those services; (iii) decentralise decision making on taxation and expenditure, entrusting local authorities with the application of the benefit approach. In the longer run, Drakos argues for a zero-base budgeting approach in the whole of the public sector, in order to increase its low and deteriorating productivity, and advocates an institutional requirement that any proposed law should be subject to a cost–benefit study, in order to limit the rent-seeking activity of special-interest groups and reduce the excessively high degree of regulation characterising the Greek economy.

A more radical line of institutional reform is advocated by G. Bitros. He argues that a cost–benefit analysis should be conducted in order to determine whether any kind of service should be left to the state or should be transferred to the private sector. No part of government economic activity should escape such an examination. Common-pool and collective goods, traditionally supplied by the state, are not to be exempted, as it is possible that a contract, voucher or even voluntary system might prove to be a preferable institutional arrangement.

In the one paper that does not unequivocally stand for the contraction of the state's economic role, M. Lambrinides and T. Pakos argue against the prevalent neo-liberal view that the expansion of the public sector is the prime cause of Greece's economic crisis. They point to a number of un-favourable, mainly international, developments which played a crucial role and conclude that drastic cuts in public expenditure are not only impractical in the short run, but also unwarranted in the long run. On the contrary, future development requires an active, and possibly enlarged, role for the state as provider of productive infrastructure and of essential social services. Such a role is also necessary for the creation and maintenance of social consensus. However they consider a gradual curtailment of public-sector employment beneficial, in the medium to long term, and favour a more immediate curtailment of public expenditure through institutional reform, with public hearings by parliamentary committees to foster trans-parency and accountability in every area of public spending. To reduce fiscal deficits, they also propose taxation reform, so as to increase state revenue by limiting tax exemption and tax evasion, as well as by strict enforcement of existing taxes while, at the same time, reducing top income tax rates and improving the structure of tax incentives.

Fiscal policy is one of the constitutent elements of macroeconomic policy, which must be related to and be consistent with the other elements of macro policy. G. Hadjimatheou reviews macroeconomic policy in the past decade, and compares the performance of the Greek economy with that of other OECD countries, drawing a parallel with the policies of the British Labour government in the mid-1970s. He paints a rather dark picture, pointing to inconsistencies in policy, and concludes that the attempt to use fiscal policy as a means of establishing a more active and permanent role for the state in the economy was responsible for many of the problems. He argues that a medium-term strategy should be pursued aimed at reducing budget deficits and inflation as well as reducing the economic importance of the state, irrespective of any cost in increased unemployment.

Until recently, monetary stability was sacrificed to the needs of a deficitary fiscal policy. L. Papademos points out that the twin objectives of monetary policy in the 1990s ought to be the simultaneous pursuit of monetary stability and financial efficiency. Monetary stability implies a choice of intermediate policy targets and of appropriate policy instruments aimed at disinflation and external equilibrium. He argues in favour of two intermediate targets, broad money (M3) and domestic credit expansion, for which target ranges should be set by the central bank over a medium-term horizon of three years. Monetary stability, combined with the deregulation and liberalisation of the financial markets, is considered essential for participation of the drachma in the exchange rate mechanism (ERM) of the European Monetary System (EMS). The 'right time' for participation in the ERM is when the falling rate of inflation, following a consistent and credible set of monetary, fiscal and labour market policies, approaches the highest level experienced by other EMS members. It would be desirable at that time to join the ERM within a six per cent band. Nevertheless due account should be taken of the possible adverse consequences that rapid disinflation and higher real interest rates that may be associated with the ERM will have on the accumulation of public debt.

The importance of the public debt and the loss of government revenue from seigniorage as a result of rapid disinflation, is an issue treated in greater detail by G. Demopoulos. He argues that, even though participation of a 'fiscally weak' country like Greece in the EMS reduces the revenue from seigniorage and causes additional budgetary difficulties, compared to the alternative of establishing equilibrium with a discretionary policy outside the EMS, participation in the EMS is preferable in terms of social welfare. The extent of macroeconomic adjustment required is also examined by Demopoulos by means of an analysis that estimates the values of the main macro variables that would have been consistent with exchange-rate stability. Though the adjustment needed is considerable and could not fail to have negative effects on real output and employment growth, whether inside or outside the EMS, it is argued that the required decrease in government expenditure growth will tend to reduce inflation and stimulate real output via a reduction of inflationary expectations. It therefore seems that the gains of reputation associated with participation in the EMS and the results of the social welfare analysis together provide support for early participation of the drachma in the ERM of the EMS.

The question of financial efficiency and the reform of the banking system is treated by E. Voloudakis. A comparison of the Greek with the Italian banking system with respect to the asset structure, the operating efficiency and profitability, the capital adequacy and financial innovations, reveals that far-reaching changes, not only by the banks themselves but also by the government and the central bank, are called for to make the Greek banks competitive in an integrated EC financial system. In Greek banks, only about one-third of deposits are not subject to control. The constraints on asset management combined with high labour costs (in terms of efficiency), inevitably result in low profitability relative to the Italian banks. Profitability would be even lower were it not for some lucrative sources of rent-type revenue from financial services, which are bound to disappear in a unified European financial market. In addition, the capital-to-risk asset ratio is below the EC rule of 8 per cent and there is a sizeable share of loans to failing enterprises. The long, though far from exhaustive, list of necessary reforms is headed by the liberalisation of central bank controls and the elimination, with the exception of EC directives, of all constraints on asset management, interest rates and pricing of financial services. The banks should rationalise their internal organisation and functioning while improving and enriching their financial services. This should be complemented and facilitated by government abstention from any interference with banking operations and decisions, including the habitual practice of appointing top officials on political criteria, and most crucially it should liberalise the labour market, to encourage flexible pay agreements and incentives.

The agreement about monetary policy being directed at disinflation is not duplicated in the area of exchange-rate policy. M. Constantopoulos develops a theoretical model to examine the effects of exhange rate policy in the presence of macroeconomic inbalance. She concludes that the role of exchange rates is to facilitate equilibrium between expenditure and income, by changing the structure of production and consumption and that 'the fight against inflation represents a misuse of exchange rate policy'. But, after 1986, exchange rate policy was used to contain the inflation created by government's overspending, thus further contributing to the distortion of production and consumption patterns. As a result, profit rates in sectors producing exportables and import substitutes were squeezed and the competitiveness of the Greek industry suffered. The drachma, currently over-valued (by almost 20 per cent relative to its 1987 level), should be rapidly adjusted downwards to restore competitiveness and macroeconomic balance. It follows from Constantopoulos' analysis, that she favours a considerably lower exchange rate for the drachma, though she is less concerned whether this should be done by means of an outright devaluation or a much faster pace of downward crawling.

The view, that the exchange rate of the drachma should be drastically lowered is strongly opposed by S. Sarantides. He uses a simple model to estimate the effects of exchange rate policy on real gross domestic product in the period 1970–86. His conclusion is that the effect of exchange rate changes on real output was negative because structural deficiencies in the economy made exchange-rate policy ineffective. Sarantides considers de-valuation or the sliding down of the drachma completely inappropriate, in view of the structural problems of the Greek economy. These problems can only be solved by appropriate domestic policies including, on the demand side, the elimination of budget deficits, strict control of money supply and restraint of wage rises so as not to exceed productivity increases and, on the supply side, encouragement of technological innovation and other structural measures to improve productivity.

While recognising the need for structural adjustment of the Greek economy, E. Pournarakis does not rule out devaluation as a useful policy move when Greece joins the EMS. Though the two devaluations of the 1980s are assessed negatively, he considers that this was largely due to the inadequate support provided by fiscal, monetary and incomes policies. All these policies were inconsistent with the achievement of equilibrium after the 1983 devaluation, while the improved outcome of the 1985 devaluation was due to the tight incomes policy, although this was not fully matched by an equally tight fiscal policy. With proper coordination of fiscal and monetary policies, and in the context of a change in the exchange-rate regime, a devaluation may prove useful. In examining the long-term outlook, Pournarakis expresses the view that the shock likely to result from full financial integration in the EC will be of such a magnitude that 'for Greece monetary union is strictly a distant future issue'. Substantial structural change is required if the country is to benefit from entry in the EMS.

Structural change has been hampered in the last 30 years by the excessive preoccupation of economic policy with industrialisation. Reorientation of resource allocation with the help of the market, rather than a misconceived industrialisation target, suggests that 'agriculture is destined to play a role of vital importance for several years while the more distant future belongs to services'.

L. Tsoukalis seems to be in agreement with Pournarakis that reorientation of resource allocation is better left to the market, mainly because of the 'acknowledged inefficiency and inflexibility of the Greek state'. The state should aim at the creation of a favourable economic climate by achieving macroeconomic stability and, above all, by establishing 'transparency and consistency in terms of the basic rules of the game'. To this end a decision to join the exchange-rate mechanism of the EMS at a relatively early stage, possibly with wider margins of fluctuation, will strengthen the state's credibility and resolve. In the period leading to this, the deteriorating competitiveness of the Greek economy may require devaluation of the drachma. Though not to be adopted lightly, devaluation should be accompanied by a restrictive set of monetary and fiscal policies as well as a dilution of the indexation system of wages. Such policies together with the curtailment of public expenditure are necessary anyway and any hardship in terms of unemployment is inevitable. The difficulties in achieving the macroeconomic adjustment and the rationalisation of both the public and private sectors of the economy, required for competitive operation within the European single market, may to a certain extent be alleviated by EC transfers, which are expected to reach 6–7 per cent of Greek GDP on a net annual basis by the end of 1992.

A. Sarris is not very optimistic about the prospects of the Greek economy in the European single market. He examines the adjustments required in four crucial areas: the industrial structure, the public sector, the labour market and the financial system. After examining the structural features of these areas and reviewing the recent patterns of adjustment, he argues that investment prospects in the medium run appear bleak. But the most difficult problem to solve will be the structure and behaviour of the public sector. Restructuring through the reduction in the overall size of the public sector and the redirection of public expenditure towards investment will entail huge sacrifices and political costs. It is therefore concluded that political stability and determination as well as improvements in the functioning of state institutions are the keys to medium-term growth in Greece.

An improvement in the functioning of the state administration resulting in 'a supportive, consultative, coordinating role for both the public and the private sector' in the implementation of technological and industrial policies is another prerequisite of economic growth insisted upon by N. Vernardakis. The required rates of technological change and productivity growth to prevent large-scale unemployment, in the face of the international trend towards deindustrialisation, cannot be left to market forces, but call for an industrial strategy and policy. Vernardakis argues that the design of this policy should differentiate between the low and medium technology sectors, where an imitative strategy is required, and high technology sectors, where an opportunistic, niche-seeking strategy is needed. In selecting sectors, it is argued that sectors using new production processes are preferable to sectors producing new products, while a larger size should be encouraged in firms. Finally measures should be taken to improve receptivity of technical change and promote the diffusion of new technologies. In particular the level of penetration of information technology and telecommunications in all areas of economic activity, especially industry, should be raised considerably. Links between universities and industry, the creation of technological parks and the development of conformance testing services are some of the means that can be used to raise the level of receptivity of technological change.

J. Hassid is concerned with the development of policy to aid and promote the efficiency of small and medium-size enterprises (SMEs), which comprise nearly 90 per cent of manufacturing industry in terms of employment, the highest level in the EC. The consequent relative absence in Greek industry of technical and managerial economies of scale presents additional difficulties for the design of an appropriate industrial policy. Hassid does not advocate the encouragement of larger-size firms. Instead he proposes institutional changes, especially of a legal nature, that will promote cooperation among firms. He nevertheless agrees with Vernardakis that the need is less for sectors producing new, high-technology products than for the spread of new, high-technology production processes throughout industry, including the traditional sectors. The design of an appropriate policy for the SMEs should take cognisance of market forces, recognise the need for competitiveness and do away with state intervention and regulations that afford protection to inefficient producers.

J. Tzoannos considers the prospects of two export-oriented sectors, shipping and tourism, both of great importance to the Greek economy. EC maritime policy, which promotes the liberalisation of maritime trade, is favourable to the interests of Greek international shipping. Nevertheless the proposed abolition of cabotage would have a serious effect on cruising as well as on coastal passenger and cargo fleets. It would require important adjustments in the shipping industry and it would certainly necessitate a fundamental revision of Greek internal transport policy. The tourist industry also requires a major adjustment to get out of its present crisis. The industry needs to upgrade its services and sell a more sophisticated and specialised product mix with the emphasis on high-income tourism and the combination of sun and sea with culture. The future trend will be for the hotel industry to organise into larger groups, through mergers and acquisitions, in an effort to rationalise operations and provide the integrated production of all tourist services.

The papers in this volume cover a very wide range of policy issues but they leave some important questions to be answered. Prominent among these are policy questions regarding demographic developments and the environment. Other issues insufficiently treated include employment policy and the role of the hidden economy, which is conservatively estimated at about one-third of official GDP.[4] Another issue which does not receive adequate treatment is the relative importance of the secondary sector in the future and whether industry or some other sector offers the most promising path for the development of the Greek economy. As noted by Pournarakis, this is a question that dominated discussions on policy making for many decades.[5] It is probably an omen of the times that it is hardly touched upon in the present volume as past dogmas lose their grip on economic and social life.

The withering away of false certainties may also be responsible for the fact that the contributors to this volume do not, on the whole, venture into offering 'vision' of the Greek economy in the year 2000. What emerges from this volume is a remarkable degree of consensus among Greek academic economists about the policies to be followed in the short and medium run, coupled with an unwillingness to speculate not only about the likely shape but even about the desirable 'vision' of the Greek economy at the turn of the century.

Notes

1. A policy based on public investment in infrastructure was advocated strongly and at considerable length in Skouras (1983).
2. Attention is here concentrated only on the two strategically crucial errors which, in my view, determined the central direction of economic policy and had the most far-reaching consequences. There were naturally other errors as well as many instances of mismanagement, but these were all of lesser importance.
3. Some of the colleagues I would have liked to participate unfortunately had other commitments at the time of the conference. Among them, Professor C.

Vaitsos and Professor L. Katseli, both at the University of Athens and both prominent in economic policy-making during PASOK's first term in office, were included in the conference programme but, at the last moment, were not able to attend.

4. Prior commitments prevented Professor P. Pavlopoulos, who conducted the main empirical study on the hidden economy, from taking part in the conference session on the Greek economy.

5. A relatively recent example of this point of view is Petras (1984a); for a critique see Skouras (1984). In English, this controversy is to be found in Petras (1984b) and Skouras (1985).

References

Petras, J. (1984a) 'The dynamic of Greek development and its industrial underdevelopment are due to rentier capital' (in Greek), *Oikonomikos Tachydromos*, 8 March.

Petras, J. (1984b) 'Greek rentier capital: Dynamic Growth and Industrial Development', *Journal of Hellenic Diaspora*, vol. 11, no. 2.

Skouras, T. S. (1983) 'Recovery and restructuring: An Investment policy proposal' (in Greek), *Bulletin of the Commercial Bank of Greece*, December.

Skouras, T. S. (1984) 'Rentier capital and economic development' (in Greek), *Oikonomikos Tachydromos*, 28 June.

Skouras, T. S. (1985) 'Rentier capital, industrial development and the growth of the Greek economy in the post-war period', *Journal of the Hellenic Diaspora*, vol. 12, no. 2.

Part I

Fiscal Problems and the Role of the State

H40   L30 L32   3-16
012 & Greece

1 Aspects of the Public Sector in Greece: Postwar Developments and Future Prospects

Theodore A. Georgakopoulos
ATHENS UNIVERSITY OF ECONOMICS AND BUSINESS

1 INTRODUCTION

Is the public sector large or small? Is it excessively or inefficiently large or is its size in line with allocative efficiency considerations? Should we go on nationalising more economic activities or start privatising activities and, if so, which ones? Is the public sector producing efficiently, in the sense of avoiding or minimising X inefficiencies? Is it producing the right mixture of goods and services or not? Is the public sector using the correct measure and choice of financial option to finance its activities, (for example, debt finance versus tax finance, or direct taxes versus indirect taxes)? Is the allocation of functions to each layer of government satisfactory or not? These are some of the questions that frequently crop up when talking about the public sector which will be addressed in this paper. Following a brief discussion of postwar developments, the present situation will be appraised, and future prospects outlined, and I will suggest where we must go in view of 1992 and 2000.

2 SIZE AND GROWTH OF THE PUBLIC SECTOR

As with other OECD countries, the public sector in Greece has grown substantially during the postwar period. Total general government expenditure as a percentage of gross national product (GNP) at market prices, a widely used index of public sector size, increased from about 23 per cent in 1948 to 50 per cent in 1987.[1] The increase has not, of course, been smooth. Four periods can be distinguished: (i) the immediate post-civil war years, 1949–53, when, as shown in Table 1.1, the ratio of government expenditure

3

to GNP fell by 4 percentage points; (ii) the long period of high economic growth, 1954–73, when the same ratio increased by only 8 per cent, all during the pre-Junta years of 1953 and 1967; (iii) the immediate post-Junta period of relatively low economic growth from 1974 to 1981 (at that time, when the country was run by a conservative government, the ratio increased by 14 percentage points in seven years); and (iv) the post-1982 years, when, under a socialist government with a stagnating economy, the public sector increased by 9 per cent in five years.

Thus government expenditure as a percentage of GNP increased slowly during the years with high economic growth, strong urbanisation and wide structural change compared to the much faster growth of the last fifteen years. These anti-Wagnerian developments in the growth of the public sector in Greece, with the economy growing more slowly, urbanisation stopped if not reversed and limited structural change, were probably the result of several factors arising, perhaps, from both the demand and supply sides of the economy.

Without wishing to enter into the controversy over the relative importance of each of these factors, a subject fully covered in the literature of economics and political science journals in recent years,[2] three factors seem to stand out as most important: (i) interest group activity resulting from the

Table 1.1   Growth of general government expenditure in Greece
in the postwar period

Period	Current prices				Constant prices			
	R_G	R_Y	$e = R_G/R_Y$	$\Delta (G/GNP)$	R_G	R_Y	$e = R_G/R_Y$	$\Delta (G/GNP)$
1949–53	16.2	20.7	0.78	–4.0	4.1	9.3	0.44	–6.2
1954–73	13.6	11.7	1.16	7.7	8.1	7.0	1.16	5.1
1954–66	13.6	10.7	1.27	7.6	8.6	6.6	1.30	6.0
1967–73	13.6	13.6	1.00	0.1	7.2	7.7	0.94	–0.9
1974–81	26.5	19.8	1.34	14.4	7.2	2.9	2.48	10.5
1982–87	24.0	20.1	1.19	8.8	4.2	0.7	6.00	8.7
1974–87	25.4	19.9	1.28	23.2	5.9	2.0	2.95	19.2
1954–87	18.3	15.0	1.22	30.9	7.2	4.9	1.47	24.3
1949–87	18.0	15.7	1.15	26.9	6.8	5.4	1.26	18.1

Notes:

R_G	= rate of growth of total government expenditure: per cent.
R_Y	= rate of growth of GNP: per cent.
e	= *ex-post* elasticity of total government expenditure.
$\Delta (G/GNP)$	= percentage change in ratio of total government expenditure to GNP.

Source: T. Georgakopoulos and J. Loizidis, *Government Expenditures in Postwar Greece: Size, Structure and Growth* (Athens 1989).

shift in power from the conservative forces, which favoured government interference rather than increased expenditure, that is tax concessions, to the more radical forces, which favoured higher government spending; (ii) the accumulation of unsatisfied desires and needs during the junta regime, when the size of the public sector remained constant; (iii) fiscal illusion, and especially debt illusion, which allowed governments to increase public expenditures without at the same time bearing the political cost of raising the necessary funds through taxation.

In addition to general government activity, the public enterprise sector also grew rapidly in postwar Greece. Before the war, public enterprises were of no importance. Even traditional activities, like electricity and transport, were wholly or partly in private hands. Utilities, as well as certain financial institutions, including a very large proportion of the banking and insurance sectors, were nationalised in the 1950s and the 1960s. However expansion of the public enterprise sector boomed in the late 1970s and continued into the 1980s, contrary to the European movement for privatisation. As a result over 75 per cent of banking activity, over 60 per cent of energy and water and more than 40 per cent of transport and communications are now produced by public enterprises. The main public enterprises, for which alone there seem to exist reliable data, contribute about 7.5 per cent to employment, 10 per cent to value-added and 20 per cent to investment in the non-agricultural sectors of the economy. If one takes into account the activities of the various subsidiaries and other firms controlled by the major public enterprises (which probably contribute a further 4 per cent to total non-agricultural employment, not to mention the activities of enterprises belonging to other lower layers of government and the activities of the newly acquired so-called problematical enterprises),[3] it is clear that public enterprises play a considerable role in the Greek economy today.

It is difficult to appraise the situation concerning public sector size in Greece because of the lack of any benchmark against which an evaluation could be made. A comparison with the other EC countries can perhaps throw some light. Table 1.2 gives government expenditure as a percentage of GDP in EC countries in certain postwar years. As Table 1.2 shows, between 1960 and 1987 the ratio for Greece increased at a faster rate than the corresponding ratio for most other member countries. The increase was particularly high in the 1980s when this ratio rose by 42 per cent in five years, compared to an increase in the average ratio for all EC countries of only 12 per cent during the same period. As a result, the Greek ratio is today about the same as the EC average, compared to only 84 per cent of the EC average in 1960. Greece today has a larger public sector than Germany, the

Fiscal Problems and the Role of the State

Table 1.2   General government expenditure as a percentage of GDP at
current market prices in EC countries 1960–87

Country	G/GDP					Growth in G/GDP to 1987	
	1960	1970	1980	1985	1987	1960 = 100	1980 = 100
Belgium	30.3	36.5	50.8	54.1	52.3	173	104
Denmark	24.8	40.2	56.2	59.3	58.3	235	104
Germany	32.0	38.6	48.3	47.5	46.8	146	97
Greece	23.0	28.5	35.5	50.4	49.2	214	139
France	34.6	38.9	46.4	52.2	51.8	150	112
Ireland	28.0	39.6	50.9	54.5	54.7[1]	195[1]	107[1]
Italy	30.1	34.2	46.1	50.8	50.7	168	110
Luxembourg	30.5	33.1	54.8	52.0[2]	52.0[2]	170	95[2]
Netherlands	33.7	43.9	57.5	59.7	60.1	178	105
Portugal	17.0	21.6	43.9[3]	43.9[3]	43.9[3]	258[3]	n.a.
Spain	13.7	22.2	32.9	42.1	41.7[1]	304	127[1]
United Kingdom	32.6	39.8	45.1	46.5	45.9[1]	141	102[1]
EEC average (12)	27.5	34.8	45.9	51.1	50.6	184	110
ECC average (10)	30.0	37.3	49.2	52.7	52.2	174	106

Notes:
1. 1986.
2. 1984.
3. 1981.

Source: OECD, *Economic Outlook* (June 1989).

UK and Spain, despite the fact that per capita income is only 25, 40 and 65
per cent of each of these countries respectively.

Although the above comparisons meet with difficult conceptual and
statistical problems, they suggest that Greece today has a relatively large
public sector.[4] Given that the size of this sector has grown rapidly in the last
ten years, resulting in severe financial difficulties, I would suggest that
government expenditure growth should be severely restrained in the coming years. This is also necessary because of the relative inefficiency of the
Greek public sector compared to that of other EC countries, which will
create problems of competitiveness within a single European market.

As regards public enterprises and the regulatory activities of the government, it appears that there is much room for contraction here. My
opinion is that the government must get rid of most of these so-called
problematical enterprises, because I am convinced that the malfunctioning
of the Greek public sector, which fails even in areas where it has some
comparative advantage over the private sector, clearly cannot succeed in
areas where the private sector itself failed, in spite of its comparative
advantage. Consequently, I do not see how the Greek public sector could

run these enterprises more efficiently than the private sector to make them successful and profitable. A careful study of all other non-basic public enterprises should be carried out, especially those controlled by other public enterprises and working in manufacturing and services, to determine which of these enterprises might be privatised, and how. This will not only improve efficiency in the country, but it will also allow the government to reduce its debt, which has grown to excessive proportions.

3 THE STRUCTURE OF ACTIVITIES

Greece's structure of expenditure has, as shown in Table 1.3, changed substantially in the last thirty-five years. As in all other European countries, transfer payments increased considerably, while expenditure on goods and services rose at a far lower rate and investment expenditure as a percentage of GNP fell. Expenditure on transfers has, in fact, been the driving force behind the increase in the public sector size in the postwar period in Greece.

Table 1.3   Structure of government expenditure in Greece in selected postwar years[*]

Group of expenditures		1950	1960	1970	1975	1980	1981	1985	1986
I	CONSUMPTION								
	EXPENDITURE	12.1	11.5	12.4	15.6	15.8	17.5	20.6	19.6
	1 Administration	–	(32.0)	(32.3)	(29.1)	(31.2)	(31.1)	(35.7)	(34.8)
	2 Defence	–	(38.0)	(36.6)	(44.5)	(35.7)	(36.6)	(30.8)	(29.8)
	3 Justice	–	(6.3)	(4.8)	(3.8)	(3.9)	(3.8)	(3.5)	(3.6)
	4 Health	–	(6.9)	(8.0)	(7.5)	(10.1)	(9.8)	(9.9)	(11.5)
	5 Care	–	(1.2)	(1.3)	(1.0)	(1.4)	(1.5)	(1.6)	(1.6)
	6 Education	–	(13.8)	(15.0)	(12.7)	(13.3)	(13.0)	(14.6)	(14.5)
	7 Other	–	(1.8)	(2.0)	(1.4)	(4.4)	(4.2)	(3.9)	(4.2)
II	INVESTMENT								
	EXPENDITURE	6.8	4.6	4.6	4.0	2.3	3.7	4.2	4.0
III	ABSORPTION								
	EXPENDITURE	18.9	16.1	17.0	19.6	18.1	21.2	24.8	23.6
IV	TRANSFERS	7.4	6.5	11.3	13.2	15.9	19.7	26.0	25.6
	TOTAL	26.4	22.6	28.1	32.9	34.3	40.9	49.2	49.2

[*]   Main groups of expenditure expressed as a percentage of GNP, while individual consumption expenditures expressed as a percentage of total government consumption.

Source: *National Accounts of Greece* (various issues).

The structure of consumption expenditure has also changed, with expenditure on health increasing while expenditure on defence and justice declined substantially. Expenditure on administration also rose slightly in terms of percentage, while expenditure on education remained fairly constant over the period.

A comparison of the structure of expenditure in Greece with that of the other EC countries, given in Table 1.4, reveals some interesting features, despite the acknowledged conceptual and statistical problems involved in making such detailed comparisons. The main conclusion is that Greece's consumption expenditure as a percentage of GNP was much higher than in most other EC countries and slightly above the EC average. On the one hand general public services and defence absorbed a much larger proportion of government consumption than in all other EC countries; on the other hand expenditure on education and health in Greece accounted for a much lower proportion of general government consumption. Total transfers in Greece as a percentage of gross domestic product (GDP) were slightly lower than the EC average. They were smaller than in most other EC countries, with the exception of Germany, the UK and the two Iberian countries. Transfers to households were the same as the EC average, while subsidies to firms were lower than the EC average. Interest payments were above the EC average but, as recent figures were not available, the data may not fully reflect the present situation. With the large increase in interest payments during the last few years, Greece probably tops all other EC countries today. Finally investment expenditure in Greece was well above the EC average, though this again may have changed in the last few years, because of the relatively low rate of increase in investment expenditure.

Thus Greece's structure of expenditure is unsatisfactory and needs to be changed. Expenditure on general administration and defence is very large, while expenditure on health and especially on education is relatively low. Resources devoted to defence are even larger, since expenditure does not give the true value. A restructuring of expenditure therefore appears necessary. Resources devoted to the first two activities will need to be restrained or reduced, while resources devoted to the other two activities will need to be increased.

4   THE FINANCE OF THE PUBLIC SECTOR

Greece had no problems financing government activities during the whole postwar period up to the middle 1970s. The high growth rates in the economy facilitated the financing of government expenditure out of current

Table 1.4 The structure of general government expenditure in EC countries (%)

Country	Consumption expenditures								Transfers					Investment expend.	TOTAL
	General public services*	Defence	Education	Health	Social security & welfare	Economic services	Other	TOTAL	To households	subsidies	Interest	Other	TOTAL		
1 Belgium (1984)	7.1	2.6	6.9	–	1.3	–	–	17.9	22.6	1.5	10.1	0.8	35.0	2.5	55.4
2 Denmark (1981)	2.2	2.6	6.3	5.5	5.7	2.2	3.3	27.8	17.8	3.0	5.3	1.7	27.8	4.2	59.8
3 France (1982)	2.1	3.5	5.3	0.5	1.2	1.2	2.4	16.2	25.7	2.2	2.2	1.3	31.4	2.9	50.5
4 Germany (1983)	2.1	2.9	4.1	5.8	2.0	0.9	2.3	20.1	17.3	1.9	2.9	1.6	23.7	4.4	48.2
5 Greece (1984)	6.7	6.5	2.9	2.1	0.3	–	0.7	19.2	18.4	2.3	5.2	0.1	26.0	4.5	52.6
6 Ireland (1983)	–	–	–	–	–	–	–	19.7	16.2	3.8	9.2	2.3	31.5	4.3	55.5
7 Italy (1982)	2.6	2.1	5.4	3.9	0.8	1.0	2.6	18.4	18.7	3.0	8.5	0.7	30.9	4.0	53.3
8 Luxembourg (1982)	–	–	–	–	–	–	–	16.9	23.4	4.6	1.0	2.5	31.5	6.7	55.1
9 Netherlands (1984)	7.5	3.1	5.4	–	0.8	–	–	16.8	28.0	1.8	7.6	2.3	39.7	5.8	62.3
10 Portugal (1979)	2.1	2.8	3.0	2.4	0.8	1.2	1.6	13.9	9.6	4.5	2.9	0.4	17.4	5.1	32.4
11 Spain (1977)	2.0	1.7	1.6	1.6	1.4	–	1.7	10.0	11.7	1.4	0.5	–	13.6	4.0	27.6
12 UK (1979)	1.2	4.4	3.9	4.1	2.5	1.1	2.8	20.0	10.8	1.9	3.6	1.9	16.3	3.6	41.6
EC average	3.4	3.2	4.5	3.2	1.6	1.3	2.2	18.0	18.4	2.7	4.9	1.4	27.1	4.3	49.5

* Data for Belgium and the Netherlands include expenditures on public order and safety, health, housing and community amenities, recreation, culture and religious affairs.

Source: OECD, National Accounts.

revenues, and especially tax revenues, leaving only a small proportion of government investment to be financed through borrowing. As a result, the size of the public debt was relatively small. Besides, the large inflows of invisibles and entrepreneurial capital outweighed the deficit on trade account, so that the need for borrowing abroad was small and external debt was low. After 1973, however, central government started generating sizeable and increasing deficits, which were for some years covered by the surpluses made by other public bodies. In the 1980s, however, the central government deficit increased substantially, while other public bodies, including most public enterprises, also went into deficit. The overall general government deficit today is estimated at 18 per cent of GDP, while that of the whole public sector including enterprises, exceeds 25 per cent. Greece seems to be the leading EC country as regards the level of deficit accounts (see Table 1.5 for developments after 1970). This means that central government debt increased from 22 per cent in 1973 to more than 80 per cent in 1989. If the debt of public enterprises is taken into account, total public debt today exceeds total GDP. External debt has also increased, mainly as a result of the huge deficits on the trade accounts which are no longer offset by inflows of invisibles and capital. External debt increased from 25 per cent of total central government debt in 1973 to the present 35 per cent.

Although similar levels of debt as a percentage of GDP occur in other European countries, there are four features of the Greek public debt that give cause for concern: (i) public debt is increasing rapidly every year, causing serious problems for the financing of the private sector; (ii) deficits and public debt mostly cover current rather than investment expenditures; (iii) most public debt is short term and can cause serious macroeconomic problems in the country; and (iv) the large size of debt, together with the relatively high interest rates, results in high debt servicing expenditure. When these expenditures total 25 per cent of the total central government budget, one really wonders about the degree of freedom the government has in conducting fiscal policy. It is therefore imperative that government should reduce the deficit in the near future. This will mean restraining the growth rate of the public sector and increasing current revenues, especially tax receipts, which, as shown in Table 1.6, are relatively small and have recently increased much more slowly than expenditures.

The question, however, is which taxes should be increased and how this should be brought about. The only answer is to increase direct taxation, especially income tax. Indirect taxes will in theory be harmonised by 1992, according to Community common rules, and this will probably reduce rather than increase the amount of revenue raised by indirect taxation. In particular, the Commission, in draft directives, proposes that all members

Table 1.5 General government financial balances in EC countries (% of GNP/GDP)

Country	1970	1980	1981	1982	1983	1984	1985	1986	1987	1988	1989	1990
Belgium	-2.0	-9.2	-13.1	-11.3	-11.7	-9.5	-8.9	-9.0	-7.2	-7.9	-6.6	-6.1
Denmark	+3.2	-3.3	-6.9	-9.1	-7.2	-4.1	-2.0	+3.4	+2.0	±0.0	+0.6	+1.0
France	+1.1	±0.0	-1.9	-2.8	-3.1	-2.8	-2.9	-2.7	-2.0	-1.3	-1.3	-1.2
Germany	+0.2	-2.9	-3.7	-3.3	-2.5	-1.9	-1.1	-1.3	-1.8	-2.0	-0.5	-1.2
Greece	-0.1	-2.9	-10.2	-7.6	-8.1	-9.9	-13.5	-11.1	-11.1	-15.3	-18.2	-19.6
Ireland	-3.6	-12.2	-13.3	-13.9	-11.9	-9.7	-12.1	-11.8	-9.9	-3.9	-5.0	-4.6
Italy	-3.7	-8.5	-11.6	-11.4	-10.7	-11.6	-12.5	-11.5	-10.5	-10.1	-9.9	-10.0
Netherlands	-0.8	-4.0	-5.5	-7.1	-6.4	-6.3	-4.8	-5.9	-6.1	-5.4	-4.8	-4.6
Spain	+0.7	-2.6	-3.9	-5.6	-4.8	-5.5	-7.0	-6.1	-3.6	-3.2	-2.9	-2.8
United Kingdom	+2.9	-3.4	-2.6	-2.4	-3.3	-3.9	-2.7	-2.4	-1.5	+0.8	+1.6	+1.7
EC average	-0.2	-4.9	-7.3	-7.5	-7.0	-6.5	-6.8	-5.0	-5.2	-4.7	-4.7	-4.7

Source: OECD, *Economic Outlook* (June 1989).

Table 1.6 Tax receipts as a percentage of GDP in the EC countries

Country	Years					Ratios		
	1965	1970	1975	1980	1986	80/65	86/80	86/65
Belgium	30.8	35.2	41.1	43.5	45.4	1.41	1.04	1.47
Denmark	29.9	40.4	41.4	45.5	50.6	1.52	1.12	1.69
France	35.0	35.1	36.9	41.7	44.2	1.19	1.06	1.26
Germany	31.6	32.9	35.7	38.0	37.5	1.20	0.99	1.19
Greece	20.6	24.3	24.6	28.6	36.7	1.40	1.28	1.78
Ireland	26.0	31.2	31.5	34.0	40.2	1.31	1.18	1.55
Italy	23.6	24.2	25.1	30.0	36.2	1.27	1.21	1.53
Luxembourg	30.4	30.2	39.2	40.9	42.4	1.35	1.04	1.39
Netherlands	33.2	37.6	43.7	45.8	45.8	1.38	1.00	1.38
Portugal	18.4	23.1	24.7	28.7	32.4	1.56	1.13	1.76
Spain	14.7	17.2	19.6	24.1	30.4	1.64	1.26	2.07
United Kingdom	30.6	37.1	35.4	35.3	39.0	1.15	1.10	1.27
EC average (12)	27.1	30.7	33.2	36.3	40.1	1.34	1.10	1.48
EC average (10)	29.2	32.8	35.5	38.3	41.8	1.31	1.09	1.43

Source: OECD, *Revenue Statistics of OECD Member Countries* (Paris, 1987).

apply VAT at only two rates: a low rate, mostly covering food and other necessities, applied within a range of 4 to 9 per cent, and a standard rate on all other goods, in the range of 14 to 20 per cent. Furthermore, all member countries will be able to apply special excise duties only on traditionally excised products, such as tobacco, beer, wine, spirits and petroleum products, at common rates. When these proposals become directives, Greece will have to abolish the high VAT rate of 36 per cent and transfer many goods to the low and the standard rates. A number of indirect taxes (such as the taxes levied on cars and the unified special consumption taxes), which are incompatible with a free market without frontiers as they require border adjustments, will have to be abolished. Finally, a number of other indirect taxes will also probably have to be abolished; I refer here to stamp duties, the tax on banking and insurance and so on which, although they do not give rise to border adjustments, are undesirable on domestic economic policy counts because they are levied only on domestic production and not on imports, but do not attract any export rebate and therefore harm the competitiveness of these goods and the trade balance from both the import and the export sides. I have estimated (Georgakopoulos, 1989), that these tax changes will reduce the total revenues raised through VAT by about 30 per cent. In order for the government to replace the revenues, VAT rates will have to be raised significantly, probably to the top rates proposed by the EC Commission. But application of the VAT at such high rates in Greece would create considerable problems and certainly increase tax evasion.

There is no other solution therefore to increasing income tax. Revenues from this tax must increase sufficiently, not only to cover part of the extensive deficits, but also to substitute for some of the loss of revenue from the reduction in indirect taxes resulting from harmonisation. Now, as Table 1.7 shows, income tax at present accounts for only a small proportion of total tax revenue in Greece, and therefore could be increased substantially. Revenue from income tax is small because of its very restricted base which results from the wide exemptions provided for by law, as well as extensive evasion. Only income from employment is effectively taxed, though this income is partly exempt. Income from other sources is either legally exempted or subject to evasion. Agricultural income brings in no revenue at all, owing to the wide concessions granted and extensive evasion by farmers. Interest revenue is not taxed, while tax on income from profits and from the professions is largely evaded. Tax revenues are further reduced because of the extensive tax expenditures granted to promote various goals of economic and social policy in the country. Problems of industrialisation and growth, income distribution, demographic problems and so on must all be dealt with via incentives provided in the income tax regulations. Concessions are at the moment so extensive that one wonders if there is a single person who does not receive some sort special treatment in the context of income tax. On the other hand, tax rates, despite their recent large reduction, continue to be relatively high. This is one reason for the high rate of tax evasion. In a country where tax evasion is a national sport and everybody, including myself, would be happy to evade tax, high tax rates are socially undesirable, since they simply punish sincere taxpayers who subsidise the evaders.

My own view is that we need a very simple income tax schedule, covering incomes from all sources and levied at relatively low and moderately graduated rates, with the highest rate set at 25–30 per cent. All exemptions, starting with members of parliament, right down to employees and farmers must be abolished. To compensate low-income employees for the reduction in their incomes, tax revenues generated from the abolition of their special treatment must be used to replace revenues from indirect taxes. This will increase the contribution of direct taxes, which is today very small, and improve the allocation of the tax burden by income class in the country. In addition tax administration will need to be totally reformed in

Table 1.7 Structure of tax receipts in the EC countries, 1986

Country	As a percentage of GDP				As a percentage of total taxation			
	Income and profits	Total direct	Goods and services	Total indirect	Income and profits	Total direct	Goods and services	Total indirect
Belgium	18.3	34.4	10.9	10.9	40.4	75.9	24.0	24.1
Denmark	28.4	32.7	17.9	18.0	56.2	64.5	35.4	35.6
France	8.0	29.9	13.0	14.3	18.2	67.7	29.4	32.3
Germany	13.0	28.1	9.5	9.5	34.5	74.8	25.2	25.2
Greece	6.4	18.0	16.7	16.7	17.5	54.4	45.4	45.5
Ireland	14.5	22.5	17.7	17.7	36.1	55.9	44.1	44.1
Italy	13.7	27.3	8.9	8.9	37.9	75.4	24.6	24.6
Luxembourg	18.3	32.0	10.4	10.4	43.2	75.6	24.5	24.5
Netherlands	12.6	33.5	11.8	11.9	27.7	73.8	26.0	26.3
Portugal	6.9	16.6	15.6	15.9	21.2	51.2	48.0	48.8
Spain	7.6	20.5	9.7	9.9	25.2	67.5	32.0	32.6
United Kingdom	14.9	26.9	12.1	12.1	38.2	69.0	30.9	30.9
EC average (12)	13.6	26.9	12.9	13.0	33.0	67.1	32.5	32.9
EC average (10)	14.8	28.5	12.9	13.0	35.0	68.7	31.0	31.3

Source: OECD, *Revenue Statistics of OECD Member Countries.*

order to make it efficient and effective. This last issue is very important and must be given special attention if evasion is to be effectively checked and revenues increased.

I realise that income tax reform, particularly certain elements such as the abolition of the special treatment of employment income or of farmers' income, probably has a high political cost, but politicians should learn to take some hard decisions, when they are so necessary and urgent. They must recognise that the inflation tax, which has been used in so masterly a way for the past ten years, though politically more convenient, is the worst tax on both economic and social counts and must be abolished.

5 CENTRALISATION OF GOVERNMENT ACTIVITY

Government activity in Greece is highly centralised. Local authorities account for only 3.5 per cent of general government current expenditure, and raise only 2.8 per cent of current revenues. Their role is therefore very limited and must be strengthened considerably in future.

6 CONCLUSIONS

The preceding analysis leads to the following conclusions. First, the size of the public sector in Greece has increased substantially in the last fifteen years and is now larger than in several more advanced EC countries. Some restraint, in the case of both general government and public enterprises, seems to be a prudent policy for the coming years. In the case of public enterprises, privatisation should be carefully considered and introduced where appropriate, especially in the manufacturing sector, particularly the so-called problematical enterprises. Second, the structure of government expenditure is not satisfactory. Expenditure on defence and general administration, which is relatively high, should be reduced, while expenditure on health and even more so on education, which is low, should be increased.

Third, the large deficits of the public sector in the last ten years have considerably increased the size of the public debt and this is now a matter of great concern. It is vital that these deficits be reduced quickly, if a macroeconomic balance is to be established. Deficits should be reduced via restraining government expenditure growth and increasing revenues. Fourth, the harmonisation of the Greek system of indirect taxes by 1992 in line with EC policy, leaves no scope for raising any extra revenue from this source. On the contrary, revenues from indirect taxes will most probably fall. Additional revenue will have to be raised from direct taxes, particularly from income tax. This will also increase the current low direct/indirect ratio and improve the allocation of tax burden by income group.

Fifth, to increase revenue from income tax, a complete reform of both the legal and administrative framework of this tax is necessary. Reform must aim at broadening the tax base and the reduction of tax evasion and the abolition of the extensive tax expenditures provided for by the law. By contrast, tax rates, which continue to be relatively high, should be further reduced. Instead of the highly complicated system, which effectively covers only part of employment income, I propose the introduction of a simplified system of income tax, which will cover everybody at moderately graduated rates. To increase progressivity, a separate low surcharge could be applied to certain types of non-employment income. Finally, because government activity is so highly centralised in Greece, steps must be taken to introduce some decentralisation into the decision-making and administrative process.

Notes

1. Data on public expenditures, given in the National Accounts of Greece have been corrected to account appropriately for civil servants' pensions and certain other transfer payments not properly dealt with in these accounts. For details see Georgakopoulos and Loizidis (1989a).
2. For surveys see Afxentiou (1979), Klein (1976), Larkey *et al.* (1981), Peltzman (1980) and Tarschys (1975).
3. These were private enterprises, with severe financial problems, which were taken under the control of the state, with the intention of the government to improve their financial position, make them viable and sell them to private hands.
4. Of the many problems such comparisons meet, the following should be mentioned: first, the downward bias resulting from the undervaluation of resources devoted to defence, since military service in Greece is compulsory and soldiers are not paid the value of their product; second, government interference in Greece takes on other forms (tax concessions, regulatory activities and so on), which are perhaps wider in Greece than in other EC countries, so that government expenditures give a downwards-biased estimate of public sector size; third, and contrary to the above, the Greek ratio of expenditures to GDP is perhaps severely upwards-biased, owing to the much larger size of the black economy in Greece as compared with other EC countries, which has resulted in downwards-biased estimates of GDP.

References

Afxentiou, P. (1979) *Patterns of Government Revenue and Expenditure in Developing Countries and their Relevance to Policy* (Athens: Center of planning and Economic Research).

Georgakopoulos, T. (1989) 'Tax Harmonisation', in Kazakos, P. (ed.), *1992: The Unified Market of the EC* (Athens: Ionian Bank of Greece).

Georgakopoulos, T. and Loizidis, J. (1989a) *Government Expenditures in Post-war Greece: Size, Structure and Growth* (Athens: School of Economics and Business Science, Center for Economic Research).

Georgakopoulos, T. and Loizidis, J. (1989b) 'Personal Income Taxation', in Provopoulos, G., *Priorities in Fiscal Policy* (Athens: Institute of Economics and Industrial Research).

Klein, R. E. (1976) 'The politics of public expenditure: American theory and British practice', *British Journal of Political Science*, vol. 6, pp. 401–32.

Larkey, P. D., Stolp, C. and Winer, M. (1981) 'Theorising about the growth of government: a research assessment', *Journal of Public Policy*, vol. 1, pp. 157–220.

Peltzman, S. (1980) 'The growth of government', *Journal of Law and Economics*, vol. 23. no. 2, pp. 209–87.

Tarschys, D. (1975) 'The growth of public expenditures: nine modes of explanation', *Scandinavian Political Studies*, vol. 10, pp. 9–31.

2 Some Lines of Action in the Greek Public Sector

George E. Drakos

PIRAEUS UNIVERSITY

L32 L50 012

Greece

Economic policy cannot be pursued in a vacuum; on the contrary it must be placed in its proper context and shaped, taking account of the circumstances and the targets that have been set. It is therefore difficult to discuss the pursuit of fiscal policy to the end of the century without, first, outlining the economic background against which specific fiscal policy should be designed and applied and, second, defining broadly the long-run target to be met.

1 THE TARGET

Dealing with the latter first, the long-run target will be defined as the fastest possible growth rate within the EC. However it is important to remember that Greece is a very small open economy relative to the rest of the world and more particularly the EC. This means *inter alia* that Greece is a price taker, or in a broader sense a policy taker in an interdependent world (Drakos, 1982). Nevertheless the Greek economy, despite its openness, remains an 'insular economy' in the McKinnon sense (McKinnon, 1981) of limited currency convertibility and restricted financial arbitrage with the rest of the world. However by the end of the century this situation is expected to have changed and harmonisation of policies within the EC could well have been achieved.

2 ECONOMIC BACKGROUND

A brief examination of Greece's recent economic performance reveals that real gross domestic product (GDP) growth was better than average world growth in the 1950s, 1960s and 1970s. In particular, Greece's rate of growth was on average 62 per cent higher than in the EC in both the 1960s and 1970s. The price deflator of GDP at market prices in Greece was on average

17

72 per cent of the EC deflator in the 1960s, but by the 1970s it had risen to 138 per cent. In Greece, total gross fixed capital formation grew at an average rate of approximately 4 per cent a year during the 1970s compared to under 2 per cent in the EC.[1] Taking the current account of the balance of payments as a percentage of GDP, the annual average deficit in the 1970s was –4.4 per cent. During the 1970s, unemployment was not really a problem in Greece.

The picture changed drastically in the 1980s. The average annual rate of growth for the years 1980–8 was 1.4 per cent in Greece compared to 1.9 per cent in the EC. That is to say that, for the first time, the gap between Greece and the EC was widening. Consumer prices during the same period increased by 20.1 per cent a year compared to 7.3 per cent in the EC. The annual average growth rate of gross fixed capital formation was negative in Greece at –1.8 per cent compared to a positive EC figure of 1.8 per cent. The deficit of the current account as a percentage of GDP was –5.2 per cent a year on average. Unemployment increased greatly, to reach EC levels.

'What went wrong in the 1980s?' is the obvious question to be answered. First, it must be remembered that as a result of the oil shocks of 1974 (which will be referred to as period A) and 1980 (which will be referred to as period B),[2] it was clear that the Greek standard of living had to decline.[3]

At both periods, Greece was living beyond her means; that is to say the value of goods demanded exceeded the value of goods produced – the difference being the deficit in the balance of payments on goods and services. Given the inelasticity, at least in the short run, of the demand for oil, this deficit was bound to increase after the oil shocks. At the same time the possibility of non-debt financing of the balance of payments deficit decreased in period B compared to period A. This development implied that foreign debt was set to rise more in period B than in period A in order to finance the increased deficit of balance of payments.

The authorities were concerned about the severe increase in foreign debt (which doubled in a few years) and they correctly sought to check this by devaluing the currency. It can be shown that currency devaluation in a small open economy can restore equilibrium at a target level of deficit in the balance of payments, *ceteris paribus*. However the cost of achieving this is a decrease in aggregate expenditure (which is a primary cause of the deficit) and an increase in the level of prices (at a lower rate than the devaluation rate depending on the degree of openness in the home country) (Drakos, 1986a).

However *ceteris* did not remain *paribus* – especially in period B. Money wages (*de facto* in period A and *de jure* in period B) were linked to the level of prices and therefore increased as well. If money wage increases were not to cause unemployment (a major problem in the 1980s) they had to be accompanied by increases in the money supply, as indeed happened. At the same time general government expenditure as a percentage of GDP increased from 28 per cent in the 1960s to 32 per cent in the 1970s and over 40 per cent in the 1980s, greatly increasing the budget deficit.

If any one of these policies – incomes, monetary or fiscal – is not tight following a devaluation it can be shown that, as far as the balance of payments is concerned, the effects will cancel out, creating a vicious circle in the economy. To summarise, this merry-go-round runs from the external shock to devaluation (in order to improve the balance of payments and restrict foreign debt), to inflation and wage increases, to money supply and public expenditure increases, which in turn lead to more inflation and a further devaluation and so on.

The situation was close to being out of control in 1985, when, in October, the authorities finally, if somewhat clumsily, announced a package of appropriate measures consisting of a devaluation together with a tight incomes, monetary and fiscal policy. Unfortunately this package was not fully applied. Fiscal policy remained very loose and monetary policy only followed later, so that the vicious circle in the economy had still to be broken.

Supporters of the 1985 measures claimed the targets could still have been achieved in spite of the loose fiscal policy.[4] However the severity of incomes policy required to break the vicious circle is not acceptable in a democratic society. So although in theory it is possible to envisage an incomes policy tight enough to counter a loose fiscal and/or monetary policy, in practice this is virtually impossible, particularly if, as happened in recent years, fiscal policy is allowed to get out of control.

The conclusion to be drawn from this discussion is that in the short and medium term a tight fiscal policy is essential and the public sector borrowing requirement (PSBR), which was running at about 20 per cent of GDP this year, must be controlled and reduced. This is a *sine qua non* condition for breaking the vicious circle operating in the Greek economy. If this is coupled with other measures designed to turn the vicious circle into a virtuous one, a higher growth rate than the EC average should be achieved.

3 IMPLEMENTATION OF FISCAL POLICIES IN THE SHORT RUN

The question arises of how to implement the necessary policy measures. My comments will be restricted to the general lines of action, which I believe should be followed in the short and long run. First, although both politicians and economists talk about the need to reduce public expenditure, I doubt if this is politically feasible, at least in the short run. A more modest and politically attainable goal would be to keep public expenditure constant in money terms and allow inflation and economic growth to take care of its relative size. I therefore intend to limit myself to discussing three broad lines of action which, if followed, should have a considerable beneficial impact in the short term.

First, privatisation. Many people take the extreme position and advocate selling every state-owned company to the private sector. Such a position not only frightens many people off and results in inaction, but may not even diminish the role of the state in the economy. A more feasible position for the foreseeable future would be to require the state to sell off any company that operates in a non-monopolisic market. This step should be taken as soon as possible.

As regards state-owned monopolies, my own view is that the question of ownership is neither important nor interesting. The important point is that they are monopolies (at least locally) and if they were to be sold to the private sector they would have to be checked, supervised and controlled by the state. Furthermore productivity will not necessarily increase if they become private monopolies as the ultimate sanction of failure will still be missing, given the fact that no government would allow them to go bust.

A more appropriate course of action, at least in the immediate future, would be to attempt to curtail their monopolistic functions to the bare minimum. This can be done by introducing techniques designed to encourage competition within the monopoly, contracting services out as far as possible and breaking the monopoly up geographically where feasible, and so on.

Second, the benefit approach to taxation. In the past, in order to avoid discriminating against the poor, many services were provided free of direct charge to everybody, as, for example, university education. This led to an increase in demand and a subsequent decrease in the quality of these services. It is time that the direct beneficiary of a service should directly bear at least a part of the cost of providing the service.

Third, decentralisation. In conjunction with the previous line of action, greater decentralisation should be encouraged. Local authorities should be allowed to decide what non-private goods they are going to offer in their constituencies and to charge the beneficiaries for at least a part of their cost.[5] Ideally an efficient decentralisation scheme would entail as many public administrations as there are non-overlapping areas over which the coverage of a particular service extends.

4 LONGER-TERM ISSUES

I now turn to some longer-term issues, and will limit myself to three points, which I consider important. First, I believe that Greek fiscal (as well as many other) institutions and tax laws will be greatly improved by EC fiscal harmonisation. This alone will be an important achievement for Greek society, because it will encourage the introduction of long overdue changes, which are currently blocked by strong vested interests or the inertia and shortsightedness of politicians.

Second, the rampant inefficiency of the public sector, together with the increase in unnecessary bureaucracy is well known. Everyone pays lip service to the need to increase public-sector productivity, and yet the situation gets worse rather than better. A major study of productivity improvement programmes is needed and all public-sector departments should adopt a zero-base budgeting approach. This could yield great benefits in the medium and long term and should, in my view, be implemented immediately.[6]

Finally, the state should begin the process of deregulation. Over many decades rent-seekers of all kinds have succeeded in persuading politicians, keen to be re-elected, to issue numerous regulations governing all facets of life, with the result that Greece today is probably one of the most over-regulated countries in the world. The technique, which has been tested numerous times, is simple. A particular group with a special interest in an issue presents its position on that issue as being beneficial to society as a whole. Politicians then adopt the position of the special-interest group in the belief that its members will vote for them at the next election, while at the same time hoping that the costs of the regulation will be spread thinly among the population generally, so that its adoption will not lose them votes.

This process has been going on for so many years that every Greek citizen belongs to one or more rent-seeking group. This has to a large extent turned the politicians into rent-supplying agents. While the cost to each citizen of a single regulation may be small, the total cost of all the existing regulations to each individual citizen is considerable. The elimination of all unnecessary regulations – that is, those which do not benefit society as a whole – should be the aim of all state officials. Furthermore, given the Greek population's high propensity to indulge in rent-seeking activities, there needs to be an institutional arrangement whereby any regulation (or law) could only be enacted if the costs are fully known and it can be proved on a cost–benefit basis that it is socially desirable. It is high time that the state limit itself to doing only those things it can do best and that the creative forces for self-determination and fulfilment be given a free rein.

Notes

1. Despite the great (25 per cent) decline in 1974 of gross fixed capital formation in Greece due to the special conditions prevailing in that year (see OECD, 1987, p. 178).
2. For a formal analysis of this question see Drakos (1986a).
3. This had to happen, especially in period A for the added reason of the increased defence expenditures which, to a large extent, involve imported materials.
4. For example, John Spraos in a paper delivered at a conference at Pantios University.
5. Local authorities are, in the final analysis, local voters. See Drakos (1986b).
6. A programme of this sort, highly appraised by an OECD experts committee, was under way in Greece in 1979–81. Some 40 technical reports had been produced and a number of recommendations were applied, with some spectacular results. See Kondylis (1980, 1981).

References

Drakos, G. E. (1982) *Foreign Banks in a Small Economy* (Paris: OECD Development Centre).

Drakos, G. E. (1986a) 'Economic Policy in Theory and Practice', in Yannopoulos, G. N. (ed.), *Greece and the EEC* (London: Macmillan).

Drakos, G. E. (1986b) 'The Socialist Economic Policy in Greece: A Critique', in Tzannatos, Z. (ed.) *Socialism in Greece* (Aldershot: Gower Publishing Group).

Kondylis, E. (1980) *Productivity Assessment and Zero Base Budgeting in the Greek Public Sector* (Paris: OECD, CT/PUMA/104).

Kondylis, E. (1981) *Aids to Policy-Markets: Council for Budget Evaluation in the Greek Public Sector* (Paris: OECD, CT/PUMA/307).

McKinnon, R. I. (1981) 'The Exchange Rate and Macroeconomic Policy: Changing Post-War Perceptions', *Journal of Economic Literature*.

OECD (1987) *Economic Outlook* (Paris: OECD, December, p. 178).

Greece

3 Structural Policies to Unwind the Greek Fiscal Tangle

George C. Bitros
ATHENS UNIVERSITY OF ECONOMICS AND BUSINESS

1 INTRODUCTION

For over a decade now, and particularly since 1980, the Greek economy has continued to defy the imperatives which derive from the country's choices in international, political and economic relations. More specifically, whereas, during the 1980s, developed nations in general, and those in the European Community (EC) in particular, tamed inflation, reduced or at least checked unemployment, balanced with relative success the accounts of their payments abroad, and achieved satisfactory rates of economic growth, Greece regressed in these most vital respects. Inflation in Greece, relative to inflation in these other countries, increased markedly, unemployment and the balance of payments worsened significantly, and the process of development came to a standstill. As a result, the gap in material welfare which separates Greece from the developed nations of the EC widened. In other words, the country lost ground at a time when the international economy flourished.

However this loss of ground *vis-à-vis* our partners and competitors may not itself be sufficient to explain the feeling of economic *impasse* which seems to prevail among informed and uninformed citizens alike. To my mind this is due to the magnitude of the fiscal problem which must be confronted in the coming years before the economy reverts to its long-term growth path. So in the remarks below I intend, first, to describe the precariousness of the situation and, second, to offer some thoughts as to how the state might deal with it in the coming decade.

2 THE ROOTS OF THE PROBLEM

In my judgement, policy makers in Greece have worked themselves into a corner because: (i) political as well as economic reasons have rendered the policy of borrowing abroad to finance public consumption unpalatable; (ii) borrowing from internal sources of funds has pushed domestic debt to prohibitive heights; (iii) under the prevailing view that public expenditure is inelastic downwards, fiscal deficits are preordained to become explosive; and (iv) in the given circumstances of Greece, traditional economic policies are ineffective. The reasons why these four conditions create an intractable fiscal problem are set out below.

2.1   The Constraint of Foreign Debt

With the external debt in excess of US\$ 22 billion, which in coming years will require about US\$ 3.5 billion annually for servicing, it is clear that the fiscal authorities have only two alternatives: either to continue the post-1981 policies of erecting an unsustainable welfare state by resorting, at all costs, to foreign borrowing, or to abandon these policies and borrow abroad only to finance investments with immediate foreign exchange-earning capabilities. Given that: (i) the former alternative is unrealistic, since under it the country would soon lose its relative political independence; (ii) only the private sector has the ability to undertake investments with the desired results; and (iii) borrowing from international economic organisations must be reserved as a possibility of last resort in case of a national emergency, it follows that the margins for raising funds abroad in order to support extravagant programmes of public consumption have all but vanished.

2.2   The Constraint of Domestic Debt

That the country was quickly approaching the limit of its capability to borrow abroad became obvious in the summer of 1985, and led to the austerity programme which was imposed in October of the same year. But, for that policy turn-around to succeed, it was necessary to bring the budget of central government together with that of the wider public sector under control. This meant that the authorities should not proceed to substitute domestic for foreign borrowing. Unfortunately this is exactly what happened. In order to maintain the public consumption programmes, initiated a few years earlier, and in view of the government's inability and/or unwillingness to raise sufficient revenue through other means, the authorities started to borrow disproportionately large amounts of funds from internal sources. As a result, the domestic debt at the end of 1988 had climbed to nearly Dr. 2 trillion, and its servicing now requires so large a chunk of overall government revenue that its size destabilises the economy.

2.3 The Constraint of So-called Inelastic Public Expenditure

From the preceding remarks it should be clear that the only way out is to eliminate the primary deficits of the public sector or, at least, to eliminate those not generated by public investment. This in turn implies that the authorities must raise revenue and/or reduce social consumption expenditure to cover public outlays adequately. Apart from the issue of raising additional government revenue, the question is whether the political system will allow the elimination of wasteful programmes of social consumption to the extent required.

Over time and through persistent education of the Greek public it may become at least possible, if not actually politically appealing, to phase out those numerous social programmes which cater to the needy only in name, while serving the interests of bureaucracy and political nomenclature. In the next few years the likelihood is that most social programmes will continue intact, since the prevailing view among policy makers is that public expenditure is inelastic downwards. Hence, whatever hope still remains is founded on the expectation that: (i) no new social programmes are initiated; (ii) the ones on the books are gradually eroded through inflation and the tightening of the standards of eligibility; and (iii) revenue raising policies, 'invariant' with respect to economic development, are designed and implemented.

2.4 The Constraint of Traditional Policies

Of the three possible policies mentioned, many would consider the last one as the easiest to adopt. Unfortunately, I cannot think of any mixture of traditional policy initiatives which would be 'economic development invariant' and at the same time effective in raising government revenues to the required extent. The rates of direct taxes cannot be increased in Greece while they are being reduced in Western countries; the rates of value added taxes are already very high; expanding the tax base to farmers is very unpopular; combating tax evasion is both difficult and extremely costly, given the structure of the Greek economy. On the other hand, recent experience with incomes policies, devaluation and direct controls has fallen significantly short of expectation. This leaves very little room for manoeuvre and it is because of these four very tight constraints and the seriousness of the economic problem which confronts us that we need to reconsider the tasks which we the people have assigned to the state.

3   THE ROLE OF THE STATE

In Greece, the public sector *produces*, *delivers* and *finances* a vast array of products and services of generally substandard quality. In other words, in contrast to the Jeffersonian dictum that 'government governs best which governs least', in Greece the government governs most and governs badly. For this reason a way out of our present fiscal problems must start from a realignment of the objectives to be pursued by the state on our behalf. To this effect I propose that, while the government should remain responsible for deciding which goods and services are to be paid for by the public, it does not have to *produce* or *deliver* them using government employees. In the words of Buchanan (1976) and Savas (1985), what our government should become is (i) an articulator of democratically expressed demands for 'laws and institutions' as well as physical public goods and services; (ii) a skilful purchasing agent; (iii) a sophisticated inspector of the goods and services purchased from the private sector; (iv) an efficient collector of fair taxes; and (v) a careful disburser of proper payments.

Should we agree that these are the only functions on which the government should concentrate, it should become fairly easy for the state to get out of its productive activities in the fields of, say, electricity, telecommunications, transportation, water supply and so on. In turn, such a policy initiative should bring about three very desirable effects. First, as production and delivery of such goods and services is turned over to the private sector, the budget will be relieved of the overwhelming deficits generated by these publicly operated productive facilities. Second, from the proceeds realised from the transfer of such assets the government can pay off large amounts of the outstanding domestic debt and, perhaps, some part of the foreign debt as well. Finally, there will be a significant spur to improve productivity, with the consequence that economic growth and, hence, government revenues will be stimulated.

Having drawn these implications from the new role of the state, I realise that many will raise the counter-arguments about economies of scale, and natural monopolies, the inherent difficulties in controlling private monopolies, or the plight of the poor and needy who may lose goods and services catering to their basic needs. In reply, I should like to stress the following points:

1. As I see it, the problem is not between public or private ownership of the assets involved in productive activities. Rather the problem is between monopoly and competition. If the choice came down to public versus private monopoly, I would be in favour of the latter because it is, at the very least, 'contestable'.

2. The claim advanced by the supporters of our over-extended welfare state, that there is nothing wrong with the public production and delivery of such goods and services, so long as public utilities are left by the politicians to operate as private enterprises, is hypocritical. Public utilities constitute part and parcel of the political game, with no possibility of operating as private enterprises.
3. The poor and needy must not necessarily lose the goods and services with which they are now provided by the state. Following the transfer of productive assets to the private sector, the state would simply purchase the necessary quantities on their behalf.
4. Welfare losses due to market failure in these sectors are dynamically less important than those inflicted on a consuming public by over-manning and other social abuses by the labour unions in public utilities.

At this point the unconvinced will ask: and what about public goods such as national defence, parks, highways, police, courts, prisons and so on? Will their production and maintenance also be left in private hands? The answer is no. Some goods will certainly continue to be owned and operated by the state because the market cannot provide them; others will continue to be owned by the state, but their operation may be left to the private sector; while yet others, which are not public goods in the proper sense, would be transferred to the private sector. Indeed, I would maintain that, after the role of the state has been revised, the category of goods to be reserved for production and distribution by the state will be quite limited. Goods and services may be classified according to the ease with which one can be denied access to consumption, as shown in Table 3.1. Since it is well known that the market handles best those goods to which access can easily be denied, the problems of supply arise mainly with respect to common-pool and collective goods. So the basic question is, how best to supply them?

Table 3.1 Definition of goods and services

	Exclusive consumption	*Common consumption*
Easy to deny access	Private goods	Toll goods
Difficult to deny access	Common-pool goods	Collective goods

To highlight this question it is helpful to look at Table 3.2 from Savas (1982). From this it is clear that common-pool and collective goods may be supplied by various arrangements besides government agency. Higher education, for example, as a common-pool good does not have to be supplied through a state university system, if it is more advantageous for society to sponsor a contract or voucher system. Or, taking another example, armaments for national defence need not be supplied by a government-owned industry if it is more advantageous to secure them through contracts with private companies. So, given that the arrangements shown in the table have advantages and disadvantages, choosing among them requires a sort of cost–benefit analysis on the basis of the objectives that could be met by each alternative.

If such a cost–benefit analysis were performed, the verdict against the provision of common-pool and collective goods through a government agency could well be overwhelming, the reason being that, for every significant advantage a government agency has, an alternative arrangement may match it. Indeed the other arrangement may well be without the disadvantages of a government agency which (i) does not promote competition; (ii) is not responsive to consumer preferences; (iii) does not relate costs to benefits; (iv) does not achieve economies of scale; (v) is not invulnerable to fraud; and (vi) does not limit the number of government employees. Before we close our minds to the possibilities that these consid-

Table 3.2 Possible arrangements for the supply of common-pool and collective goods

	Common-pool goods	Collective goods
Government agency	X	X
Contract	X	X
Franchise		
Voucher	X	
Market		
Voluntary	X	X

Source: Savas (1982).

erations hold for solving Greece's fiscal problems, as socially minded analysts we owe it to ourselves to consider seriously why a programme of policies as outlined above should not be adopted.

4 CONCLUSION

Owing to the rapid expansion of the public sector, particularly in recent years, the Greek economy faces insuperable fiscal problems which cannot be confronted with Keynesian, neo-Keynesian or other traditional-type macroeconomic policies. As a result, to get out of this economic *impasse,* the role of the state should be reconsidered so that some of its functions may be assigned to the private sector. Through the 'privatisation' of large chunks of government operation the burden of public debt will be alleviated, economic growth will be resumed and state operations will become more streamlined and efficient, without loss to the genuine poor and needy. Finally it is false and hypocritical to claim that only the welfare state as we know it in Greece can, and that a strong market economy therefore cannot, be adequately humane.

References

Buchanan, J. M. (1976) 'Public Goods and Natural Liberty', in Wilson, T. and Skinner, A. S. (eds), *The Market and the State: Essays in Honour of Adam Smith* (Oxford: Oxford University Press).
Savas, E. S. (1982) *Privatizing the Public Sector* (Chatham NJ: Chatham House).
Savas, E. S. (1985) 'Privatization: A Powerful New Tool for Government', *The Privatization Review* (Chatham NJ: Chatham House) vol. I, pp. 4–6.

4 Fiscal Deficits and the Role of the State in the Greek Economy

Matthew J. Lambrinides and Theophanis B. Pakos

PANTION UNIVERSITY, ATHENS

1 FISCAL DEFICITS IN THE 1980s

There is almost universal agreement that the expansion of public-sector indebtedness has been one of the most serious problems plaguing the Greek economy during the 1980s. As can be seen from the figures on public expenditure and taxes presented in Table 4.1, the large increase in fiscal deficits occurred after 1981. This has been a period of deepening crisis for the Greek economy, as evidenced by the marked deceleration in economic growth and private investment activity.

The figures in Table 4.1 also show that the increase in public indebtedness was primarily due to to the very marked increase in the share of the gross domestic product (GDP) accounted for by public expenditure after 1981, whereas the period 1974–81 was characterised by a more modest and stable rate of increase. The aggregate tax burden also increased during the same period, but not sufficiently to offset the increase in public spending.

Some indication of the socioeconomic factors underlying the trend in aggregate expenditure can be obtained by looking at the structure of public expenditure given in Table 4.2. It will be seen that the increase in total government expenditure as a proportion of GDP was primarily due to the increase in transfer payments and, to a lesser degree, to rising government consumption. The increase in transfer payments included both payments to households and interest payments on the public debt.

Table 4.3 shows the functional breakdown of total government consumption. It will be noted that social security was the category whose share of GDP grew fastest after 1974, whereas social expenditure on health and education increased more moderately. Expenditure on defence also expanded rapidly from 1974 onwards, as a result of Turkey's invasion of Cyprus and the continuing conflict over the status of the Aegean Sea.

30

Table 4.1   Fiscal deficits and economic growth, 1962–87

Years	Public expenditure/GDP per cent (1)	Taxes/GDP per cent (2)	Expenditure – taxes/GDP per cent (3)	Real GDP growth rate· per cent (4)	Real fixed private non-residential invest-ment per cent growth (5)
1962	25.0	20.8	4.3	0.6	14.6
1963	24.4	21.3	3.2	10.1	12.5
1964	25.5	22.0	3.5	7.5	27.8
1965	26.4	21.8	4.6	9.2	14.3
1966	27.2	23.5	3.7	5.3	7.9
1967	29.7	24.4	5.3	4.7	–3.1
1968	29.8	25.4	4.4	5.7	19.6
1969	29.4	25.3	4.1	9.3	14.1
1970	29.1	24.9	4.2	8.3	10.8
1971	30.6	25.1	5.6	8.0	2.8
1972	30.5	24.9	5.6	9.1	8.3
1973	28.9	23.6	5.3	8.3	20.5
1974	31.7	24.3	7.5	–1.8	–12.9
1975	32.5	25.1	7.5	5.1	–8.3
1976	33.0	27.4	5.6	6.1	9.3
1977	33.1	28.0	5.1	2.9	10.5
1978	35.2	28.6	6.5	6.4	0.3
1979	35.4	28.8	6.6	3.6	10.7
1980	36.1	28.3	7.8	2.1	–3.6
1981	41.9	27.2	14.7	0.2	–2.0
1982	42.9	30.8	12.2	0.6	–4.7
1983	45.2	31.9	13.3	0.4	–12.8
1984	47.7	32.2	15.0	2.9	–9.3
1985	51.8	32.6	19.2	3.4	3.7
1986	49.7	33.8	15.9	1.3	–3.3
1987	49.4	35.7	13.7	–0.4	5.1

Notes:
1. The share of public expenditures and taxes to GDP is computed at current prices.
2. (3) = (1) – (2)

Source: Hellenic Republic, *National Accounts of Greece* (various issues).

Table 4.2 Public expenditure share of GDP: selected economic categories, 1962–1987, per cent at current prices

Years	Public consumption	Public investment	Transfer payments	Transfers to households	Interest on public debt
1962	11.6	6.6	6.8	6.0	0.4
1963	11.3	5.7	7.4	6.4	0.5
1964	11.7	5.7	8.1	6.6	0.6
1965	11.7	5.6	8.9	7.0	0.7
1966	11.8	5.6	9.7	7.4	0.6
1967	13.0	6.1	10.6	8.0	0.7
1968	12.9	6.2	10.7	8.4	0.8
1969	12.7	6.9	9.8	8.0	0.8
1970	12.6	6.7	9.8	8.0	0.9
1971	12.5	7.9	10.2	8.0	1.0
1972	12.2	8.4	9.9	7.6	1.0
1973	11.5	7.8	9.7	6.8	1.0
1974	13.8	6.7	11.2	7.2	1.3
1975	15.2	5.8	11.5	7.4	1.4
1976	15.1	5.7	12.3	7.7	1.6
1977	16.0	5.1	13.1	8.5	1.5
1978	15.9	5.3	14.0	9.2	1.7
1979	16.3	5.7	13.4	8.8	2.2
1980	16.4	5.6	14.2	9.2	2.4
1981	18.0	5.9	18.0	11.0	3.2
1982	18.3	6.0	18.7	13.0	2.6
1983	18.8	7.0	19.4	13.4	3.7
1984	19.5	7.5	20.7	14.0	4.6
1985	20.4	8.1	23.3	14.9	5.4
1986	19.4	6.9	23.4	14.8	5.7
1987	19.5	5.6	24.2	14.6	7.2

Source: Hellenic Republic, *National Accounts of Greece* (various issues).

Table 4.3   Public expenditure share of GDP: functional breakdown 1962–87, per cent at current prices

Years	Administration	Defence	Public order	Health	Social security	Education	Other
1962	3.9	4.0	0.7	1.8	5.3	1.6	0.2
1963	3.9	3.7	0.7	1.6	5.7	1.7	0.2
1964	4.1	3.5	0.8	2.1	5.7	1.9	0.2
1965	4.0	3.6	0.7	2.2	6.1	1.9	0.2
1966	4.1	3.6	0.7	2.2	6.5	1.9	0.2
1967	4.2	4.6	0.7	2.2	7.1	2.0	0.2
1968	4.2	4.6	0.7	2.1	7.5	2.0	0.2
1969	4.1	4.7	0.7	2.1	7.1	1.9	0.2
1970	4.1	4.6	0.6	2.1	7.0	1.9	0.3
1971	4.1	4.5	0.6	2.2	7.1	1.9	0.2
1972	4.0	4.4	0.6	2.2	6.6	1.8	0.2
1973	3.9	4.0	0.5	2.1	5.9	1.8	0.2
1974	4.2	5.6	0.6	2.1	6.1	1.9	0.2
1975	4.4	6.8	0.6	2.3	6.4	2.0	0.2
1976	4.5	6.4	0.6	2.6	6.5	2.0	0.2
1977	4.6	6.6	0.6	2.9	6.8	2.2	0.2
1978	4.6	6.8	0.6	3.0	7.7	2.4	0.2
1979	5.0	6.6	0.6	3.1	7.5	2.3	0.2
1980	5.1	6.4	0.6	3.4	7.7	2.2	0.7
1981	5.6	6.8	0.7	3.6	9.4	2.4	0.8
1982	5.8	6.6	0.7	3.9	11.2	2.5	0.7
1983	6.0	6.5	0.7	3.9	11.8	3.8	0.7
1984	6.8	6.4	0.7	3.8	12.5	2.7	0.7
1985	7.3	6.5	0.7	3.7	13.1	3.0	1.2
1986	6.6	6.5	0.7	4.0	12.4	2.8	1.3
1987	6.3	6.0	1.1	3.9	12.7	2.8	1.3

Source: Hellenic Republic, *National Accounts of Greece* (various issues).

In Table 4.4 we trace the evolution of the share of GDP accounted for by selected economic categories of public expenditure at constant prices. These data are interesting for the following reasons:

1. The increase in the share of government expenditure at constant prices was less marked than at current prices, clearly reflecting the relative price effect due to the relative low growth in productivity in the government sector, as well as the zero productivity growth assumption implicit in national income accounting conventions.

2. The share of government expenditure on goods and services, that is government consumption plus investment, increased only slightly from 19.4 to 20.6 per cent in real terms between 1980 and 1987. The bulk of this increase in the share of real expenditure derived from transfer payments.

Table 4.4 Public expenditure share of GDP, 1962–87, per cent at constant prices

Years	Consumption	Investment	Transfer payments*	Total
1962	14.2	7.4	6.6	28.2
1963	13.4	6.4	7.1	26.9
1964	13.5	6.6	7.9	27.9
1965	13.5	6.6	8.6	28.6
1966	13.5	6.2	9.5	29.2
1967	13.8	6.5	9.6	30.0
1968	13.1	6.6	10.5	30.2
1969	12.9	7.4	9.7	30.0
1970	12.6	6.7	9.8	29.1
1971	12.4	8.0	10.3	30.6
1972	12.0	8.3	10.1	30.4
1973	12.0	7.5	10.2	29.7
1974	14.0	6.2	11.8	32.0
1975	14.8	5.5	12.0	32.3
1976	14.6	5.3	13.0	32.9
1977	15.0	4.6	14.0	33.6
1978	14.6	4.6	14.9	34.1
1979	14.9	4.9	14.6	34.5
1980	14.7	4.7	14.9	34.3
1981	15.6	4.7	18.4	38.8
1982	15.9	5.0	19.8	40.7
1983	16.2	5.7	20.7	42.6
1984	16.3	6.1	22.5	44.8
1985	16.3	6.5	25.2	47.9
1986	16.1	5.2	24.9	46.2
1987	16.4	4.2	25.8	46.4

* Includes debt interest deflated by the implicit private consumption deflator.

Source: Hellenic Republic, *National Accounts of Greece* (various issues).

From the statistical evidence presented in this section, we have concluded that the rise in public indebtedness derived primarily from the expansion of current expenditure, with social security payments accounting for the major part of this increase. The trend in social security payments is associated not only with Greece's ageing population structure (Polyzos, 1981; and Emke-Poulopoulou, 1985) but also with the very marked increase in the level of most pension categories which, until 1982, had been held down at near subsistence level. During this period, the pensions of the better-off and more privileged social groups increased relatively slowly.

The timing of the largest increases in government expenditure coincided with elections: both 1981 and 1985 were years in which general elections were held which threatened the party in power. However the rationale of the longer-term trend goes beyond the winning of elections and is closely associated with the establishment of a minimal welfare state. This is an area of institutional development where Greece still lags behind its EC partners, especially in the provision of health and education services. It is noteworthy that the share of social expenditure in GDP started to rise in the 1960s, as shown in Tables 4.2 and 4.3. This process was arrested during the period of the military dictatorship (1967–73), but resumed with the restoration of democratic government in 1974.

2 IMMEDIATE POLICY OPTIONS

There is universal agreement among Greek economists that the alarming increase in the fiscal deficit, and especially the increasing recourse to borrowing in order to finance current expenditure, makes it imperative to introduce without delay a series of policy measures designed to reverse recent trends.

It is unlikely that the next two or three years will see any pronounced growth in productive activity. This means that the curbing of the proportion of government deficit relative to GDP will depend on reducing the rate of growth of public expenditure and/or increasing the aggregate tax burden. The exact measures proposed differ according to the analytic background of the economist and his diagnosis of the deeper underlying causes of the problem. At the end of this section we present a summary of measures which would appear to produce reasonably quick results, while at the same time allowing the Greek fiscal system to be rationalised and streamlined. At present, the fiscal system is not only generally obsolete compared to other European countries but is heavily geared to enable the government budget to be used to secure economic benefits for the political clientele of the ruling party.

On the expenditure side, many analysts of the economy have stressed not only the need to expand the minimal transparency and accountability which characterises the process of determining the structure and level of public expenditure but also the importance of monitoring the execution of large spending programmes. This would require the setting up of parliamentary committees to hold public hearings into the government's budget proposals and subsequently monitor their implementation. These committees could, we believe, produce rapid results in controlling excessive public expenditure, which in the past has benefited special-interest groups. Furthermore they could curtail the unwarranted increase in public-sector employment, particularly before an election.

The powers of these committees need not be limited to vetting the government budget and employment practices, but could be extended to the monitoring of the corresponding activities of numerous public corporations and other public bodies. The increased transparency and accountability, which these parliamentary committees should quickly achieve, might include various areas where the reduction in public expenditure is currently considered both possible and essential, as for example:

1. the rationalisation of the pension system, including cuts in early retirement and in the level of pensions, where they exceed the last remuneration at work;
2. the rationalisation of the system of benefits, including a reduction in the number of occupations designated as dangerous and unhealthy;
3. the curtailment of lavish and ostentatious expenditure by government or the civil service;
4. the strict curbing of the illegal use of public monies for the enrichment of individuals, such as members of the government, civil servants or private citizens, or for adding to the coffers of the governing party – which in recent years have assumed scandalous proportions.

The institutionalisation of public hearings by parliamentary committees could also help to secure a national social consensus for the speedy implementation of several badly needed reforms to the tax system, including the following:

1. the removal or at least radical limitation of the web of tax exemptions currently permeating the Greek tax system;
2. a thorough re-examination of the structure of tax incentives;
3. the simplification of the income tax structure, including decreases in the high income and marginal tax rates, coupled with the implementation of measures aimed at ensuring that social categories other than wage and salary earners pay appropriate levels of income tax;

4. the reorganisation of the VAT collection system to make firms pay VAT dues faster than at present;
5. the institutionalisation of a substantive property tax, linked to income tax, in order to limit income tax evasion (by using property acquisition as income indicators);
6. the implementation of various measures, which have been proposed in the past, for limiting tax avoidance, which is extensive in Greece owing to the large number of self-employed persons.

The impact of the measures outlined above has been extensively analysed by Tatsos (1988), Georgakopoulos and Loizides (1989) and Pavlopoulos (1989). It seems likely that almost all these measures could produce rapid results. The problem regarding their implementation is basically political, in that the government that had to enforce them would undoubtedly incur a heavy political cost and the actual opposition of those social groups whose vested interests would be threatened by their implementation.

3   MEDIUM- AND LONG-TERM POLICY STRATEGIES

The relative concensus of the Greek economists' views regarding the immediate policy does not extend to longer-term policy strategies for limiting the public sector's indebtedness. In the longer term, both economic growth and the tax share of GDP at given tax rates can accelerate. As a result the share of government deficit in GDP could be curtailed without a major deceleration in the real growth rate of government expenditure. Economists are accordingly divided, depending on their views of the conditions necessary for accelerating economic growth.

In recent years, the neo-liberal view has won increased acceptance among economists in Greece, as in other western countries. Neo-liberals regard the expansion of the public sector as the prime cause of the current economic crisis, because of the relatively low productivity inherent in state, as compared to private, economic management. They argue that drastic cuts in public expenditure and the concomitant restriction of government economic activity should form the focal point of the economic restructuring that would lead the economy out of the crisis.

Pavlopoulos (1989) recently put the neo-liberal view regarding fiscal management most succinctly, arguing that the high growth rates experienced in Greece until 1973, together with the subsequent deceleration, showed that the size of the public sector compatible with fast economic growth entails a share of approximately 35 per cent for current expenditure plus investment expenditure (excluding interest on the public debt) compared to a corresponding share of 56 per cent in 1987. It therefore follows that the resumption of fast economic growth presupposes cuts in public expenditure relative to GDP of approximately 37 per cent.

Even though we would agree that there is wide scope for a significant reduction in public expenditure growth, as well as for improving the efficiency of the public sector, we consider that Pavlopoulos's argument in favour of limiting expenditure to such a degree is not well founded.

The weakness of the neo-liberal argument is most evident when the causes of the Greek economic crisis are examined. In our view the current crisis is the result of a process that goes back to 1974 and beyond. The root of the crisis lies in the accumulation of increasingly serious problems concerning the functioning of the development model on which the high rates of growth experienced up to 1973 were based. These problems were particularly acute as a result of the international economic crisis, for a number of reasons.

First, the international economic crisis caused a deceleration of activity in several key sectors of the Greek economy, such as shipping, tourism and export-oriented industries (particularly textiles and metals). Second, the crisis in Europe resulted in a significant decline in remittances from abroad which, together with tourism and shipping, were the main source for financing Greece's permanent and sizeable trade deficit. Third, the fall in remittances contributed to the decline of investment in housing, which throughout the postwar period had significantly exceeded investment in manufacturing in value terms.

In addition to these problems there were other difficulties. In the first place there was the abnormal development of labour costs, which had been held down at low levels until 1974, as a result of the suppression of the freedom of labour from the end of the civil war in 1949 until the end of the rule of the military junta. This subject has been examined by Karayeorgas and Pakos (1986), who analysed the impact of this low wage policy on unit labour costs. The restoration of the democratic process in 1974 inevitably resulted in high wage increases at a time when economic growth started to slow down, as the unions tried to make up for lost ground, particularly during the years of dictatorship. This led inevitably to a deterioration of Greece's international competitive position. Furthermore the delay until 1974 in the institutionalisation of the welfare state in Greece meant that the restoration of democracy entailed significant increases in social expenditure, just when economic growth began to falter.

Greece's full membership of the EC, irrespective of immediate and future benefits, caused a sizeable reduction in the industrial sector's overall rate of protection and created uncertainty regarding Greece's prospective position in the international division of labour, which could not fail to have a negative effect on business investment. It is worth noting that real investment in manufacturing is still below the peak level reached in 1974. Finally, as Yannitsis (1986) and Lambrinides (1989) have shown, the vacillations in government policy, especially after 1981, undoubtedly constituted a further counter-incentive to private investment and contributed to the deepening of the economic crisis.

In our opinion the causes of Greece's economic crisis cannot be attributed solely, or even primarily, to the expansion of the public sector. On the contrary, the crisis was due to the multi-faceted decline of the development model, which had been the corner-stone of the fast economic development up to 1973. In addition, we believe that the resumption of fast growth presupposes the elaboration of a new development model or strategy, which would be free of all the blockages that led to Greece's economic decline. In the first place this would entail a restructuring of the private sector, to encourage new leading sectors to develop and/or to ensure that the old sectors would be freed from all inhibiting malpractice. In a capitalist economy, such as Greece's, government policy cannot play an active role in bringing this about. What government policy can do, however, is to provide the stable environment in which private business, both Greek and foreign, can look at the future and make a reasonable estimate of the return on their investment. One very important aspect of this will be the finalisation of Greece's position in the European division of labour, and this is an area where both the government and the EC authorities can help.

What are the implications of our analysis for the size and role of the public sector in this new economic development model, which we are confident could take the economy out of the present crisis? First, the sort of limitation on expenditure envisaged by Pavlopoulos seems to us quite unrealistic. Any fundamental restructuring of the productive potential will require expenditure on large public works, such as the expansion and improvement of the road and rail network, at least one new major airport, the Rio-Antirio bridge and so on. As a result public investment expenditure, which has stagnated for a long time, will be set to rise significantly.

Second, with regard to social expenditure, even though there is scope for rationalising the existing services, their level and quality are by European standards still very low for large sections of the population. We regard a decent well-functioning national health service and a social security system that guarantees more than a minimum subsistence pension for the majority of the population to be of critical importance, both for the purpose of increasing labour productivity and for ensuring a social consensus, which restructuring will make difficult under the existing configuration of political power. Furthermore we consider it difficult to expect any major restructuring of production without modernising the education system, especially higher education. This will probably require a reduction in the number of university admissions, as well as increased expenditure on university infrastructure.

Third, while we agree that limiting public-sector employment is a desirable public policy goal in the medium to long term, we note that the expansion of public-sector employment in the 1950s and 1960s, while it could not be justified on any efficiency criteria, was undertaken to avoid social turbulence which might have developed in the post civil-war period. Thus this policy was directed at providing employment for the large proportion of high-school and university graduates who could not be absorbed into the private sector and who would otherwise have been unemployed. At the same time, the high proportion of the labour force with poor educational qualifications, who were also unable to find employment in the private sector, often emigrated. Most of the emigration was to western Europe. Tsoukalas (1986) has analysed the relationship between public-sector employment, emigration and the political, social and economic developments of the period. As it is clear that emigration is no longer a feasible solution to Greece's unemployment problem, we consider that any sudden cut in public-sector employment, as advocated by Pavlopoulos, would create such a severe unemployment problem, particularly among the better-educated section of the labour force, that it could lead to social unrest and prevent the creation of the social consensus so essential for a major restructuring programme to succeed.

Bearing this in mind, we conclude that any cutback in employment should be a gradual process, conditional on the creation of new employment opportunities in the private sector. In the long run, the solution to the problem of public-sector deficits in capitalist economies must lie primarily in the resumption of fast growth in the private sector; the role of government must be to help and support this process, but not to lead.

References

Emke-Poulopoulou, I. (1985) 'Demographic Ageing in Greece and its Consequences', in *The Demographic Crisis in Greece* (Athens: Greek Society for Demographic Research) in Greek.

Georgakopoulos, T. and Loizides, J. (1989) 'Income Taxation', in Provopoulos, G. A. (ed.), *Priorities for Fiscal Policy* (Athens: Institute for Economic and Industrial Research) in Greek.

Karayeorgas, S. and Pakos, T. (1986) 'Social and Economic Inequality', in Manesis, A. *et al.* (eds), *Greece in Transition* (Athens: Exantas) in Greek, pp. 272–35.

Lambrinides, M. J. (1989) 'Economic Crisis and Stabilisation Policy', *Themata* (Athens: Regional Development Institute, Pantion University) in Greek, pp. 26–41.

Pavlopoulos, P. G. (1989) 'Tax Burden, Size of Public Sector and Shadow Economy', in Provopoulos, G. A. (ed.), *Priorities for Fiscal Policy* (Athens: Institute for Economic and Industrial Research) in Greek, pp. 25–9 and 44–51.

Polyzos, N. (1981) *Demographic Challenge: Low Fertility and Ageing in Greece* (Athens: Exantas) in Greek.

Tatsos, N. (1988) 'The Tax System as a Means for Implementing Social Policy: The Concept of Tax Expenditures', in *Essays in Memory of Sakis Karayeorgas* (Athens, Pantion University), in Greek.

Tsoukalas, C. (1986) *State, Society and Labour in Postwar Greece* (Athens: Themelio) in Greek, pp. 82–126.

Yannitsis, T. (1986) 'Greece: Industrialisation in Crisis', in Manesis, A. *et al.* (eds), *Greece in Transition* (Athens: Exantas), in Greek.

Part II

Monetary Policy and Banking Developments

5 Macroeconomic Performance and Policies: Recent Past and Prospects

George Hadjimatheou
CITY OF LONDON POLYTECHNIC

1 RECENT COMPARATIVE PERFORMANCE OF THE GREEK ECONOMY

A brief assessment of the macroeconomic performance of the Greek economy in the 1980s and an examination of the thrust of macroeconomic policy in the same period seems to be a good starting-point for assessing the prospects and potential path of the economy in the 1990s. Looking at the stylised facts and the fiscal policies of the PASOK governments would also help to identify policy mistakes and to suggest a medium-term strategy that would appear to serve the needs of the economy for the next decade. Table 5.1 provides data to enable some useful comparisons to be made. First, in terms of economic growth, the performance of Greece in the 1980s, both in terms of its own past and relative to other countries, has been poor. More specifically, out of twenty-four OECD countries Greece does better only than Ireland. In relation to the 1970s, when Greece achieved high rates of growth, both in absolute and relative terms, the performance of the 1980s appears far worse.

Second, with the exception of Turkey and Iceland, Greece has the worst inflation record in the OECD. The rate of increase of consumer prices rose from an average 15.9 per cent in 1975–80 to an average 19.5 per cent in 1981–8. Furthermore, with the exception of Portugal whose performance is nearly as bad, Greece in the 1980s experienced more than double the inflation rate of its EC partners.

Third, the unemployment rate rose from 2.1 per cent in the years 1975–80 to an average of about 7 per cent in 1981–8. Inadequate data and definition differences prevent a direct comparison, in terms of levels, with other OECD countries but there is no doubt that the 1980s mark a relative deterioration in unemployment. The number of unemployed in the late 1980s is at least three times as large as that of the late 1970s.

Fourth, with the exception of 1985 and 1988, total fixed capital formation was substantially negative in the 1980s. In this respect, Greece's record is the second worst of the OECD countries and, with the exception of Ireland, who did slightly worse, it bears no comparison with EC rates. It also compares badly with Greece's performance in the 1970s.

Fifth, with the exception of Iceland and Turkey, who performed worse, Greece in the 1980s experienced the most persistent and most substantial depreciation of its currency. A continuous depreciation has been recorded since 1974, but the rate accelerated in the 1980s, so that the effective exchange rate dropped from 52.9 in 1980 to 18.0 in 1988.

Sixth, despite the substantial fall in the value of the drachma, there was a considerable worsening of the current balance of payments which, for the period 1980–8, appears to be the second worst in Europe. It must be said, however, that in this aspect of the economy there has been a gradual and considerable improvement since 1985, when the current account deficit reached a record 9.8 per cent of GDP.

Seventh, another exceptional development was the tremendous increase in public sector activity. Total government outlay as a percentage of GDP rose from 30.5 in 1980 to over 44 per cent in 1988. No other OECD country appears to emulate Greece in this respect in the same period, although Sweden recorded a similar rise in the 1970s. The unusual increase in public spending was accompanied by a significant rise in government revenue. Nevertheless increases in receipts by the state did not match the rise in expenditures, with the consequence that substantial budget deficits were recorded. Thus the general government financial balance as a percentage of GDP rose from 2.5 in 1975–80 to 10.9 per cent in 1981–8. The Greek budget deficits were among the largest in Europe, but not as large as those of Italy, Ireland and Belgium.

Finally, productivity declined slightly between 1979 and 1985. According to the 1987 OECD Survey of the Greek economy

> this contrasts sharply with developments elsewhere in the OECD area, where sizeable productivity gains were recorded over this period principally as a result of labour shedding in low productivity or loss-making firms and accelerated capital-for-labour substitution. As a result, the large productivity gap *vis-à-vis* trading partners has further widened since the end of the 1970s (p. 29).

All in all, Greece's economic record in the period 1981–8 is one of the poorer, if not the poorest, of the OECD countries. The remarkable thing about Greece in this period is that its economic performance is bad across the board, as will be seen from the economic indicators given for Greece in

Table 5.1 and for the OECD in Table 5.2. There does not seem, for example, to be a trade-off between inflation and the rate of growth of the economy or even unemployment. It is true that the rate of unemployment in Greece, although increasing threefold between 1979 and 1988, was throughout the period lower than the EC average. But comparison of levels is difficult, given that a standardised rate of unemployment for Greece, in line with EC practice, is not available. However the increase in the rate of unemployment between 1979 and 1988 was as large as in any other EC country. Even more interesting is that the performance of the Greek economy is on the whole worse than the performance of Spain and Portugal, Greece's nearest EC partners in terms of economic development and political stability. Both of them achieved enviable GDP and capital formation growth after 1985 (on average about 4 and 10 per cent respectively) and managed to reduce their inflation rates well below Greek price inflation, as well as sustaining more manageable external and internal balances. OECD projections for Greece

Table 5.1   Macroeconomic indicators: Greece, 1975–88

	U	P	G	BP	EER	I	GE	RE	GFB
1975–80	2.1	15.9	4.7	−4.3	83.5–52.9	3.7	28.9	29.7	−2.5
1981	4.0	24.5	0.1	−6.5	49.2	−7.5	35.9	29.1	−10.9
1982	5.8	21.0	0.4	−4.9	44.8	−1.9	37.0	32.3	−7.6
1983	7.9	20.2	0.4	−5.4	38.6	−1.3	38.2	33.6	−8.1
1984	8.1	18.4	2.7	−6.3	32.5	−5.7	40.2	34.8	−9.9
1985	7.8	19.3	3.9	−9.8	28.6	5.2	43.7	34.6	−13.5
1986	7.4	23.0	1.2	−4.2	22.3	−5.7	42.1	35.6	−11.1
1987	7.4	16.4	−0.4	−2.6	19.3	−3.2	43.0	37.2	−11.1
1988	7.6	13.5	3.5	−1.9	18.0	10.0	n.a.	n.a.	−15.3

Notes: U = unemployment rate; P = percentage change in consumer price index; G = rate of growth of real GDP; BP = balance of payments current account as a percentage of GDP (deficit); EER = effective exchange rate; I = rate of growth of gross fixed capital formation; GE = government expenditure as a percentage of GDP; RE = current receipts of government as a percentage of GDP; GFB = general government financial balance as a percentage of GDP.

Source: OECD, *Economic Outlook*.

Table 5.2 Macroeconomic indicators: OECD, 1975–88

	U	P	G	BP	EER[1]	I	GE	RE	GFB[2]
1975–80	5.6	11.6	2.3	−0.1	92.7–43.7	0.9	44.8	41.1	−1.3
1981	8.3	12.1	0.2	−0.6	43.6	−4.3	48.0	42.6	−3.9
1982	9.4	10.3	0.8	−0.6	39.21	−2.0	48.9	43.4	−5.6
1983	10.4	8.3	1.8	0.2	31.5	0.6	49.1	43.8	−4.8
1984	10.8	7.5	2.6	0.6	25.3	2.1	49.1	44.1	−5.5
1985	11.0	6.6	2.6	0.8	23.3	2.7	49.3	44.5	−7.0
1986	10.9	4.0	2.6	1.3	21.6	4.1	49.0	44.3	−6.1
1987	10.5	3.9	2.7	0.7	20.0	5.1	49.9	45.4	−3.6
1988	10.1	4.9	3.5	0.3	19.0	7.2	n.a.	n.a.	−3.1

Notes:
1. Includes Portugal.
2. Includes Spain.
3. Key as in Table 5.1.

suggest a marked deterioration of the public sector borrowing requirement (PSBR) for 1989, a worsening of the trade balance and an upward move in inflation.

2 MACROECONOMIC POLICIES IN THE 1980s

2.1 Plans and Intentions

The type of socialism advocated by PASOK was clearly different from the 'paternalistic, state socialism of the eastern block' (Papandreou, 1979) and from the social programmes of west European social democratic parties. PASOK's socialism was aiming at a radical, structural and institutional change of society. The professed transformation of the economy and society envisaged the achievement of a reasonable growth of the economy with a more equal distribution of income. The state was expected to play a more active and important role through an economic stabilisation programme and the pursuit of developmental policies. A five-year plan for the period 1983–7 was considered an indispensable part of economic and social policy. According to Katseli (1986) although there had been plans in the past, these had been abandoned, with the consequence that no real planning took place. Katseli suggests that

> the preparation of the 1983–7 Economic and Social Plan was the first step towards consolidation of a planning process whose future critically depends (a) on the creation of a minimum social consensus around targets and methods of implementation, (b) on a political commitment to a medium and long term restructuring of the economy and (c) on the undertaking of broad and bold reform measures to create the institutional apparatus conducive to planning. (p. 65)

Democratic planning was so defined as to require a minimum level of decentralisation and autonomy in decision making, based on socialisation and self-management. The planning process involved a credible investment programme that was expected to 'increase present and future productivity, to diversify the productive base, to enhance international competitiveness and to mitigate inequities and distortions' (Katseli, 1986, p. 69). The need to pursue policies to shift resources from consumption towards investment was something emphasised by many PASOK economists in the early 1980s (Vaitsos, 1986; Corliras, 1986). In this context, the lack of sufficient investment in the 1970s was held responsible for the increase in unemployment in the 1980s. Other issues considered and expected to be addressed were the external and internal imbalances, including inflation. It seems that it was also fully recognised that a prerequisite of success of the new more active role of the state in economic matters was a much more efficient public sector. Finally, it was suggested that, along with the removal of institutional impediments, there was an urgent need to tackle the issue of developing the quality of Greek human capital which was seen as a major constraint.

According to Corliras (1986) a complicated policy package was needed which

> rejecting the short term trade-off between inflation and unemployment . . . must strive to reduce both by a mixture of demand-management and supply-oriented policies. The latter does not mean, however, the naive 'supply-side economics' of the *laissez-faire* type. On the contrary, it means the implementation of planned intervention at the industry level by means of (a) planning agreements between the state and particular large firms, (b) selective credit policies and controls, (c) setting certain industrial sectors under public control, (d) encouraging investments under

mixed private/public ownership, and (e) expanding the activities of the state-controlled enterprises. (Corliras, p. 37)

The 1983 OECD Survey of the Greek economy notes the five-year plan but notes also the following pertinent factors: the absence from the plan of sufficient quantitative macroeconomic targets and of the precise mechanisms to be put in place to achieve the plan goals; a too optimistic projection for GDP and capital formation growth; the need for greater adjustments to achieve certain goals; the need to recognise the importance of the external deficit as a constraint; and a need to reverse detailed microeconomic intervention by the state, which creates rigidities, reduces competition and generates a multitude of rent situations.

2.2 Implementing Policy: Constraints and Failures

In the light of information currently available it seems that the PASOK governments (i) for one reason or another, did not implement the package of policies that were thought necessary to achieve the set targets in a sufficient and consistent way; (ii) probably misjudged the effects of their policies on the economy – especially the rapid expansion of the public sector and its adverse effects on productive activity in the private sector; (iii) under-estimated the importance of sufficiently reducing both internal and external imbalances as prerequisites for achieving developmental targets; (iv) over-estimated the ability or willingness of the private sector to respond to fiscal stimulus by increasing production; and (v) eventually ended up with an economy in a worse state than in 1981.

As we have already seen the PASOK socialist government coincided with a huge increase in the public sector. In terms of the components of public expenditure there was a drastic increase in government transfers which rose by 70 per cent in 1981. The other component that increased more than the rest of public expenditure was investment which, in nominal terms, increased by 51 per cent in 1981. The relative importance of public consumption declined, as did, at least initially, the servicing of public debt. But, after six or seven years of persistent deficits and public borrowing, the latter item represented a much higher component in the total, while investment reached a maximum in 1984 and then declined in relative importance. What is more important, in view of the above discussion, total gross fixed capital formation as a percentage of GDP at constant prices, fell from an average of 22.8 in 1975–80 to 18.9 in 1981–6. The public-sector equivalent, for the same periods, increased slightly from 5.6 to 6.2 per cent respectively. But, despite the exceptional increase in public spending, revenue from taxation relative to GDP remained unchanged, with the result that the financial deficit of government bore the brunt of the increase in spending. According to the OECD (1983) the PSBR soared to 19 per cent in 1981 (up eight percentage points from 1980). The substantial fiscal stimulus, combined with large increases in minimum wages and salary rates and the establishment of a formal indexation system (both initiated by the in-coming government), a depreciating drachma, shorter working hours, longer holidays and excessive wage increases in relation to productivity changes meant increasing unit labour costs. In terms of the level of economic activity, despite the considerable increase in both private and public consumption, there was a substantial jump in unemployment, big reductions in fixed capital formation and static real GDP. Although there is insufficient reliable evidence to establish a causal link, it would appear that the exceptional expansion of the public sector and simultaneous increases in labour costs contributed to a serious squeeze in profitability and in private investment in the period 1981–5.

According to the 1987 OECD survey,

> apart from the failure of the private sector to adjust to changing patterns of demand and external supply shocks, crowding-out mechanisms may have become stronger as public sector claims on real and financial resources rose rapidly to high levels. Fast growth of public sector employment, with wage and salary levels above the national average, must have shifted upwards the supply curve of labour, pushing up labour costs in the private sector (p. 37).

The public-sector expansion also meant a high rate of growth of domestic credit expansion to the public sector.

The following quotation from the same survey raises very interesting issues:

> Even allowing for stronger crowding-out effects on private sector activity than in the past, the disappointingly weak supply response of the private sector to the economic challenges of the two oil shocks and of Greece's entry into the EC remains puzzling. Complex socio-political rather than straightforward economic reasons seem to have been largely responsible. One worrying aspect is the extent to which Greek society exhibits features typical of a 'rentier' mentality. Sizeable foreign-exchange inflows from Greeks living abroad, the recent large EC payments and fast-growing government transfers to households, have apparently

created a climate of complacency, dissociating income from work effort, reducing work incentives and favouring consumption. Up to mid-1985, the development needs of the economy would seem to have been subordinated to the aspirations of the population for continuing rapid increases in living standards at the expense of capital accumulation and external equilibrium. This consumer mentality has been reflected in a marked decline of the gross national saving ratio from 25 per cent in 1979 to some 12 per cent in 1985. It is also witnessed by the low priority attached to the up-grading of the structure and methods of production after the two oil shocks and in response to growing foreign competition, notably from EC members and newly industrialised countries (p. 38).

A somewhat similar mentality has probably afflicted the PASOK governments!

The pace, in terms of fiscal policy, set in 1981 was little changed until after the general election of 1985. Government revenue increased somewhat, leading to a modest fall in budget deficits but public spending as a percentage of GDP increased, on top of the exceptional rise in 1981, by another seven to eight points between 1981 and 1985. The major imbalances, both internal and external, did not alter very much between 1981 and 1984 but showed a distinct deterioration in 1985. At the same time the rising unemployment did not seem to have any favourable effect on inflation, which between 1981 and 1986 was confined in the narrow range 18–24 per cent.

The ideological commitment of PASOK to a higher profile of the state in the economic and social process made it difficult to reverse policies in the light of the deteriorating economic situation between 1982 and 1984. Even if it is assumed that the need for substantial corrective deflationary measures was recognised, any serious attempt to change course was prevented by the impending general election of 1985. This meant that any policy change to improve the situation was too little and too late. It seems clear that the need to do well at the general election dictated economic policy in 1984 and early 1985. The implication was a deterioration of the existing macroeconomic imbalances: 1985 marked a distinct worsening in both the budget and balance of payments deficit and in the rise in inflation. Valuable time was lost, and when the austerity measures were announced they appeared excessive and gave rise to industrial conflict. Furthermore the lack of consistency and persistence in pursuing these measures – probably as a result of disagreements between rival factions in the party and a lack of courage to accept the short-term political cost of unpopular policies – sustained this lack of credibility in government policies.

2.3   The Greek and British Experience Compared

It is interesting at this stage of the discussion to draw a parallel between the Greek experience as described above and the developments in the British economy in the mid-1970s. The electoral commitments of the Labour Party in 1974, following a period of social strife and a bitter confrontation between the trade union movement and the Conservative government, were largely responsible for the initial inflationary policies of the Wilson Labour government. The economic background in early 1974 was leading towards economic recession, rapidly rising prices and a rejection of attempts through incomes policies to moderate wage settlements. The Labour government to a large extent gave in to wage demands and at the same time implemented extensive subsidies in an attempt to help the lower-income sections of society. As a result of these and other policies government expenditure as a percentage of GDP rose from 41 in 1973 to 48 in 1975. This led to a substantial swelling of the PSBR. At the same time there was a deterioration of the balance of payments, while the rate of inflation rose to a record 25 per cent. These developments, in conjunction with sustained pressure on sterling and the need to borrow from the IMF to replenish depleted foreign reserves, led to a reversal of policies. After a great deal of socialist soul-searching the Labour government implemented a programme of drastic cuts in public expenditure and a biting incomes policy. Thus, by 1977, the public expenditure ratio was down to 42 per cent, leading to a substantial fall in the PSBR. At the same time a fall in real incomes was experienced by the majority of employees, leading to an improvement in UK trade competitiveness and a sizeable reduction in the current account deficit. Finally there was a gradual reduction in inflation from around 25 per cent in 1975 to about 9 per cent in 1978. It is worth noting that the deflationary policies of this period were implemented while unemployment was rising and when economic activity was just picking up after two years of negative growth rates. This reference to British economic history contrasts with the Greek predicament.

In the case of Greece the 'corrective' measures were implemented in the aftermath of the 1985 election. But they were neither as extensive nor as lasting as those described above for the British case. The ratio of public expenditure, after a slight fall in 1986, bounced back in 1987–8. Budget deficits have proved very difficult to suppress. The incomes policy has led to an improvement in unit labour costs and, in combination with the sliding drachma, to some gains in competitiveness which led to a substantial improvement in the current balance. Inflation was reduced from about 22 per cent in 1986 to around 14 per cent in 1988, unemployment has remained around 7.5 per cent for the last three years, while investment and GDP growth in 1988 exhibited an encouraging recovery. OECD estimates suggested that, following a substantial fall in shares of profits in the 1970s and 1980s, there was some recovery in the last two or three years. These improvements, however, must be put in perspective and judged in relation to the rest of Europe. When this is done a clearer picture emerges of the distance that Greece has to cover to compete with its EC partners.

2.4   OECD Reviews of the Greek Economy

Repeated OECD surveys, in unusually candid terms, point to the serious problems of the Greek economy in the 1980s and to the need for certain policy measures. The 1983 survey, for example, points out that

> the continuation of strong expansionary policies up to 1982 has moved Greece out of phase *vis-à-vis* its main economic partners – an unsustainable situation for a small open economy – while insufficient adaptation of the structure of production and external trade to changing world economic conditions has limited the potential benefits from accession to EC membership in 1981. As a result the Greek economy is faced with major economic imbalances (OECD, 1983 p. 51).

The same survey goes even further in its criticism of the Greek government's management of the economy by suggesting that, 'apart from the macro-economic coherence of policies, . . . it is important for promoting a climate of confidence to define as clearly as possible the "rules of the game", namely a stable institutional and regulatory environment for the activities of the private and public sectors' (p. 53). The 1986 survey observes that

> lack of competitiveness, market rigidities and the associated misallocation of resources have weakened the response of the Greek economy to domestic and external stimulus. It is indeed striking that, in spite of an increase in the PSBR of the order of 6 per cent of GDP, and distinctly faster expansion of export markets, real GDP grew by only 4 per cent in the two years to 1985 (OECD, 1986 p. 65).

This lack of responsiveness is attributed to a number of factors: 'institutional bottlenecks, bureaucratic attitudes, labour market rigidities, failure to innovate, poor management and inefficient use of financial resources are important obstacles undermining the growth potential of the economy and perpetuating inflationary pressures' (p. 66). The same survey concludes by raising the issue of credibility, pointing out that:

> much will depend on the behaviour of economic agents and on the extent to which confidence will improve. For lasting results to be achieved, adjustment policies will have to be pursued over several years. Chances of success would be enhanced if there was a better recognition by the general public that the national collectivity cannot continue to live beyond its means and, accordingly, greater willingness to accept the needed sacrifices (p. 67).

The 1987 survey hammers the message home that structural and institutional impediments must be removed and that there is a need for 'a relative shift of resources from public and private consumption to investment and from sheltered activities to the exposed sectors' (OECD, 1987 p. 52). Until these conditions are achieved and in the presence of macroeconomic imbalances, restrictive demand-management policies are recommended. It is unfortunately the case that little progress has been made in implementing these suggestions. So much so that, as recently as July 1989, the EC Commissioner Henning Christophersen used unusually dramatic expressions to describe the state of the Greek economy which, he said, 'is today critical and unless the necessary stabilisation measures are taken it will not be possible to prevent an explosive increase of the public debt and to restore the conditions necessary for healthy growth' (translated from Greek quotation in *Oeconomicos Tachydromos*, 27 July 1989). Finally, in a report on the state of the Greek economy, the governor of the Bank of Greece estimated that the borrowing needs of the public sector in 1989 were likely to go up by four percentage points, reaching or even exceeding 20 per cent of GDP. He suggested that domestic loanable funds would be inadequate to meet this demand and expressed his concern about the potential size of monetary expansion and the need to maintain high interest rates, despite their adverse effect in crowding out private investment.

3 LESSONS FOR THE FUTURE

3.1 False Expectations

The PASOK experiment appears to have been a failure. The evidence suggests a misplaced reliance on fiscal policy – not simply as a means of economic stabilisation and income redistribution, but also as a manifestation of a more active and permanent role of the state in the economy. The potential adverse effects of budget deficits and of increasing taxation in the form of higher inflation, falling profit margins and crowding out of private capital formation have not been fully addressed. Quick changes in policy, lack of clear direction, the absence of a consistently pursued medium-term strategy and a systematic and reckless manipulation of the economy for electoral success are not the means by which a government gains in credibility or inspires confidence. The poor public-sector productivity, laggard bureaucracy and widespread political expediency are not good omens for increased efficiency when the public sector is expanding in an attempt to replace parts of the private sector. Although reliable evidence is hard to come by, it appears that great expectations placed on the concept of socialisation, industrial subsidies and the bailing out of companies on the verge of bankruptcy were not justified by the results. On the contrary it seems that the takeover of 'problematic' companies by the state has increased the burden on the public budget. The economic viability of most of these companies is in doubt, but no resolution on their future was made because of the obvious impact on unemployment and the resistance of the employees. Another manifestation of political expediency was the unnecessary and hurried expansion of public-sector employment just before the general election earlier this year.

3.2 Proposed Government Action

In the light of 1992 it is urgent that the existing imbalances in the economy be removed. An efficiency and rationalisation drive in the public sector must lead to substantial economies which, in conjunction with a simplified tax system and a reduction in tax evasion, would lead to a fall in budget deficits and in the public-sector share of expenditure. An incomes policy could be applied until the rate of inflation is brought down in line with EC inflation rates. The above would help in extending deregulation of the banking and financial markets.

The most fundamental problem of productivity and restructuring is not one that can be improved substantially in the short run. But the state can help in a number of ways. First, it should adopt a medium-term fiscal and financial strategy that avoids excesses, provides a feasible measure of stability and reduces uncertainty; the strategy could allow for a response to external shocks and the implications of business cycles, especially in terms of the appropriate fiscal stance. Second, it should pursue a cost–benefit approach towards the abolition of those regulations and controls that introduce rigidities and substantial inefficiencies in labour, financial and trade markets in general. Third, it should introduce a more up-to-date and sufficiently responsive educational system to meet the needs of a rapidly changing technology, training and retraining programmes as well as systematic programmes for replicating good practices and technological innovations originating in other countries; the aim of the latter measures should be to reduce spells of unemployment and increase labour mobility. The social dimension of the state's role will include redistributive policies, the provision of a decent level of income for the victims of economic recession and economic restructuring.

The failure of macroeconomic management has meant that the Greek economy approaches 1992 in a bad state. A major contributing factor to this failure was the inability or unwillingness of the PASOK governments to pursue the policies repeatedly recommended by the OECD. Similar policies were adopted by Greece's EC partners with some success. In the course of implementing such policies some sacrifices, especially in the form of increased unemployment, were accepted as inevitable. It appears that Greece in the 1980s was not prepared to accept such inevitable economic consequences. In the light of past experience, the institutional discipline implied by the forthcoming European integration may be especially beneficial to Greece. Such institutions as the exchange rate mechanism (ERM) and eventually the adoption of a single currency and a European central bank will be dominated by countries that are more successful economically and, it may be added, more mature politically than modern Greece. In other words the loss of sovereignty implied by integration and seemingly resisted by some EC countries, especially the UK, may not be bad for Greece. For example, full membership of the EMS by Greece would mean that the relative ease with which high inflation and a sliding currency were tolerated will no longer be an option. The cost of a strict monetary or fiscal policy with the probable fall in employment would seem to be more acceptable if it appeared to be imposed by external bodies. But a reduction of the power and discretion of the Greek state may also be helped by an increase in the relative autonomy of some internal institutions, such as the banking sector, the Bank of Greece, national television and radio.

The gap between Greece and the rest of the EC, in terms of standards of living, productivity and efficiency of markets, has grown wider in the last eight years. Macroeconomic mismanagement and little, if any, progress on the supply side of the economy are the main reasons. As a result the prospects for the future of the Greek economy do not seem to be very encouraging at the moment. Unless these issues are addressed in a serious and rational manner Greece will lag further behind its EC partners.

3.3   Medium-Term Strategy

In the light of the above and in view of the fast approaching integration of Greece into the Single European Market the degrees of freedom of any government are limited. Thus, in the short term, a medium-term strategy should be adopted, announced and pursued consistently. The aims should include the following measures:

- a gradual but substantial reduction in budget deficits and inflation; in the short run taxation may need to go up and public expenditure should be reduced; the reduction of inflation could be achieved either through an incomes policy or monetary restraint, or both;
- supply-side measures, such as education and training programmes, should be introduced; unnecessary regulation and controls, especially those relating to the labour and financial markets should be abolished; this does not of course include regulations in cases of market failures, as with, for example, public goods, externalities, monopolies or environmental issues;
- privatisation of a large part of publicly owned companies;
- reduction of overmanning in the public sector and initiation of a concerted efficiency drive;
- increased confidence in the government and reduced uncertainty – both necessary for increasing capital formation in the private sector.

An increase in unemployment in the short run may be an inevitable cost of such a strategy. But the experience of the UK, Spain and Ireland indicates that the political cost to the party that pursues such a policy may not be unduly high – indeed there may be a gain in popularity in recognition of its political courage and forthrightness.

Drawing a long-run scenario – or attempting a long-run forecast – is a much more difficult task. The scale of government intervention in the economy should obviously depend on the quality and efficiency of government as well as the parameters set in the context of the EC. If Stages 2 and 3 of the Delors Plan are implemented, questions of monetary, regional and industrial policy may not be the unlimited prerogative of national governments. However, in terms of economic prospects, recent experience from small EC countries suggests that, as long as serious imbalances are substantially improved and gains in competitiveness and the confidence of the private sector are achieved, standards of living can exhibit a satisfactory upward trend.

References

Corliras, P. (see also Koliras, P.) (1986) 'The economics of stagflation and transformation in Greece', ch. 3 in Z. Tzannatos, (ed.), *Socialism in Greece* (Aldershot: Gower).

Katseli, L. (1986) 'Building a Process of Democratic Planning', in Tzannatos, Z. (ed.), *Socialism in Greece* (Aldershot: Gower).

OECD (1983, 1986, 1987) *Surveys of the Greek Economy* (Paris: OECD).

Oeconomicos Tachydromos (1989) Athens, 27 July, p. 6.

Papandreou, A. (1979) *Transition to Socialism* (Athens: PASOK Press Office) in Greek.

Vaitsos, C. (1986) 'Problems and Policies of Industrialisation', in Tzannatos, Z. (ed.), *Socialism in Greece* (Aldershot: Gower).

6 Monetary Policy and Financial Markets in the 1990s

E 52

Lucas Papademos

BANK OF GREECE AND UNIVERSITY OF ATHENS

1 INTRODUCTION

This paper deals with certain fundamental issues concerning the formulation and conduct of monetary policy in Greece over the coming years. In the 1990s monetary policy should have two central objectives: monetary stability and financial efficiency. The first macroeconomic objective calls for rapid disinflation and restoration of external balance. The second objective, which is microeconomic in nature, requires the further liberalisation and development of domestic financial markets and their integration in the European financial system. The attainment of these two objectives is of vital importance for the stabilisation and recovery of the Greek economy. It is also essential for the country's participation in the process of economic and monetary union (EMU) in the European Community (EC). During the first stage of EMU, beginning on 1 July 1990, the drachma was to participate in the European monetary system (EMS) exchange rate mechanism (ERM) and the Greek financial markets were to be integrated in the single European financial area.

The twin objectives of monetary stability and financial efficiency need to be pursued simultaneously. That is necessary not only because these goals are equally urgent, but also because the effectiveness with which monetary policy can achieve its macroeconomic objectives depends on the structure and efficient functioning of the financial markets. It should be stressed, however, that, in the short run, certain conflicts and trade-offs might arise between the two goals. Policy action must be timed carefully and prudently to avoid inducing instability in the financial markets, which could result from liberalisation measures taken at a time when financial markets were in a state of severe disequilibrium and uncertainty concerning economic policy.

The paper has been organised as follows. Section 2 deals with issues relating to the design and conduct of monetary policy aimed at disinflation and external equilibrium. It discusses the choice of final and intermediate policy targets, the use and effectiveness of policy instruments and the constraints imposed on monetary management by fiscal policy. Section 3 addresses issues relating to the participation of the drachma in the ERM of the EMS. In particular, it discusses the likely effects of full EMS participation on the effectiveness of monetary policy, the revenue from seigniorage and the debt accumulation process. It also examines the implications of further planned deregulation of domestic financial markets and the abolition of exchange controls for the timing of the ERM entry. Section 4 focuses on the financial markets and institutions and outlines a programme of financial liberalisation to promote monetary stability and the process of European financial integration.

2   TARGETS AND INSTRUMENTS OF MONETARY POLICY

2.1   Final objectives: Disinflation and External Equilibrium

The primary objective of monetary policy over the coming years should be the reduction of inflation to a rate close to the Community average. In addition, monetary policy should contribute to the restoration and main-tenance of equilibrium in the balance of payments. The importance of these final policy objectives is obvious for a country that has experienced con-tinuous high inflation, persistent balance of payments disequilibria and rapidly rising external debt over the previous ten years. Inflation rates in the 1980s, despite the progress made in containing inflationary pressures over certain periods, remained consistently above the average rate of the member states of the EC, especially those participating in the ERM. Similarly, the current account deficit as a percentage of GDP remained large in most years of the past decade, causing a fast rise in external debt.

The attainment of monetary stability, both internal and external, as the fundamental macroeconomic objective of monetary policy needs to be stated publicly and explicitly in order to avoid misunderstandings concerning the role and responsibility of monetary policy, and to avoid any potential conflict from the pursuit of other policy goals. It is, of course, recognised that other policies, especially incomes policy, can affect the inflationary process more directly and promptly than monetary policy in the short run. Moreover monetary policy cannot by itself contain inflationary pressures successfully unless it is accompanied by compatible fiscal and incomes policies. Nevertheless the price level and average inflation are fundamentally determined by monetary factors in the long run. Fiscal and other economic policies can influence inflation in the long run only through their effects on average output growth and trend velocity. Consequently monetary policy should be made primarily responsible for the control of inflation, the variable over which it exercises a dominating influence in the long run.

Monetary policy should support the other general government economic policies, without jeopardising the commitment to the objective of monetary stability. Monetary policy has occasionally been employed, both in Greece and in other countries, to stimulate investment and output growth, and in certain cases to foster the development of specific activities or sectors. This usually implies pursuing a policy of low real interest rates and/or the imposition of credit rules to channel financial resources into specific economic activities or sectors at preferential terms. But low real interest rates cannot be maintained for long periods without jeopardising the attainment of monetary stability, both internal and external. The level of real interest rates is determined in the long run primarily by real factors, including the demand for real financial resources; it cannot be controlled permanently by regulating the nominal supply of financial aggregates. Consequently, although monetary policy can influence the level of real interest rates in the short run, it cannot control it effectively and systematically in the long run. Indeed the level of real interest rates can be influenced more effectively by fiscal policy, that is, by influencing the demand for real credit by the public sector and through appropriate changes in the policy mix. As regards the role and efficiency of specialised credit rules and regulations to support specific economic activities, the experience in many economies, including Greece, has not been favourable, at least not in the medium term. Moreover specialised credit controls are economically inefficient and in the future it will be impossible to enforce them in the context of a unified European financial market.

2.2   Intermediate Targets and Policy Instruments

To attain the final policy objectives it is essential that the rate of monetary and credit expansion should be steadily reduced over the coming years to levels compatible with the planned deceleration of inflation and nominal income growth. It is also necessary to pursue an exchange rate policy that is consistent with the projected convergence of domestic and foreign inflation, the targeting of monetary aggregates and the requirement for external balance.

The choice of the appropriate intermediate monetary targets depends critically on the stochastic stability of the relationship between these targets and the final policy objectives. It also depends on the extent to which the intermediate targets are controllable by the instruments of policy. Empirical analysis suggests that, in the case of Greece, a broad monetary aggregate bears a more stable relationship to nominal income than the narrower measures of the money stock. On the basis of the criterion of its stochastic stability to nominal GDP, broad money (M3) can be a useful intermediate target and policy indicator.[1] Nevertheless this broad monetary aggregate is not sufficient as an intermediate target; nor is it likely that it can continue to be an efficient policy indicator in the future. The insufficiency of an M3 target is due to the effects of the external sector on money creation.

For the Greek economy, which is characterised by persistent external imbalances, the twin final targets of nominal GDP growth and equilibrium in the basic balance of payments requires the adoption of two intermediate targets: M3 growth and domestic credit expansion (DCE). These two intermediate targets together allow for the joint monitoring of nominal income and balance of payments developments and provide a better means for assessing the stance and likely effects of monetary policy on the economy. However the efficiency of the M3 aggregate as an intermediate target and indicator is likely to be impaired in the coming years by the ongoing financial deregulation, the abolition of exchange controls and the development of non-bank financial markets. These developments, by affecting the structure of the financial markets and the behaviour of market participants, will undermine the stability of the relationship between M3 and nominal income. The monitoring and targeting of a broad monetary aggregate should not be abandoned, but the choice and use of an intermediate monetary target should be made carefully, taking into account the need for flexibility and, both *ex ante* and *ex post*, the effects of changes in the economy's financial structure. The chosen broad monetary target should be monitored and interpreted in conjunction with other financial aggregates and indicators.

It would be useful to adopt target ranges for the intermediate objectives of monetary policy over a medium-term horizon of three years. A medium-term 'monetary programme', consistent with the projected deceleration of inflation and the minimum requirement of equilibrium in the basic external balance, would contribute to a better coordination of monetary and fiscal policies, especially in the light of the Greek government's recently announced fiscal consolidation programme. It could also contribute to the disinflation process by favourably influencing inflationary expectations and the decisions of participants in the labour and capital markets. However the announcement of a medium-term monetary programme would have a positive effect on expectations and the process of disinflation only if it were perceived as credible and if it were successfully enforced over time.

The credibility of a monetary policy formulated in terms of intermediate monetary targets depends on the ability of the central bank to achieve these targets, or at least minimise the extent to which outcomes deviate from targets within a range determined by uncontrollable and unanticipated events. This in turn depends on three factors: the existence of policy instruments which can be effectively employed to control the evolution of the targeted financial aggregates, the credibility of fiscal policy, and the stability of the relationships between the final and intermediate targets and the instruments of policy. In the event of uncertainty about fiscal policy in the medium term, or if there is reason to believe that the economy's financial structure and the behaviour of market participants will not be stable owing to the planned deregulation and development of the domestic financial markets and the removal of exchange controls, the announcement of a medium-term monetary programme is unlikely to be credible or enforceable. In that case it should be avoided. Nevertheless the adoption of such a programme internally by the central bank would prove useful for monitoring and interpreting monetary developments and policies, and provide the means of ensuring the consistency of the fiscal consolidation programme aimed at disinflation and external balance.

Exchange-rate policy can and should contribute to disinflation by maintaining its anti-inflationary orientation, but without inducing systematic losses in competitiveness. An important requirement for the conduct of an anti-inflationary exchange rate policy is that it be consistent and co-ordinated with incomes policy and aggregate demand management. The significant loss of competitiveness over the last two years, however, raises an important question deserving further analysis, namely the sustainability of an anti-inflationary exchange-rate policy, given the prevailing level of the effective exchange rate and the projected containment of aggregate demand pressures.

3   EMS, EMU AND MONETARY POLICY

Monetary and financial policies in the 1990s will have to evolve within the framework of the EMS and be consistent with Greece's participation in the process of EMU in the Community. This process gained considerable momentum in 1989. The report of the Delors Committee (1989) proposed concrete stages leading towards the progressive realisation of EMU. The European Council, at its meetings in Madrid in June 1989 and Strasbourg in December 1989, decided that the first stage of EMU would be launched on 1 July 1990, followed by an inter-governmental conference in December 1990 to prepare a new Treaty for the implementation of the second and final stage of EMU.

The first stage of EMU aims at greater convergence of economic policies and performance within the existing institutional framework. In the monetary field, the principal objectives are: (i) the creation of a single financial area, in which all monetary and financial instruments can circulate freely and all financial services are offered uniformly; and (ii) the inclusion of all Community currencies in the ERM. In addition all impediment to the private use of the ECU will be removed and, in order to strengthen the coordination of monetary policies, the mandate of the Committee of Central Bank Governors will be broadened in scope, the status of the Committee will be strengthened and its work will be supported by the creation of a research unit and three sub-committees on monetary policy, foreign exchange policy and banking supervision policy. Thus the main, urgent tasks ahead for Greece in the monetary field are participation of the drachma in the ERM and enforcement of the Community directives concerning the full liberalisation of capital movements and the free provision of financial services.

There are two essential prerequisites for participation in the ERM and the full liberalisation of capital movements: the convergence of nominal magnitudes and further liberalisation and development of domestic financial markets. The monetary strategy outlined above and the programme for financial deregulation and reform described below are designed to establish the essential conditions for a successful and viable participation in the first stage of EMU. Given the prevailing macroeconomic imbalances and the state of financial markets, it is envisaged that the necessary preconditions for ERM entry could be established by 1993. The remaining part of this section addresses a number of policy issues pertinent to the choice of the 'right approach' and the 'right time' for the drachma's participation in the ERM, which have been discussed more fully by Papademos (1990).

3.1 Discipline, Credibility and Disinflation

Full membership in the EMS should provide the change to the system necessary for imposing 'discipline' on economic policies, limiting political business cycles and facilitating the attainment of monetary stability in Greece. It could be argued that the immediate accession of Greece to the

EMS as a full member would accomplish these aims by inducing changes in the behaviour of both the public and the policy makers, by influencing expectations and making disinflation policy more credible and thus more effective. The positive role of the EMS in imposing monetary discipline and promoting disinflation is generally accepted. It is supported by the experience of a number of countries, including France, Italy and Ireland, where ERM participation served as a catalyst for disinflation, as ably discussed by Giavazzi and Pagano (1988), although some analyses of the empirical evidence yield rather mixed conclusions; see, for example, Collins (1988), De Grauwe (1986), Giavazzi and Giovannini (1988) and Russo and Tullio (1988).

The extent to which early ERM entry will enhance the credibility of economic policies and force nominal convergence depends on a number of factors, notably the magnitude of divergence before entry, the structure and functioning of labour markets, and the prospects for introducing a consistent package of fiscal, monetary and structural policies. In the case of Greece, imbalances are very large and require substantial policy adjustment, especially in the fiscal area. If the necessary radical change in the stance of fiscal policy cannot take place promptly, then premature full EMS membership could undermine the credibility of economic policies and lead to instability. Moreover it is doubtful whether the behaviour of the labour unions would be sufficiently affected by ERM entry if inflation were substantially higher than the Community average. In a country with a long history of high inflation, trade unions are not likely to respond appropriately and promptly to the new exchange-rate regime, especially if fiscal consolidation appears uncertain. This would result either in financial instability or in substantial and prolonged unemployment, in the event that policy became restrictive contrary to expectations.

Given the present state of the Greek economy, the right approach to full EMS membership is first to achieve greater convergence by implementing a consistent, credible set of economic policies and then to participate in the ERM. This approach does not imply that it would be optimal to postpone participation until inflation is reduced and stabilised at the average level of the ERM countries. Although an overdose of EMS discipline could be hazardous to the economy if applied before sufficient convergence is achieved, Greece should take advantage of the discipline that the EMS can impose on domestic policy as soon as this is deemed feasible and viable. Thus, as inflation approaches the highest level experienced by other ERM members, it would be desirable to join the ERM within the wider 6 per cent band, provided that consistent economic policies are pursued. It would be more effective to join as soon as feasible so as to consolidate the progress made towards inflation convergence, rather than postpone entry with the aim of joining within the narrow band. Early participation within the wider band would also help minimise potential employment losses, which could be substantial in an inflation-prone country. The Irish experience has amply demonstrated that, although a hard-currency policy can ultimately be successful, it may entail high unemployment costs over a long period as shown by Dornbusch (1989).

3.2 Public Finance and the EMS

Another issue which is relevant to the choice of the 'right time' for a country like Greece to become a full member relates to the effects of ERM participation on public finances, in particular the revenue from seigniorage and the debt accumulation process. This issue has recently been emphasised by a number of economists, notably Dornbusch (1988), who pointed out that in southern Europe 'the quest for disinflation has been pursued without recognition of the long-term budget consequences'. He has argued that, in a country with a debt problem, which is presumably related to an inefficient tax structure, there is scope for financing a large budget deficit by means of relatively moderate rates of inflation, provided the velocity of high-powered money is low. Rapid disinflation, by reducing the revenue from money creation, would accelerate the growth of debt, unless compensated by fiscal measures. Moreover a higher degree of exchange-rate fixity could require a higher level of real interest rates, which would further speed up the debt accumulation process both directly, by increasing the interest payments on debt, and indirectly, by reducing the demand for high-powered money and the growth rate of output. Dornbusch therefore concluded that it would not be optimal for a 'low-velocity' country with a debt problem to aim at achieving average ERM inflation, at least not until appropriate fiscal measures were adopted to lower the 'optimal' inflation rate.

This view has been challenged by, among others, Gros (1989) and Thygesen (1988). Gros noted that the benefits from seigniorage rest on the assumption that a country is in a position to choose the optimal amount of seigniorage. In a country with high public debt, however, the authorities have an incentive to reduce the real cost of debt servicing through unanticipated inflation. On the other hand, an informed public aware of this incentive would expect higher inflation, which would prevent the authorities from choosing the 'optimal' inflation rate. Thus, for a country with high public debt, which is usually much larger than the monetary base, the potential revenue from unanticipated inflation is more important than the revenue from seigniorage. Consequently such a country would gain from ERM participation which would effectively eliminate the use of surprise inflation to reduce the real cost of public debt. In addition Thygesen (1988) has argued that a country, by joining the ERM, might be able to lower real interest rates, thus enhancing the sustainability of public debt. If a country did not join the ERM and instead adopted a 'crawling peg' exchange-rate policy, the burden of ensuring the stability of inflation would be borne by domestic monetary policy.

In the case of Greece, a country with high public debt, where money creation is a relatively important source of government revenue, ERM participation could destabilise the debt accumulation process, with serious implications for the conduct of monetary policy. Over the last decade, the revenue from seigniorage has been significant, estimated at 2–3 per cent of GDP (Dornbusch, 1988; Giavazzi, 1989). To reduce the deficit and money financing by raising tax revenue is a formidable task, which could take a long time to achieve, as it requires the broadening of the tax base rather than an increase in the already high tax rates on incomes and transactions. In addition, since the maturity of the public debt is very short, unanticipated inflation would not help reduce the debt burden significantly. These facts lend support to the argument made by Dornbusch that, for a country like Greece, it would not be 'optimal' to aim at early ERM entry. However this argument should not be interpreted as implying that policy makers face a trade-off between relatively high inflation, which is optimal from a public finance point of view, given the prevailing tax structure, and the lower inflation implied by participation in the ERM. The long-term benefits from full EMS participation clearly outweigh the short-term gains from the inflation tax and the political cost of tax reform for a country with a narrow tax base and a high public deficit. The problem that must be faced as a result of the loss of seigniorage after joining the ERM is important, but primarily relevant during the transition towards lower inflation and a more efficient and equitable tax structure. To prevent the rapid accumulation of further debt, it is essential to reform the fiscal system and reduce the public deficit substantially before the drachma enters the ERM. The disinflation required for ERM entry should be achieved with a policy mix that does not rely excessively on monetary policy, so as to avoid high real interest rates which would aggravate the debt accumulation problem. It has also been suggested that a country that relies on the inflation tax and faces difficulties in changing its tax structure promptly could increase reserve requirements during the transition period so as to widen the base of seigniorage and thus compensate for the lower inflation (Giavazzi, 1989).

To assess quantitatively the implications of alternative policies for the debt accumulation process and the convergence of inflation towards the ERM average, the model presented in Papademos (1990) specifies the determinants of the dynamic behaviour of public debt and the mechanism through which changes in the economy's financial and fiscal structure affect the means and cost of financing the public-sector deficit.

3.3 Financial Deregulation and Exchange Controls

The ongoing deregulation of domestic financial markets and the planned progressive abolition of exchange controls have important implications for the drachma's entry into the ERM. With respect to financial deregulation there are two interrelated issues. First, financial deregulation must be completed before ERM entry so as to improve the functioning of money and foreign exchange markets and allow the central bank to influence them more effectively through market-oriented control instruments. Despite substantial progress towards the deregulation and liberalisation of the financial system in recent years, there are a number of key regulations and constraints which still impair the efficient functioning of markets and undermine the effectiveness of monetary policy. Although interest rates on government securities are more market-related than in the past, they are still set by the fiscal authorities and do not fully reflect market conditions. This limits the central bank's capacity to influence the general level of interest rates promptly and efficiently or to counteract the effects of the public-sector deficit on money creation. Following the drachma's entry into the ERM, the monetary authorities should be in a position to employ interest rate policy flexibly so as to maintain the exchange rate within the permitted fluctuation range. Full EMS membership requires that interest rate policy be assigned primarily to the attainment of exchange-rate stability and be implemented efficiently so as to offset transitory exchange-rate fluctuations in the short run and help establish the monetary conditions necessary for exchange-rate stability in the long run.

A second implication of the process of financial deregulation is the desirability of full EMS participation at an early stage, as it will tend to improve the effectiveness of monetary policy in reducing unpredictable fluctuations in nominal income. Financial deregulation and liberalisation inevitably affect the stability of the relationships between monetary and credit aggregates and nominal income. In the presence of financial shocks, monetary policy can achieve a nominal income objective more effectively by employing the exchange rate rather than a monetary aggregate as an intermediate target (Artis and Currie, 1981). On the other hand, financial liberalisation – in particular the abolition of restrictions on bank portfolios and the market determination of interest rates on government securities – is likely to result in higher interest rates, with unfavourable consequences for the debt accumulation process. Financial liberalisation must be advanced before ERM entry. This in turn will enhance the efficiency of monetary management, but also underscores the importance of accelerating the efforts for tax reform and fiscal consolidation.

The Greek economy is still subject to considerable constraint on capital movements. Exchange controls are to be progressively abolished by 1992 and domestic financial markets will be integrated into the single European market. Some restriction on short-term capital movements may be retained until 1995, subject to the approval of the European Commission, provided that this is warranted by unfavourable economic conditions. Exchange controls allow monetary authorities a certain degree of independence in the conduct of monetary policy within the EMS. The extra room for manoeuvre could be helpful in the period immediately after ERM entry, especially if fiscal policy and wage and price setting behaviour failed to adapt to the requirements of the ERM. If capital controls were removed before the drachma's entry into the ERM, economic policies would have to be fully compatible with the ERM or would have to be adjusted appropriately and promptly in the face of speculative pressures to prevent a realignment. It could thus be argued that ERM entry before the removal of all capital controls offers certain advantages. However this is not necessary, especially if credible and consistent economic policies are pursued when the drachma joins the ERM. Moreover the opposite argument could be made, namely that exchange controls should be fully abolished before the drachma joins the ERM, as the economy could adapt better to the liberalisation of capital movements if the exchange rate were allowed to move flexibly and absorb the effects of potentially sizeable portfolio shifts, which could occur in a country with a long history of strict exchange control.

The effects of financial deregulation and capital liberalisation before and after ERM entry depend on the economy's financial structure, the behavioural characteristics of market participants, expectations and the stance of actual and anticipated economic policies. An assessment of these effects is possible using the simulation model constructed by Papademos (1990), a model which approximates the present financial structure of the Greek economy and its evolution following the gradual liberalisation of domestic financial markets and the abolition of exchange controls.

4 THE FUTURE FOR FINANCIAL MARKETS AND INSTITUTIONS

The financial markets and institutions in Greece have been transformed during the last decade, nevertheless further change will be required to ensure their efficient operation and ability to assume an important role in the single European financial market. In the early 1980s, the Greek financial system was strictly regulated, exhibiting all the characteristics usually associated with a 'repressed financial system'. The salient features were:

1. A very small capital market and non-existent non-bank money market. About 90 per cent of private savings were channelled through the banking system, the only effective source of finance for both the private and public sectors.
2. An oligopolistic and largely state-controlled banking industry. In 1985 it comprised thirty-three commercial banks (fourteen Greek and nineteen foreign) and eight specialist credit institutions. The three largest financial institutions (the National Bank, the Agricultural Bank and the Commercial Bank) together accounted for 61 per cent of total private deposits and 62 per cent of all loans to the private sector. Eight of the commercial banks, including the three largest, and all the specialist credit institutions were state controlled.
3. Interest rates on all categories of bank deposits and loans were set centrally. The monetary authorities did not always respond promptly or consistently to changing market conditions, which frequently resulted in negative real rates over long periods.
4. The allocation of financial resources by the banking system was determined according to a complex set of rules and regulations. These included a general portfolio allocation requirement that commercial banks earmark a specific proportion of their deposits for investment in government securities, to finance public enterprises as well as small and medium-sized firms, and long-term loans to industry. In 1985, these portfolio requirements restricted the allocation of 71 per cent of deposits; in addition to which, commercial banks were also subject to a primary reserve requirement of 7 per cent of total deposits. The amount of credit commercial banks could extend to various sectors of

the economy or types of economic activity, and the loan terms were subjected to additional conditions other than the interest rate. The overall credit expansion of the specialist credit institutions was subject to quantitative ceilings, while some of these institutions operated under special regulations and were heavily dependent on the central bank for funds.

5. All foreign exchange transactions were strictly controlled. Long-term and short-term capital movements by Greek residents were not generally allowed.

These features of the financial system, which were interrelated, were largely a consequence of the existing regulatory economic environment. In particular, the administrative setting of interest rates and the quantitative restrictions on credit allocation restricted competition, the development of the money and capital markets and required strict credit rules, and a complex system of reserves and rebates on bank assets. The increasingly large fiscal deficits of the first half of the 1980s influenced the setting of interest rates and the retention of compulsory investment in treasury bills by commercial banks. During this period, the public sector deficit was financed exclusively by the domestic banking system and foreign borrowings.

Since the mid-1980s, a series of financial liberalisation measures have substantially improved the functioning of the financial markets. Financial liberalisation was a gradual process. It involved: (i) the raising of interest rates on deposits, loans and government securities to market-clearing levels; (ii) the simplification of credit rules; (iii) the partial abolition of interest rate ceilings; (iv) the partial elimination of quantitative restrictions on credit allocation; and (v) the progressive easing of foreign exchange controls, first on non-residents and second on residents. A more detailed description of the process of financial reform over the last five years is given in Chalikias (1987) and in various issues of the *Annual Report* of the Bank of Greece.

As a result of these liberalisation measures, the financial system is now far less controlled or regulated than five years ago, and interest rates on most categories of bank deposit and loan have been liberalised. Virtually all specialised credit rules and regulations have been abolished; the complex reserve–rebate system on bank loans has been dismantled; some of the general restrictions on bank portfolios have been lifted – for example, the requirement that commercial banks allocate 15 per cent of their deposits to long-term loans to industry at preferential rates. The domestic financial system has been opened up to capital flows by non-residents and in part by residents; and the non-bank money and capital markets have developed considerably. Lastly, the government has reduced its reliance on the banking system to finance its deficit.

Nevertheless, despite this progress, the Greek financial system is still subject to severe restrictions, which cause distortions, inhibit the development of a competitive environment, impair the efficient functioning of the financial markets and reduce the effectiveness of monetary policy instruments.

The general level and structure of interest rates are still influenced by the central setting of interest rates on government securities and general restrictions on bank portfolios. Although since 1987 the government has paid high, market-related rates on its securities, the rates on three-month treasury bills, held primarily by banks, do not fully reflect market conditions. Consequently, banks are still required to invest a proportion of their deposits in such securities and the central bank has to finance, at least temporarily, the residual part of the government's deficit, which cannot be financed by banks or the market at the set interest rates. However this is limited by a law which prohibits the outstanding amount of central bank advances to the government from exceeding 10 per cent of budgeted expenditure. Nevertheless, the flexibility and effectiveness of monetary policy are still impaired by this compulsory financing of the public sector deficit by the commercial banks at preferential interest rates, together with the mechanism of making central bank advances to government which temporarily solves the government's borrowing requirement. The inflexible setting of interest rates on government securities, the existence of minimum interest rates on savings deposits and bank loans, and the compulsory investment ratios cause serious distortions in the system. One undesirable consequence is that the private sector subsidises the public sector, by paying higher interest rates because of the enormous size of the public sector deficit.

The first priority, therefore, in the process of financial reform must be a radical change in government funding policy. The fiscal deficit should be financed at rates that fully reflect market conditions; that is prices, and thus yields from government securities, should be adjusted to equate demand by the public and the banks with the government's borrowing requirement. Minimum interest rates on savings deposits and bank loans could be abolished once the yield on government securities is market determined and the central bank is able to influence the general level of interest rates through open market operations.

A second important objective of financial reform in the 1990s should be the elimination of general portfolio requirements imposed on commercial banks. These requirements, as distinct from the largely abolished special controls and regulations, are still very high. Since the beginning of 1990,

49 per cent of all commercial bank deposits (in drachmas and foreign exchange) have been earmarked to finance government and public sector enterprises and organisations, and 10 per cent of drachma deposits have been earmarked for loans to small and medium-sized firms. In addition to these portfolio requirements there is an 8 per cent primary reserve requirement imposed on total commercial bank deposits in order to control the broad measure of the money stock. This means that 67 per cent of all deposits remain subject to control. The most onerous and distorting restriction is that compelling commercial banks to invest 40 per cent of all their deposits in treasury bills. The compulsory financing of public enterprises is less binding in practice and does not adversely affect bank profits in general, since interest rates on loans to public enterprises are already freely set by the banks. The earmarking of commercial banks' deposits for the financing of small and medium-sized firms at preferential rates could be eliminated without causing serious difficulties, because banks are at present reluctant to lend to such firms (following the liberalisation of most interest rates on loans and the dismantling of the reserve–rebate system which equalised the effective return to banks on different types of loan).

Compulsory investment requirements should be eliminated as soon as possible, so that Greek banks can adapt to and compete freely in the single European financial market. The elimination of compulsory investment requirements implies a simultaneous change in the government's funding policies as outlined above. An immediate and complete elimination of compulsory investment in government securities is not feasible at present, because of the sizeable claims of the commercial banks on the government. Moreover although the public sector borrowing requirement (PSBR) is likely to remain substantial for some time, it should be gradually reduced. This reduction could initially be applied to the increment of bank deposits, in order to eliminate compulsory investment at the margin within one or two years. Clearly the banks' holdings of government securities associated with the outstanding stock of deposits when the marginal reduction in portfolio requirement begins, will progressively decline as a percentage of the growing stock of deposits. The outstanding stock of treasury bills held by banks could be converted into medium-term marketable debt instruments, possibly of different maturities to be traded freely by banks.

In order to improve the efficiency of the financial markets in the 1990s some financial institutions will need restructuring, together with fundamental changes in the general environment in which financial institutions operate. Competitive conditions need to be enhanced. To perform efficiently in the competitive integrated financial market of the 1990s, some state-controlled banks must restructure their portfolios, strengthen their capital base and improve their management techniques. They should also be allowed to function on the basis of economic criteria without political interference. For example specific forms of intervention, such as the subsidisation of interest rates on categories of assets and liabilities of the specialist credit institutions, or the imposition of a specific tax on banks' interest income should be abolished. More importantly, the administrations of state-controlled banks should not be subjected to political pressure adversely affecting the management of both their portfolios and their labour resources. The high level of non-performing assets at present held by some state-controlled banks largely reflects decisions taken on political rather than banking criteria. Experience in many countries has amply demonstrated that political intervention is not compatible with the efficient functioning of financial institutions.

The liberalisation of Greek financial markets and their integration into the European financial market will also pose new challenges for the Bank of Greece. Monetary policy will in future have to rely exclusively on market-oriented, indirect means of monetary control. The supervisory role of the Bank must be further enhanced by effective supervision of the financial institutions in the new deregulated environment. In the past, the task of the supervisory authorities was to ensure that the specific rules and regulations constraining bank operations were complied with. There was less emphasis on assessing the quality of a bank's portfolio or any comprehensive evaluation of its capital adequacy. A change of orientation is obviously needed. A new supervisory framework has already been designed but not yet implemented. The implementation of an effective supervisory system is essential for the efficient functioning and stability of the financial system in the new, deregulated and competitive environment of the 1990s.

5   CONCLUDING REMARKS

In the past decade, monetary policy aided the containment of large and persistent macroeconomic imbalances, while the Bank of Greece introduced a series of important structural measures aimed at the gradual deregulation of the financial system. In the 1990s, with the EC march towards economic and monetary union, the monetary authorities will need to pursue with vigour the twin objectives of monetary stability and financial efficiency.

This paper has addressed various issues relating to the challenge facing monetary policy in the 1990s. Section 2 focused on topics associated with the formulation and implementation of a stability-oriented monetary policy, as for example the effectiveness of monetary aggregates as intermediate targets or the role of exchange rate policy in the disinflation process. Section 3 dealt with issues pertaining to the participation of the drachma in the EMS exchange rate mechanism and discussed the conditions essential for successful and viable participation in the ERM. It examined the implications of full EMS membership on the anti-inflationary monetary policy, the dynamics of the debt accumulation process and the monetary-fiscal policy mix; and it considered the consequences of the deregulation of domestic financial markets and the progressive abolition of exchange controls for the conduct of monetary policy and the timing of the drachma's entry into the ERM. Section 4 outlined the principal features of the Greek financial system, the progress in recent years towards deregulation, the major steps required to complete the process of financial liberalisation and the conditions needed to restructure the Greek financial system.

Two general conclusions emerge from this analysis. First, financial reform and a stability-oriented monetary policy ought to be pursued simultaneously. However full liberalisation of the financial markets and the complete abolition of all capital controls in the presence of macroeconomic disequilibria and uncertainty regarding the direction of economic policy could lead to further financial instability. In particular, the rapid liberalisation of the financial markets before reducing the public sector deficit to sustainable levels could be risky. On the other hand, the process of financial reform must not become hostage to the public sector deficit or a fiscal policy reluctant to adopt the required structural measures for fiscal consolidation, because of the preferential treatment the public sector currently enjoys from financial regulations and exchange controls. Although the timing of financial liberalisation measures should be compatible with the stabilisation of the economy, the pace of financial reform should progress fast enough to enable market forces to act as a catalyst to the speeding up of the stabilisation effort by exerting greater discipline on economic policy. Further, the completion of the single European financial market by the end of 1992 imposes an important time constraint which will influence the pace of the financial liberalisation and restructuring process.

The second general conclusion is that the effectiveness of a stability-oriented monetary policy in Greece will depend on its consistency and credibility. These aspects would be strengthened by an improved policy mix designed to reduce the excessive burden on monetary policy, together with institutional reforms aimed at freeing the central bank from political interference. Confidence in monetary policy would be enhanced by both these factors, and aid the attainment of low inflation and external balance, without jeopardising economic growth.

Note

1. Narrow monetary aggregates are not reliable indicators and cannot serve as effective intermediate targets. In particular, currency in circulation is not a useful intermediate target owing to the instability of its velocity relation to nominal income and also because it cannot be effectively controlled, being demand-determined.

References

Artis, M. J. and Currie, D. A. (1981) 'Monetary Targets and the Exchange Rate: A Case for Conditional Targets', *Oxford Economic Papers*, 33, Supplement, pp. 176–203.

Chalikias, D. (1987) *Financial Reform and Problems of Monetary Policy*, Papers and Lecture Series, No. 59 (Athens: Bank of Greece).

Collins, S. M. (1988) 'Inflation and the European Monetary System', in Giavazzi, F., Micossi, S. and Miller, M. (eds), *The European Monetary System* (Cambridge: Cambridge University Press) pp. 112–36.

De Grauwe, P. (1986) 'Fiscal Policies in the EMS: A Strategic Analysis', International Economics Research Paper, no. 53, Catholic University of Louvain.

Delors Committee for the Study of Economic and Monetary Union (1989) *Report on Economic and Monetary Union in the European Community*.

Dornbusch, R. (1988) 'The European Monetary System, the dollar and the yen', in Giavazzi, F., Micossi, S. and Miller, M. (eds), *The European Monetary System* (Cambridge: Cambridge University Press) pp. 23–41.

Dornbusch, R. (1989) 'Credibility, Debt and Unemployment: Ireland's Failed Stabilization', *Economic Policy*, no. 8, pp. 173–209.

Giavazzi, F. (1989) 'The Exchange Rate Question in Europe', in Bryant, R. C. *et al.* (eds), *Macroeconomic Policies in an Interdependent World*, (Washington DC: The Brookings Institution, the Centre for Economic Policy Research and the International Monetary Fund) pp. 283–304.

Giavazzi, F. and Giovannini, A. (1988) 'The Role of the Exchange Rate Regime in Disinflation: Empirical Evidence on the European Monetary System', in Giavazzi, F., Micossi, S. and Miller, M. (eds), *The European Monetary System* (Cambridge: Cambridge University Press) pp. 85–107.

Giavazzi, F. and Pagano, M. (1988) 'The Advantage of Tying One's Hands: EMS Discipline and Central Bank Credibility', *European Economic Review*, vol. 32, no. 5, pp. 1055–82.

Gros, D. (1989) 'Seigniorage and EMS Discipline', paper presented at the Conference on 'The EMS in the 1990s', Athens, 31 August–2 September 1989.

Papademos, L. (1990) 'Greece and the EMS: Issues, Prospects and a Framework for Analysis', in De Grauwe, P. and Papademos, L. (eds), *The European Monetary System in the 1990's* (London: Longman) pp. 251–82.

Russo, M. and Tullio G. (1988) 'Monetary Policy Coordination within the EMS: Is there a Rule?', in Giavazzi, F., Micossi, S. and Miller, M. (eds), *The European Monetary System*, (Cambridge: Cambridge University Press) pp. 292–356.

Thygesen, N. (1988) 'Introduction', in Giavazzi, F., Micossi, S. and Miller, M. (eds), *The European Monetary System* (Cambridge: Cambridge University Press) pp. 1–20.

7 Financial Liberalisation, the EMS and the Consequences for Greek Macroeconomic Policy*

George D. Demopoulos
ATHENS UNIVERSITY OF ECONOMICS AND BUSINESS

1 INTRODUCTION

This paper studies the entry of Greece into the European Monetary System (EMS) under two alternative methodologies. The first, dealing with the necessary conditions of a possible entry of a country into the EMS, provides a series of processes in obtaining estimates of economic variables that would have been consistent with exchange-rate stability as discussed by Korteweg (1980). However this approach does not differentiate the economies which participate in a monetary union according to their structural characteristics.

The economies of the member states of the European Community (EC) and especially those of southern Europe display different structural characteristics from those of the northern EC countries. The former may be characterised as 'fiscally weak' countries because of their high budget deficits and large public debt, inefficient tax-collection systems and extensive underground economies. These special structural characteristics can be better analysed in the context of a second methodology which deals with the welfare gains of a country from the EMS discipline (Giavazzi, 1989; Gros, 1989; Torres, 1989).

This paper is organised as follows: Section 2 discusses briefly the European internal market and the European financial area as proposed by the Single European Act of 1985. Section 3 refers to Greece's position regarding its participation in the EMS. Section 4 studies the necessary conditions of a possible entry of Greece into the system. Section 5 explores the welfare gains of the country under two alternative policy scenarios: (i) a monetary discipline – the EMS, and (ii) a discretionary regime. The policy conclusions are reported in the last section.

2 THE EUROPEAN INTERNAL MARKET AND THE EUROPEAN FINANCIAL AREA

The Single European Act adopted in December 1985 has set a target of 1992 for the completion of the internal market.[1] For goods and services this means the removal of physical, technical and fiscal barriers within Europe. 'The detailed measures of these non-tariff barriers were set out in a White Paper which specified the precise programme, timetable and methods for creating a unified economic area in which persons, goods, services and capital would be able to move freely.' Free trade in goods and services will increase gains from trade and specialisation as well as competition. It will promote efficiency and choice.

The economic arguments which point to benefits from the mobility of labour are known. The Single European Act reaffirmed the need to harmonise working conditions with respect to health and safety standards, to promote dialogue between management and labour, to establish rules for the co-ordination of national social security systems and to prevent migrant workers from within the Community suffering discrimination or loss of cumulative benefits. The question of the convergence of labour costs is vital in the context of increasing monetary integration. However these labour market issues might insulate insider workers from direct competition in the labour market and hence encourage them to press for even higher pay. In competitive industries such efforts may drive the firm out of business.

The Single European Act establishes the European Financial Area. The latter rests on two sets of reforms now under way. The first is complete liberalisation of capital movements within the Community, establishing a single market in financial assets. The second is free competition in the provision of financial services within the Community (both implemented by 1 July 1990, except for the three newest member states which are expected to join by the end of 1992).

But, with the full freedom of capital movement and integrated financial markets, incompatible national macroeconomic policies could quickly translate into exchange rate tensions and put an increasing and undue burden on monetary policy. The EMS cannot continue operating as before. Once Europeans accepted the abolition of controls on capital movements, they were formally committed to strengthening the EMS arrangements. This presupposes a much greater coordination of monetary and interest rates policies.

A tighter EMS may pave the way for the monetary union to which EC governments are already formally committed. A monetary union cannot be accomplished without a third condition, namely 'the elimination of margins of fluctuations and the irrevocable locking of exchange rate parities'. As a result of this condition, national currencies would become increasingly close substitutes and their interest rates would tend to converge.

The establishment of a monetary union presupposes the need for a common monetary policy. Responsibility for the single monetary policy would have to be vested in a new institution: the so-called European System of Central Banks. The monetary union also presupposes the full participation of all currencies of member countries in the exchange rate mechanism (ERM) of the EMS.

Whether we have a tighter EMS or a monetary union, national autonomy in the conduct of economic policy will be sacrificed for a cooperative exchange rate and cooperative monetary policy. That is, the objectives of national economies will become more dependent on a cooperative approach to policy making.

3   GREECE AND THE EMS

The entry of Greece into the EMS is one of the important issues the Greek authorities have to face in the very near future. Since September 1984, the drachma is part of the basket of European currencies which constitute the European currency unit (ECU); but it does not participate in the main feature of the EMS, the ERM.

The participation of the drachma in the ECU obliges the Greek government to follow a policy of converging the growth of the Greek economy with that of the other member states of the EC. This is interpreted to mean that the Greek government has to follow an economic policy that will minimise the disequilibrium differences that now exist in various macroeconomic aggregates between the Greek economy and the economies of the other member states. This will entail the following: a drastic reduction of the current account deficit; the reduction of the public sector borrowing requirement to gross domestic product (PSBR/GDP) ratio; the reduction in inflation differences, and so on.[2]

On the other hand, participation of the drachma in the ERM presupposes that it is always feasible to have a stable exchange rate relationship of the drachma versus EMS currencies. This imposes a restriction that cannot be met unless the causes that lead the Greek currency to a continuous devaluation *vis-à-vis* the EMS currencies disappear altogether.

In the next section, the economic and financial situation in Greece and the necessary conditions of possible entry into the EMS are discussed.

4 THE NECESSARY CONDITIONS OF A POSSIBLE ENTRY OF
GREECE INTO THE EMS

4.1 Monetary and Exchange Rate Developments

Monetary developments in Greece in recent years have been dominated by
the PSBR, which derives from the financial needs of general government
and public enterprises (Demopoulos, 1983).

The explosion of the PSBR since 1981 (it increased from 8.4 per cent as
a percentage of GDP in 1980 to 16.0 per cent in 1988) was partly financed
by increased recourse to external borrowing corresponding to a growing
current account deficit in the balance of payments, but it also led to a
substantial acceleration of the money supply. The authorities sought to
retain some control over the situation by holding back bank credit to the
private sector (it was reduced from 30.8 per cent on an annual basis in 1981
to 15.2 per cent by the end of 1988). This implies that since 1981 the larger
share of bank credit expansion has gone to the public sector. This is also
confirmed by the ratio of domestic credit expansion in the private sector to
the total bank credit (private and public) which has decreased from 45.7 per
cent in 1981 to 34.0 per cent in 1988.

The monetary financing of the PSBR has consequently led to an acceleration of the money supply (M3) since 1981. This excessive expansion of
the money supply has had undesirable effects on domestic balances, increasing the differential consumer price inflation rates between Greece and
EMS countries from 8.5 per cent for the period 1974–80 to 13.5 per cent
during the period after 1981.

As for exchange rates, the widening of the differential inflation rates
induced nominal depreciation of the drachma, as competition tends to
ensure that prices of tradable goods, expressed in a common currency, will
be the same everywhere.

In Table 7.1 actual inflation rates are compared with the inflation rates
that would have been consistent with nominal exchange rate stability of the
drachma given the German inflation rate. Consistent inflation rates are
calculated by subtracting from the German inflation rate the real exchange
rate changes of drachma against the Deutschmark (DM) (Korteweg, 1979,
1980).

It is obvious that actual inflation rates are expected to be much higher
than those which would have been consistent with stable nominal exchange
rates of the drachma against the DM. If Greece had joined the EMS in 1988,
one could say that the inflation differential would have stabilised around

Table 7.1   Actual, consistent and excess inflation rates (annual percentage change)

Year	Actual inflation rates	Consistent inflation rates	Excess inflation rates
1981	24.5	19.9	4.6
1982	21.0	8.7	12.3
1983	20.2	− 5.1	25.3
1984	18.4	3.5	14.9
1985	19.3	0.8	18.5
1986	23.0	−14.5	37.5
1987	16.4	− 0.5	16.9
1988	13.5	6.3	7.2
Period average	19.5	2.4	17.2

Source: IMF, *IFS Yearbook 1988* (May 1989).

6 per cent for the stability of the nominal exchange rate of the drachma against the DM.

Let me turn now to the monetary policy followed by the Greek monetary authorities. The first two columns of Table 7.2 summarise the past record of growth of the money supply (M1) and the growth of real GDP respectively, while the third column gives the monetary expansion in excess of output growth.

This excess monetary expansion, given the velocity of money, translates itself on average into inflation to the extent shown by the 'inflation-money multiplier' in the last column of Table 7.2.

Dividing the consistent inflation rates by the inflation-money multiplier we obtain the money growth per unit of output which would have been roughly consistent with stable exchange rates of drachma against the DM. These figures are given in Table 7.3.

It is evident that the Greek monetary authorities have pursued too loose a monetary policy relative to the policy that would have been consistent with exchange-rate stability. On average, actual money growth per unit of output has been higher than the consistent growth by almost 15 percentage points.

The above analysis clearly indicates that participation of Greece in the EMS means, first of all, that the Greek authorities will have to commit themselves to coordinating monetary policy with that of the other member countries, in order to establish inflation rates consistent with nominal ex-

Table 7.2   Monetary growth (M1) per unit of output in Greece
(annual percentage change)

Year	Actual monetary growth	Output growth	Monetary growth per unit of output	Inflation-money multiplier
1981	18.3	0.1	18.2	1.35
1982	24.8	0.4	24.4	0.87
1983	12.5	0.4	12.1	1.67
1984	15.0	2.7	12.3	1.50
1985	21.4	3.1	18.3	1.06
1986	16.0	1.2	14.8	1.55
1987	16.7	−0.4	17.1	0.96
Period average	17.8	1.1	16.7	1.3

Source: IMF, *IFS Yearbook 1988* (May 1989) and Commission of the European
Communities, *European Economy* (May–June 1989).

Table 7.3   Monetary growth (M1) per unit of output consistent with exchange
rate stability (annual percentage change)

Year	Consistent monetary growth per unit of output (1)	Excess monetary growth per unit of output (2)
1981	14.8	3.5
1982	10.0	14.4
1983	−3.1	15.2
1984	2.4	9.9
1985	0.8	17.5
1986	−9.2	24.0
1987	−0.5	17.6
Period average	2.2	14.6

Source: Tables 7.1 and 7.2.

change rate stability; that is, inflation differences that will exactly compensate for movements in the real exchange rate of the drachma.

4.2 Trade and the Balance of Payments

Another condition for possible entry of a country into a monetary union is related to the structural characteristics of the current account balance. Before considering that, let us describe the developments in the exchange rate of the drachma. Table 7.4 gives the average annual bilateral exchange rate changes of the drachma against the US and EC currencies, both in nominal and in real terms.

The exchange rate changes for the period before 1981 reflect the choices of the Greek monetary authorities rather than real economic factors relating to the state of the Greek economy. Particularly in the case of real exchange rate changes of the drachma, the interpretation of the data is not clear and

Table 7.4   Exchange rate of drachma against foreign currencies
(average annual percentage change)

| | *Nominal* | | *Real* | |
	1975–80	*1981–8*	*1975–80*	*1981–8*
US$	6.2	17.0	–0.7	2.2
Belgian franc	11.3	13.5	2.8	–1.2
Danish kroner	7.5	14.2	1.9	1.2
Deutschmark	12.5	17.2	1.0	0.1
French franc	8.6	10.3	3.4	0.2
Dutch florin	11.6	16.8	2.4	–1.0
Irish punt	4.1	12.3	3.4	1.7
Lira	1.6	85.6	1.6	1.9
Luxembourg franc	11.3	13.5	2.2	–1.4
£ sterling	6.5	13.0	6.6	–2.1

Notes:
1. Real exchange rate changes are the nominal exchange rate changes minus the rate of domestic consumer price inflation plus the rate of foreign consumer price inflation.
2. A positive sign indicates depreciation of drachma against the currency shown, while a negative sign indicates an appreciation.

Sources: IMF, *IFS*, various issues; OECD, *Economic Outlook* (June 1988).

straightforward, since we cannot know, *a priori*, the extent to which *ex post* changes in real exchange rates reflect changes induced by endogenous real factors rather than specific exchange rate choices by the Bank of Greece. However the evidence presented for the post-1981 period is of much greater interest, since during this period the parities of the drachma were mainly determined by the exchange market.

During the period 1975–80 a policy was pursued of devaluation of the drachma, both in nominal and in real terms (with the exception of the real appreciation of the drachma against the US dollar). The nominal devaluation of the drachma increased sharply after 1981; devaluation in real terms was, on the other hand, rather slight, while in the case of parities against the Belgian franc, Dutch florin, Luxembourg franc, and pound sterling, the drachma experienced a real appreciation.

Furthermore the devaluation of the drachma in terms of the nominal effective exchange rates against 19 countries reported in the European Economy was 7.74 per cent on average for the period 1975–80, while it increased to 14.36 per cent for the period 1981–6.

The devaluation of the drachma against the European currencies and the US dollar reported above was theoretically expected to improve the competitiveness and the balance of payments position of the Greek economy. However the evidence does not seem to confirm this theoretical argument. Table 7.5 shows the division of the growth of trade (measured as a percentage of GDP at current market prices) between intra-Community and extra-Community trade. These developments have been rather unfavourable; the growth of exports of goods and services declined after 1981, while the

Table 7.5   Average annual growth of trade in Greece
(percentage of GDP at current market prices)

	1974–80	1981–8
Growth of exports of goods and services	5.95	1.44
Growth of intra-community exports of goods	4.35	6.47*
Growth of extra-community exports of goods	9.64	−4.52*
Growth of imports of goods and services	0.61	2.69
Growth of intra-community imports of goods	1.45	6.31*
Growth of extra-community imports of goods	6.82	−4.21*

* 1981–7.

Source: Commission of the European Communities, *European Economy* (November 1988).

growth of imports increased during the same period. Relative to the growth of exports and imports of goods and services, intra-Community trade growth increased after 1981, while extra-Community trade growth declined dramatically, leading to negative growth rates of exports and imports.

Let us now turn to the balance of payments position of the Greek economy. Table 7.6 shows the current (goods, services and transfer payments) and trade balances. Both the trade balance and the current balance have been in deficit since 1974. Both deficits have increased in the post-1981 period.

These unfavourable developments, which were undoubtedly a restraining factor in the growth process in Greece, can be considered the result of the destabilising economic conditions that prevailed in the world economy (and to which Greece is more vulnerable than other EC countries) and the structural deficiencies of the Greek economy. It has been argued (Drakos, 1984; Demopoulos, 1989) that the inadequate management of the devalua-

Table 7.6 Trade balance and current balance of Greece (billions US$)

	Trade balance	Current balance
1974	−2.885	−1.141
1975	−3.042	−0.953
1976	−3.333	−0.933
1977	−3.903	−1.075
1978	−4.343	−0.949
1979	−6.178	−1.907
1980	−6.809	−2.211
Average 1974–80	−4.356	−1.309
1981	−6.697	−2.409
1982	−5.927	−1.891
1983	−5.386	−1.879
1984	−5.351	−2.122
1985	−6.268	−3.280
1986	−5.686	−1.670
1987	−6.942	−1.220
1988	−7.631	−1.010
Average 1981–8	−6.236	−1.935

Source: Bank of Greece, *Report of the Governor* (various issues); OECD, *Economic Outlook* (June 1989).

tion policy of the drachma as a means of restraining the balance of payments deficits must be attributed to the policy of continuous monetary expansion; the final outcome of this combination of policies has been a 'vicious circle' of devaluation–inflation, with a sharp increase in the latter. This is why Korliras (1985) and Demopoulos (1989) have argued that an active policy of controlling the endogenous mechanisms that cause the inflationary process to be 'self-feedback' should be in effect, if the exchange rate policy is to be effective in restraining the balance of payments deficits and stabilising the economy.

5   WELFARE GAINS FOR GREECE FROM THE DISCIPLINE OF THE EMS

It has been argued (Giavazzi and Pagano, 1988) that high inflation countries may find it worthwhile to join a system promoting monetary stability such as the EMS, because of the gain derived by linking their currencies to the currency of a low inflation country. For the high inflation countries, participation in the EMS discipline could be a better means to pursue disinflation than a flexible–discretionary anti-inflationary policy, on the grounds of the gain of reputation derived from the EMS.

On the other hand, the costs of high inflation countries in embracing a low inflation monetary arrangement like the EMS arise from the loss of their freedom to follow flexible discretionary policies; if the costs are too high, embracing the EMS may lead to a deterioration in welfare in the participating country. These costs depend, however, on the structural characteristics of the economy of the specific country.

Indeed countries with inefficient tax-collection systems and a large public debt, called 'fiscally weak' countries, may not require monetary discipline since they can derive seigniorage revenues to finance their increasing expenditures through the exercise of their discretionary and unanticipated policies. Therefore, it has been argued, particularly by Dornbusch (1988) and Giavazzi (1989) that the EMS is worth joining if the authorities do not seek to extract seigniorage revenue from their fiscal system. It has even been argued that, for 'fiscally weak' countries, a quick convergence to a low inflation EMS may cause distortions to the existing tax system by raising marginal tax rates. Thus 'fiscally weak' countries should, if they choose to remain in the EMS, adopt a 'crawling-peg' policy *vis-à-vis* the fiscally strong members that would allow for a higher inflation rate and an optimal level of seigniorage (Dornbusch, 1988; Gros, 1989; Torres, 1989).

Greece, like Italy, Spain and Portugal, is classified as a 'fiscally weak' economy with high budget deficits and a large public debt, an inefficient tax-collection system, rampant tax evasion and an extensive black economy. Those structural characteristics have become a major source of concern for Greece in terms of designing a stabilisation programme for the economy and examining possible entry into the EMS. High public debt levels and money creation remain a significant source of government revenue. The possibility that participation in the EMS may substantially reduce the revenue from seigniorage, and thus destabilise the budget, is an important argument against possible participation of the drachma in the ERM of the EMS.

The observation made by Gros (1989) and Torres (1989) that even 'fiscally weak' countries can gain from the EMS discipline in terms of welfare relative to a flexible discretionary policy outside the EMS gives rise to the analysis that follows.

5.1   The Greek Public Debt Dynamics

The necessity for 'fiscally weak' countries to manage a discretionary policy with the purpose of deriving seigniorage revenues through higher inflation can be shown by studying the government's budget constraint (Giavazzi 1989; Gros 1989; Torres 1989) using the following equation:

$$D(B_t) = (G_t - T_t) + rB_t - D(H_t)/P_t \tag{1}$$

Dividing (1) by GDP we obtain,

$$D(b_t) = (g_t - t_t) + (r - n)b_t - D(H_t)/P_t Y_t \tag{2}$$

where the left-hand side of this equation represents the growth rate of the public debt to GDP ratio (b_t), while the right-hand side gives the sources of the increase in the debt to GDP ratio, as follows: (i) the primary deficit (spending g_t minus interest and debt amortisation payments minus taxes t_t) as a proportion of GDP; (ii) the debt service ratio, that is, the *ex post* real interest rate, which is equal to interest payments r as a percentage of GDP net of GDP growth rate n, multiplied by the debt to GDP ratio; and (iii) the seigniorage revenue which is equal to the change in the monetary base $D(H_t)$ as a proportion of GDP.

Table 7.7 gives the dynamic evolution of the Greek public debt for the period 1980–8. The growth rate of the public debt to GDP ratio does not remain constant. The sustainability of the public debt equation relies,

Table 7.7 The Greek debt accumulation equation

	$D(b_t)$ (1)	$(g_t\text{-}t_t)$ (2)	$(r\text{-}n)b_t$ (3)	$D(H_t)/GDP$ (4)	Residual (5)
1980	42.3	4.3	7.5	4.4	34.9
1981	75.0	12.0	47.0	7.2	22.3
1982	−13.6	8.6	30.5	5.3	−47.4
1983	−10.2	8.8	39.9	2.1	−56.8
1984	35.1	8.2	30.8	5.5	1.6
1985	16.2	10.5	44.7	1.1	−37.9
1986	−21.7	7.3	67.2	3.2	−93.0
1987	−5.7	7.5	102.9	4.5	−111.6
1988	−21.2	10.7	−	−	−

Notes:
(1) is the growth rate of PSBR as a proportion of GDP.
(2) is the primary deficit as a proportion of GDP.
(3) is the interest rate (interest payments as percentage of GDP) net of GDP growth rate multiplied by the PSBR/GDP ratio.
(4) is the change of monetary base as a proportion of GDP.
(5) is the residual of the equation, namely the difference between actual and fitted values of public debt: (5) = (1) − (2) − (3) + (4).

Source: Bank of Greece, *Monthly Statistical Bulletin* (various issues).

however, on the ability of the government to generate primary surpluses to keep the debt to GDP ratio constant. The evidence shows that the primary deficit as a proportion of GDP keeps increasing, resulting in a substantial increase in the size of the residuals as shown in column 5.

The main destabilised source of the size of the Greek public debt to GDP ratio is the growing positive contribution of the debt service ratio $(r - n)b_t$ shown in Column (3). This suggests that the ratio has reached an almost uncontrollable situation. The explosion of the debt (PSBR) since 1981 was partly financed by increased recourse to external borrowing, but it also led to a substantial acceleration of the money supply. Column (4) suggests that the loose monetary policy exercised produced seigniorage revenues.

On the other hand, the low GDP growth rates experienced point to the structural weaknesses of the Greek economy and to problems in stabilising the debt service ratio.

In summary, the data presented above suggest that Greece relies on seigniorage revenues to service the debt and that it would have to sacrifice a percentage of its GDP on seigniorage if it were to join the EMS discipline.

The next section discusses whether the loss of seigniorage revenue from the EMS discipline also represents a welfare loss.

5.2 Minimisation of Welfare Loss: Discretionary Equilibrium versus EMS Discipline

In order to answer the question of whether a 'fiscally weak' Greece can gain from the EMS discipline we follow the methodology adopted by Gros (1989). Starting from the basic theoretical principles of optimal control, Gros's methodology employs a comparative analysis of costs and benefits, in terms of social welfare, that are derived from a country's participation in a currency area – such as the EMS. He formulates and solves two different dynamic problems of economic policy planning which are related to two alternative regimes: (i) under a monetary discipline – the EMS, and (ii) under a flexible discretionary policy. Both are solved by the method of optimisation, that is, minimisation of the social welfare loss function subject to the government's budget constraints.

In other words, the decision of a 'fiscally weak' country to participate in the EMS presupposes a comparative analysis of the minimal welfare loss for the country under either a discretionary regime or an EMS discipline. If the minimal loss is lower under the second policy than under the first one, then the country will obtain substantial benefits by entering the EMS.

Applying Gros's methodology to the relevant data for Greece in 1987, we find that the welfare loss to the Greek economy from participation in the EMS would have been about 9.1 per cent lower than if it had remained under a discretionary regime.[3]

Given that the public debt to GDP ratio for Greece is projected to be about 86 per cent by 1990, it is calculated that the welfare loss to the country from joining the EMS would have been even lower – by 17.2 per cent. This indicates that Greece's participation in the EMS would lead to a substantial welfare gain relative to a discretionary equilibrium outside the EMS.

6   POLICY CONCLUSIONS

The participation of the drachma in the ERM of the EMS needs macroeconomic stabilisation policies that would adjust the Greek economy to the level compatible with that of its partners by 1992.

Of course, a strong anti-inflationary policy might have negative effects on the real development of the economy, a fact that would make such a policy politically unpopular. On the other hand, participation in the EMS could be a better means of implementing such an anti-inflationary policy at a lower political cost – as in the case of France and Italy – on the grounds of the gain in reputation derived from the EMS and the Bundesbank. In this case, however, the Bank of Greece should follow a policy of real exchange rate appreciation of the drachma, especially with respect to the Deutschmark.

However this gain in reputation is only one aspect of embracing the EMS arrangements (Fratianni, 1988); the final outcome crucially depends on the loss in competitiveness implied by real exchange-rate appreciation, the value of the inflation tax and the present value of real output loss due to inflation variability.

These forces should be very seriously considered in deciding on EMS membership for Greece. A loss in Greece's competitiveness, as implied by the real appreciation of the drachma, would worsen the already unfavourable balance of payments position. In addition a cut in the inflation tax would be quite a serious problem since the Greek authorities seem to extract considerable revenues from inflation. Finally a loss in real output due to high inflation variability would slow down the already unsatisfactory growth performance of the Greek economy, with consequent adverse effects on employment.

Thus what seems to be of great interest is the examination of the disinflation possibilities in Greece through stabilisation policies which will not have negative effects on real output and employment growth, as well as on the competitiveness of the Greek economy. A 'soft-landing' scenario could be the adoption of an early disinflation policy, say by a reduction in budget deficits. The latter could also be thought of as a necessary condition for establishing the feasibility of Greece's entry into the EMS, since the implied loss in monetary autonomy implies that the government will lose its power to extract unlimited amounts of money from the banking system to finance its budgets.

The question to be answered is whether the reduction in budget deficits could be achieved without a loss in real output and employment. Alexander and Demopoulos (1989) argue that a permanent decrease in government expenditure growth in Greece can have only positive stabilisation effects. It reduces inflation and stimulates real output via a reduction in inflationary expectations. This seems to be a very tempting starting-point for a disinflation process. Stabilising the Greek inflation rate at the level of its EC partners would allow the Greek economy to experience a desirable reduction in the exchange-rate variability, resulting in a more stable real exchange rate.

An alternative policy to guarantee a permanent reduction in the growth rate of government expenditure could be the earliest participation of the drachma in the ERM of the EMS. This does not necessarily mean that the inflation differential and the differential in the labour cost per unit of output between Greece and the EMS countries must first be reduced to zero. These arguments refer to the necessary conditions of a possible entry of a currency into a monetary zone, as analysed in section 4 of this paper. This method of analysis, however, does not differentiate economies according to their structural characteristics.

Greece is characterised as a 'fiscally weak' country and, consequently, the proposition of early participation of the drachma in the EMS discipline is also supported by the findings of this paper, which point to substantial welfare gains for the Greek economy relative to a discretionary equilibrium outside the EMS.

Notes

*   This is part of a research project on 'Greece and the EMS' financed by the Economic Research Center, The Athens School of Economics and Business. Special thanks should be expressed to my former graduate students Sophia Lazaretou, P. Kapopoulos and Z. Psaradakis for their research assistance and valuable suggestions.

1.   This section draws heavily on the Delors Report (1989) and Begg's paper (1989).
2.   For a detailed analysis of the macroeconomic aggregates of the Greek economy see Alexander and Demopoulos (1989), and Demopoulos (1989).
3.   These data have been taken from IMF: IFS, *Statistical Yearbook 1988*, lines 14, 99b, 99bip, 81; and OECD: *Economic Outlook*, 1989.

References

Alexander, V. and Demopoulos, G. D. (1989) *Stabilization Policies in Greece in the Context of Modern Macroeconomic Theory* (Berlin: Duncker and Humblot GmbH).

Begg, David (1989) '1992 and the European Financial Area: Consequences for Macroeconomic Policy', inaugural lecture given at Birkbeck College, London, 9 February.

Delors, J. (1989) *Report on Economic and Monetary Union in the European Community*. Committee for the Study of Economic and Monetary Union, 12 April.

Demopoulos, G. D. (1983) 'Financial Markets and Institutions in Greece', *European Economy*, no. 15, March, pp. 145–55.

Demopoulos, G. D. (1989) 'Stabilisation Policies in Greece in the Context of the Economic and Monetary Union in the European Community', a lecture delivered at The Chamber of Commerce and Industry, Thessaloniki, 24 November (in Greek).

Dornbusch, R. (1988) 'The EMS, the Dollar and the Yen', in Giavazzi, F., Micossi, S. and Miller, M. (eds), *The European Monetary System* (Cambridge: Cambridge University Press).

Drakos, G. E. (1984) 'Economic Policy in Theory and the Greek Practice', *Eleftheri Kinonia*, Sept.–Oct. (in Greek).

Fratianni, M. (1988) 'The European Monetary System: How Well has it Worked?', discussion paper, no. 384, Indiana University.

Giavazzi, F. (1989) 'The Exchange Rate Question in Europe', Economic Papers, no. 74. Commission of the European Communities, Directorate-General for Economic and Financial Affairs, Brussels.

Giavazzi, F. and Pagano, M. (1988) 'The Advantage of Tying One's Hands: EMS Discipline through Central Bank Credibility', *European Economic Review*, vol. 32, no. 5, June, pp. 1055–82.

Gros, D. (1989) 'Seigniorage and EMS Discipline', prepared for the joint CEPS/Bank of Greece Conference on the EMS, Athens, 31 August–2 September.

International Monetary Fund, *International Financial Statistics* (Washington DC) various issues.

Korliras, P. (1985) 'The Balance of Payments in Greece', Archive of Studies and Speeches, no. 50, (Athens: Bank of Greece) in Greek.

Korteweg, P. (1979) 'The European Monetary System: Will it Really Bring more Monetary Stability for Europe?', Working Paper, Institute for Economic Research, Erasmus University, Rotterdam, May.

Korteweg, P. (1980) 'Exchange-Rate Policy, Monetary Policy and Real Exchange Rate Variability', Essays in International Finance, no. 40, International Finance Section, Princeton University.

Torres, F. (1989) 'Portugal, the EMS and 1992: Stabilization and Liberalization', prepared for the joint CEPS/Bank of Greece Conference on the EMS, Athens, 31 August–2 September.

8 Some Thoughts on the Current State and Prospects of the Greek Commercial Banking System

Evangelos A. Voloudakis

DEREE COLLEGE, ATHENS

1 INTRODUCTION

The commercial banking system in Greece cannot be said to have developed in a competitive environment, particularly during the postwar period, when it was forced to operate under tight credit rules, not to mention endless political interference, which finally led to its quasi-nationalisation. From being a mere distributional network of the financial resources – new money and counterpart funds of foreign aid – of the Bank of Greece, unable to mobilise private savings mainly as a consequence of wartime hyperinflation, it turned into a highly liquid banking system as saving deposits poured in at spectacular rates with the stabilisation of the economy and a steep rise in the deposit interest rate in 1956.

This financial affluence and its role as the main vehicle for the sectoral allocation of resources helped it to maintain a dominant influence on the country's financial system, though at the cost of having to comply with an ever-expanding maze of rules and regulations. As a consequence, the Greek commercial banking system, protected from foreign competition and oligopolistic in its structure, passive in its funding and highly constrained in its asset management, remained until recently innocently unaware of the revolutionary changes that have been taking place since the mid-1970s in the international banking industry.

Partly through emulation, but mainly as a result of the pressure that followed Greece's membership of the European Community (EC) and the prospective economic and financial integration of the European market by the middle 1990s, a slow but quite visible process of liberalisation and readjustment has started. This paper attempts to evaluate the current state of the Greek commercial banking system and the progress made so far; to draw some basic inferences with respect to its future prospects within the new financial environment of the 1990s; and to make some policy suggestions for a smoother process of readjustment.

The paper is organised as follows: section 2 highlights some of the salient features of the Greek banking system and compares the Greek with the Italian system, which is similar in many respects. The focus is on four major topics: the asset structure, operating efficiency and profitability, capital adequacy and, finally, financial innovations. In section 3, proposals are put forward for amending the Greek banking system, indicating the areas in which improvements are most urgently needed and suggesting some policy steps. The paper closes with a word of caution which brings the whole issue closer to current Greek economic reality.

2 SOME SALIENT FEATURES OF THE GREEK COMMERCIAL BANKING SYSTEM

2.1 Asset Structure, Liquidity and Earning Capacity

The asset structure of the Greek commercial banking system has changed dramatically during the last two decades. As Table 8.1 shows, while in 1970 the basic structure of total assets of the commercial banks was quite close to international standards (compare the first and last columns), in 1988 it exhibited a highly distorted pattern. Thus the share of government securities, already relatively high, doubled between 1970 and 1988 to exceed 30 per cent. Furthermore the ratio of total liquid assets (which include cash in vault and required and other reserves in drachmas and foreign exchange) to total assets almost tripled. These increases were at the expense of the share of loans, which dropped from 62 per cent in 1970 to only 32 per cent in 1988. This diminution of the private sector was the result of the Bank of Greece's credit policies, which were aimed mainly at accommodating the steadily increasing public sector borrowing requirement and, to a lesser extent, at promoting the finance of especially favoured sectors, such as small-scale industries or public enterprises.

Without underrating the importance of recent steps towards liberalisation as, for instance, the abolition of the complex system of reserves on credit and the proportion of deposits earmarked for long-term financing of industry under special terms, the room for free asset management remains extremely limited, since only about one-third of deposits are not subject to any control. The ratio of primary reserve requirements is 8 per cent, the

Table 8.1   The asset structure of commercial banks (per cent)

	Assets	1970	Greece 1980	1988	Italy 1988	USA 1988
1.	Reserves etc.	8.5	16.2	25.6	12.6	7.4
2.	Government securities	15.2	22.1	32.1	2.6	11.4
3.	Loans	61.9	51.4	32.3	53.6	67.8
4.	Other securities	5.2	3.1	4.0	22.5	6.8
5.	Other assets	9.2	7.2	6.0	8.7	6.6

Sources: Bank of Greece, *Long-term Statistics of the Greek Economy* (1989); Bank of Italy, *Annual Report for the Year 1988*, (1989); W. Brocci (1989); *Federal Reserve Bulletin* (June 1988).

secondary reserve requirements ratio in treasury bills is 38 per cent, the ratio earmarked for financing small-scale industry is 10 per cent and the corresponding ratio for financing public enterprises stands at 10.5 per cent. To a varying degree, all these assets earn an interest rate smaller or at best equal to the nominal cost of funds collected by the banking system. The heavy hand of the Bank of Greece on their profitability is a constant complaint of most banks – particularly the quasi-nationalised (National Bank of Greece, 1989). Indeed their loans to deposit ratio was close to 37 per cent in 1988, compared to 66–77 per cent for the Italian banks (Brocci, 1989), suggesting a much smaller earning capacity.

From another point of view, the Greek commercial banking system appears to be one of the most liquid systems. Compared with the Italian commercial banks, for instance, the total sum of the primary and secondary liquidity ratios is about three times higher than in the Italian case (54 per cent as against 17 per cent in 1988). Still this high liquidity ratio scarcely reflects the effective liquidity of banks in Greece, since not only is a reserve ratio required but also, because of the shallowness of the treasury bills market, any attempt to liquidate a significant portion would have been rather costly, if possible at all. This situation has been somewhat ameliorated by the recent introduction of repurchase agreements (RPs) in treasury bills among banks, but this liquidity improvement refers, of course, only to individual banks, not to the system as a whole. Further, as is pointed out below, this lopsided asset structure is likely to have had another important effect on the banks' portfolio as far as its performance is concerned.

2.2 Operating Efficiency and Profitability

All indicators suggest that the operating efficiency of the Greek commercial banks is still well below international standards. Although efficiency is one of the most difficult attributes to measure, some evidence can be drawn from indices such as the value of intermediate financial resources per employee, resources per unit of personnel cost or resources per unit of total operating cost. These indices for the five major Greek commercial banks and the corresponding ratios for the Italian banking system are presented in Table 8.2. It should be noted that the figures for the group of five Greek banks are representative of the whole Greek commercial banking system, since their assets account for about 90 per cent of its total assets. The relative size of the individual banks in the sample was as follows: National Bank 56.2 per cent, Commercial Bank 14.8 per cent, Ionian Bank 8.0 per cent, Credit Bank 7.5 per cent and Ergo Bank 2.8 per cent.

Although these indices are only indicative, two conclusions seem to emerge from the table. First, the 'factor productivity' of the Greek commer-

Table 8.2 Indices of bank operating efficiency

Index	National Bank	Commercial Bank	Ionian Bank	Credit Bank	Ergo Bank	Italian banks
Resources per employee (drachmas m.)	199	118	140	139	152	318[*]
Resources per unit of personnel cost	66	44	54	57	65	45
Resources per unit of operating cost	55	35	42	42	46	33

* Computed using the official exchange rate.

Sources: For Greek banks, *Annual Reports for the Year 1988* (1989); for Italian banks, Bank of Italy, *Annual Report for the year 1988* (1989).

cial banks exhibits a V-curve pattern, if any at all, when plotted against the bank size. This is particularly evident in the second index, where the denominator may be taken as an efficiency-weighted personnel index (weighted relative salary rates). No clear evidence can be drawn, therefore, of the existence of economies of scale, at least for the range and size of bank in the sample used. Second, the Italian banks seem to be much more efficient on the basis of the first index – the simple labour productivity index – and relatively less efficient on the basis of the other two indices, where the relative money cost is taken into account. One explanation for this apparently conflicting evidence is that the latter indices also reflect relative standards of living, and a more meaningful comparison might have been obtained if the indices had been standardised in terms of per capita income. Indeed, by deflating the corresponding indices, the superior efficiency of the Italian banks is clearly confirmed.

The lower operating efficiency of Greek banks naturally has a serious bearing on their profitability, particularly as far as their revenue from regular banking business is concerned. Additional important profit-determining factors, besides costs, are the interest rate spread and the size of non-interest revenues. In Table 8.3, data on costs and revenues are presented as ratios for the five Greek banks in our sample, as well as for the Italian banking system.

Based on these figures, a number of interesting observations can be made. First, the cost per employee appears to be positively correlated with the size of bank. This perhaps reflects differences in staff composition in terms of seniority, since salary differentials in the banking sector have been practically eliminated by collective agreements in recent years. Private banks also seem to have a significantly lower cost per employee, even for banks of the same size and efficiency.

Second, gross profitability (that is operating surplus per unit of intermediate resources) by contrast exhibits a negative relation with size of bank, in a stepwise fashion. Bottom is the National Bank, with a rate of 2 per cent, followed by the two larger, nationalised commercial banks with a rate averaging 3.4 per cent. Topping the list are the two, smaller, private banks with a rate exceeding 4 per cent. This inverse relationship is more evident in the net profits rate, which ranges from a mere 0.1 per cent for the National Bank to a rate slightly higher than 1 per cent for the Credit Bank and an impressive 2.4 per cent for the Ergo Bank. As the last row of the table indicates, differences in personnel costs account for this strengthened negative correlation. The proportion of the operating surplus absorbed by personnel costs is about 77 per cent for the National Bank, dropping to only

Table 8.3 Cost and profitability ratios, 1988

Ratios	National Bank	Commercial Bank	Ionian Bank	Credit Bank	Ergo Bank	Italian banks
1. Annual cost per employee (drachmas 000s)	3 080	2 712	2 594	2 416	2 345	6 940[*]
2. Operating surplus/ resources (%)	2.0	3.5	3.3	3.8	4.5	4.7
3. Net profits/ resources (%)	0.1	0.2	0.6	1.0	2.4	1.0
4. Interest revenue/ resources (%)	–	–	–	1.8	1.4	3.5
5. Other revenue resources (%)	–	–	–	2.0	3.3	1.2
6. Personnel cost/ operating surplus (%)	77.2	66.4	55.6	46.1	33.1	46.9

[*] Converted at the official parity rate.

Sources: Basic data from Greek banks, *Annual Report for the Year 1988* (1989); Bank of Italy, *Annual Report for the Year 1988* (1989).

33 per cent for the Ergo Bank. Considering that the corresponding difference in the cost per employee is smaller, the degree of over-manning should be even larger.

Third, according to the available data, which refer to the two private banks only, the major source of revenue comes from the item 'other revenue', that is a non-interest revenue source. In effect, more than 50 per cent of total gross revenue for the Credit Bank and more than 70 per cent for the Ergo Bank originates from that source. This is a surprisingly high percentage compared to international standards, considering that the range of financial services offered by the Greek banking system still lags far behind in variety and size. Even some of the common financial services supplied are sometimes under-priced. It is thus clear that the Greek commercial banking system has enjoyed some quite lucrative sources of rent-type revenue. In fact it is hardly an exaggeration to say that, under normal competitive conditions, banking business in Greece today is probably a non-profitable enterprise. Working within a narrow spread – at least until recently – and being excessively involved in retail banking, heavily constrained in their asset management and exposed to a lethal combination of oligopolistic non-price competition and an over-demanding labour union, most commercial banks have retained a façade of profitability only by end-of-year arrangements with the central bank and rent seeking. This is particularly true of the two larger nationalised commercial banks, for which the token 0.1 per cent or 0.2 per cent net profit rate on total resources implies that their revenue account from regular banking business must have been in the red.

Fourth, compared to Italian banks, the cost per bank employee is much lower, even if the per capita income differences are taken into account. Despite that, the proportion of operating surplus absorbed by the personnel cost is in general much higher in Greece. This observation suggests that bank employees in Italy, while they are better paid, have an efficiency edge which over-compensates for the increased cost per employee.

Fifth, the structure of revenue sources in Italy is also at variance with the Greek pattern. Contrary to the Greek case, about 75 per cent of total revenue is generated from interest revenue sources and only about one-quarter from 'other revenue', a more normal situation, indicating much lower rent seeking. Finally, the net profit rate on total resources in Italy is around 1 per cent, which is considered satisfactory by international standards. In our sample of Greek banks this profit rate was attained only by the two private banks.

The overwhelming influence of the Bank of Greece on the profitability of the banking system has already been mentioned. This is exercised either by granting direct subsidies or by changing the interest rates paid on reserves, or charged on the banks' current account, or by setting some basic deposit or lending rates or, finally, by varying the reserve requirement ratios. This is clearly an anomaly, which is aggravated by two uncommon facts. First, the Bank of Greece's decisions are sometimes shaped with an eye to its own profitability and, second, the commercial banks generally assume that at the end of the year, the central bank will save them from the embarrassment of showing a loss to their shareholders and thus upsetting the capital market or shaking public confidence in the soundness of the Greek banking system (Bank of Greece, 1989).

2.3 Capital Adequacy

The problem of capital adequacy has recently received considerable attention in discussions concerning the unification of the EC rules and regulations on bank supervision (Filios, 1988; Zavos, 1989). An 8 per cent minimum capital/risk asset ratio has been proposed for 1992. Though higher than in some cases, the EC rule of 8 per cent would not appear to be a severe constraint on the banks' expansion leverage, considering that the corresponding ratio in the US banking system is close to 13 per cent.

The Greek commercial banking system has for years been below international standards. The overall capital/asset ratio has been around 2–3 per cent, compared to 4–6.5 per cent in the UK (Lomax, 1987) and 7 per cent in the USA. Most Greek banks have only recently taken steps to improve their capital adequacy, mainly by capitalising reserves generated from revaluations of their fixed capital assets. As a result, the two private banks in our sample have reached the 8 per cent limit and one of the big nationalised banks (the Commercial Bank) has come close to it, according to the results of our calculations based on EC criteria, which are presented in Table 8.4.

The first observation is that the capital/risk asset ratio is generally twice the simple capital/asset ratio in the Greek case, while in Italy the difference is substantially smaller. This is almost exclusively owing to the fact that the component of liquid assets with zero risk weight is much larger in the Greek banking system because of the high compulsory reserve requirements in treasury bills.

The second observation refers to the fact that, despite the steps taken to raise the capital adequacy ratio, the overall weighted capital/risk asset ratio remained essentially unchanged, owing to the worsening of the corresponding ratio of the National Bank, which dropped by almost one percentage

Table 8.4 Capital adequacy ratios (per cent)

Bank	Capital/asset		Capital/risk asset	
	1985	1988	1985	1988
National	3.13	3.61	6.13	5.35
Commercial	4.06	4.90	6.52	7.83
Ionian	3.87	4.12	6.50	6.85
Credit	2.32	4.81	3.84	8.06
Ergo	3.38	4.30	6.25	8.24
All five banks (weighted)	3.31	3.99	6.08	6.16
Italian banks	6.27	7.66	8.01	10.17

Source: Own calculations based on data from annual reports of individual Greek banks and the Bank of Italy.

point during this four-year period. The problem, therefore, is currently only with the National Bank, but because of the bank's dominating position it has had serious overall repercussions. In effect, if the National Bank had decided to meet the standard, by raising the necessary capital from the Stock Exchange, it would have to float new shares of a value equal to its present equity capital within the next three years. Having in mind the current conditions of the capital market and their short-run prospects, such an attempt would almost certainly cause a serious disruption in the market. On the other hand, considering the low profitability of the bank, and that it seems to have scraped the bottom of the barrel in capitalising hidden reserves, it would have to seek other resources, domestic or foreign. Excepting the two private banks – assuming that they maintain their present high profitability – the same problem is likely to be faced by the other two large nationalised banks if they keep expanding their total risk assets at recent rates.

Despite their obvious usefulness, the capital/asset ratios are only indicative of the degree of protection against bank insolvency, because they fail to reflect the 'inner' soundness of the bank loan or share portfolio. This may be of critical importance if the share of loans to problematic enterprises is sizeable, as is the case for some Greek commercial banks, for instance. It is not without significance that the provision for loan losses of the two larger banks (the National Bank and the Commercial Bank) dropped significantly in 1988, as a percentage of total intermediate resources, and today stands at 0.2 per cent as against 0.3 per cent for the other banks, including the Italian banks.

The problem of ailing enterprises is quite complex as far as its causes is concerned. Besides extraneous factors, such as the prolonged stagflation and the political arm-twisting, banks were led to expose themselves to an increased degree to moral risk and an unwise selection of customers by two major factors. First, the system of state guarantees for small-scale industrial firms was virtually automatic and the granting of loans to this category of customer was practically done under coercion. For loans to very large firms the case was different, but had essentially the same result. In case of difficulty, and for the allegedly serious social and political problems involved, some sort of bailing out was, as a rule, undertaken by the authorities. Second, the compulsory large proportion of deposits kept in highly liquid, low-yielding riskless assets must have induced banks to compensate by trying to maximise the yield on the unconstrained part of their portfolio, without having due regard to the corresponding risk. It is also true that banks were caught, to some extent, in the vicious circle of what Stiglitz called 'lousy customers'; that is, they continued to extend loans to failing enterprises in the hope that, by keeping them alive, they might retain some chance of recovering their total claims if these firms managed to survive on their own in the future.

2.4 Financial Innovations

Considerable progress has been made in modernising the Greek financial markets during the last two years, particularly as regards the introduction of new financial instruments and institutions. There is no doubt that the introduction of certificates of deposits (CDs), RPs or institutions such as leasing or factoring are substantial steps forward. In some cases these changes were quite bold as, for instance, in allowing banks to pay interest on cheque deposits, a measure which apparently supersedes the negotiable orders of withdrawal (NOWs) accounts revolution in the US financial markets.

Without underrating their importance, the effectiveness of such innovations in transforming the Greek financial markets into a modern financial system is still in doubt. It remains an open question whether they can trigger a process towards a genuine transformation or will simply become an artificial 'superstructure' which may inflate financial speculation and distort the yield–risk relationship, to the detriment of the sound financing of the economy. In other words, it is not clear yet whether these new instruments will serve as a complement or as a substitute to real capital accumulation. Banks are reporting, for instance, that enterpreneurs are becoming so preoccupied with these new investment opportunities in the new lucrative and liquid financial assets that they may abandon or postpone their plans for new production or investment initiatives.

The possibility of such an apparently undesirable outcome should not be under-estimated, since the introduction of these innovations was not endogenous to the commercial banking system – a reaction to pressing funding needs – as was the case in foreign financial markets. Rather they were the result of initiatives by the central bank intended to serve specific purposes, such as to accommodate the financing of the ever-expanding budget deficit, or to facilitate compensatory finance of the balance of payments deficits or to provide banks with alternative, non-interest, means to raise their profitability (leasing) or, finally, to allow private firms to indulge in some rudimentary cash management. Perhaps the only innovation initiated by the commercial banking system was the use of RPs in treasury bills among its member banks.

Although it is perhaps too early to judge the pace of the innovating process, it appears that the Greek banking system still lacks the dynamism necessary to catch up the fast readjusting European financial markets. After some initial promising response to the central bank's initiatives, the process seems to have lost momentum. It is notable that the National Bank, which usually sets the tone in the market, has shown very little interest in these financial innovations. There may be several explanations for such a lack of enthusiasm, but one is probably crucial. As long as the structure of interest rates is not left to be determined by market forces and, particularly, the saving deposit rate is kept at artificially high levels, neither will the public show an interest nor will the banks be willing to offer any other more attractive financial prices.

3   TOWARDS A GENUINE READJUSTMENT OF THE GREEK COMMERCIAL BANKING SYSTEM

The analysis in the previous section provides sufficient evidence that the Greek commercial banking system has certain serious weaknesses, which render its prospects for withstanding competition in a unified European financial market rather bleak, unless significant progress is achieved on several fronts. While its dominance in retail banking may not be in danger, because of the extensive network of branches all over the country, its share in wholesale banking will be effectively challenged, and its profitability will be further impaired by the unavoidable elimination of rent-type revenue sources.

To meet the challenge the Greek banking system has to undertake major readjustment and modernisation. There are four main areas of banking in which innovative changes are urgently needed, particularly in view of the anticipated financial conditions in 1993 and beyond. The first two are external and the other two are internal to the commercial banking system.

First, the formal environment of monetary and credit rules and regulations within which the Greek banking system operates as a result of central bank policies. These measures not only define the space and delineate the size of the banks' operations but also have an important bearing on their profitability and thus on their capacity to survive in a competitive set-up.

Second, the scope of government intervention and, particularly, the degree of the banks' involvement in the sectoral allocation of resources and the attainment of the government's social and political goals. It is common knowledge that, for some banks, direct or indirect government intervention has been a critical factor in shaping the soundness of their portfolio or in determining their operational efficiency. A major issue in this context is, of course, the degree of privatisation or the effective form of nationalisation that can be envisaged.

Third, the array of monetary assets and financial institutions available for asset or liability management. It should be remembered that, while financial innovations would normally increase the flexibility and efficiency of the banking system, they may lose their potency or degenerate into simple speculative instruments unless proper conditions are established in the first place.

Fourth, the internal organisation and functioning of the individual banks and the structure and operation of the banking industry as a whole. As was pointed out above, the operating efficiency of Greek banks leaves much to be desired and their profitability is relatively low or depends mainly on sources generated by market imperfections which will be difficult to maintain under the expected competitive conditions of 1993. The industry's oligopolistic structure, on the other hand, precludes innovation and entails suboptimal financial output. According to existing evidence, the large banks have failed to reap economies of scale, while the small banks have shown a remarkable ability to exploit sectors of the financial market where high rents can be gained.

Accordingly a genuine readjustment of the Greek commercial banking system would require a combined and consistent effort from all three parties concerned; that is, the central bank, the government and the banking system itself. The following is an indicative list of pertinent policy steps to be taken, grouped according to the origin of the action.

3.1 Policy Actions by the Bank of Greece

1. Phase out all constraints on banks' portfolio management and asset structure and save the required cash reserve ratio which may be retained as a monetary tool, at least until it is adjusted to EC rules and partially replaced by RP operations. By this action not only will commercial banks be able to rationalise their portfolio but the central bank will also be able to get rid of a complex and costly system of cross-subsidisation. Fears that the abolition of the secondary reserves in treasury bills will create havoc with the market seem unfounded. In the first place, readjustments to the banks' portfolio are bound to be gradual, since the banks are locked in, as any attempt to liquidate a large portion of their portfolio might entail significant capital losses. Secondly, if the saving deposit interest rate is liberalised (as dis-

cussed below), the burden of adjustment will shift from the treasury rate to deposit rates. The net outcome would be a more normal distribution of treasury bill holdings between the general public and the banking system.

2.   Liberalise all interest rates and consequently let the interest rate margin (lending and funding rates spread) be determined by market forces. This will allow banks to improve their profitability and substitute this augmented interest revenue for some of the current rent-type sources, which cannot be sustained beyond 1993 and which should be eliminated well before that date.

3.   Abolish all direct or indirect subsidies to the banking system and thus let the yield of each financial asset reflect the underlying fundamental factors.

4.   Allow banks to price their services to all customers (private or public) on competitive terms, according to their marginal cost conditions, and induce banks to be much more cost- and risk-conscious in providing financial services or opening new branches.

5.   Speed up the process of elimination of all – or most – remaining specific credit controls, with the exception, perhaps, of those related to consumption expenditure and transactions in securities.

6.   Strengthen bank control and supervision by setting specific rules with respect to capital adequacy and liquidity, along the lines of the EC directives, and exercise a systematic inspection on the banks' portfolio to ensure that proper banking criteria are applied and its soundness is properly safeguarded.

7.   Set stricter rules for the conditions of the opening, buying or merging of banks or bank branches. Again the EC directives or proposals should serve as the main guidance for action and decisions should be taken without unnecessary delay.

3.2   Policy Steps by the Government

As might be expected, government actions refer mainly, but not wholly, to the quasi-nationalised banks which, as they dominate the market, will ensure that these actions have a far-reaching impact. A far from exhaustive list of policy steps is suggested below.

1.   Reduce direct or indirect government involvement in banks' policies, particularly as far as the sectoral allocation of resources or the attainment of social objectives is concerned. These objectives should be pursued through budgetary policies.

2.   Select and appoint top bank officials, using non-political criteria; that is, base the selection on qualifications (knowledge, experience, status

and so on) similar to those required for corresponding positions when establishing new private banks.

3. Relax all constraints with respect to the acquisition of modern computing equipment and software packages. According to current terms of public-sector procurement, the acquisition of large-scale computing hardware or expensive software packages by nationalised banks is conditional upon an extensive bureaucratic procedure.

4. Permit labour union collective bargaining on an individual bank basis and abandon the unified salary scale which kills the employees' incentive for advancement based on efficiency differentials. Permit special rewards based on performance.

5. Review the existing system of granting guarantees to small-scale industrial firms which has, to a large extent, been misused, causing an avalanche of failures.

3.3 Actions by Commercial Banks

The main burden of the readjustment falls naturally on the commercial banks themselves. The necessary policy steps can be grouped into two categories: those referring to the production and pricing of financial services and those that concern the banks' internal organisation and functioning. These are outlined in the following sections.

3.3.1 Financial services

1. Review and rationalise the portfolio composition in the new context of a more liberal asset management policy. Gradually establish the necessary norms for liquidity and solvency.

2. Enrich the package of financial services offered by making use of the newly established institutions, such as leasing or factoring, or by introducing new ones, such as trust fund or financial consulting services.

3. Price financial services on a marginal cost basis but exploit the fact that banking is a differentiated product industry.

4. Review the bank branching policy pursued by applying a careful cost and benefit analysis.

5. Embark upon an active liability management policy, exploiting the possibilities opened by the recent central bank initiatives. With a more normal interest rate structure and a more flexible money market this source of funding will become not only feasible but indispensable.

6. Prepare the ground for closer cooperation with other domestic or foreign banks for syndicated loans, other joint ventures or risk sharing.

7.   Expand horizons towards internationalisation of banking operations, especially towards the EC area, and undertake the necessary groundwork (train personnel and so on) for an active presence in European capital markets.

3.3.2   *Internal organisation and functioning*

1.   Upgrade the quality of personnel through an intensive retraining programme, suitably structured and organised. Efforts so far have had rather poor results, probably because of an inappropriate selection of persons retrained, or because of insufficient interest on the part of re-trainees owing to the lack of incentives.

2.   Reshuffle the employed personnel and utilise the surplus workforce (which in some banks is reported to be almost one-half of the total) in new departments or in independent but affiliated institutions providing new financial services.

3.   Re-establish a salary scale and a scheme of penalties and rewards to promote efficiency and penalise indifference and laziness. Review the existing system of personnel evaluation.

4.   Seek and hire top-level experts to undertake the highly specialised jobs of modern financial markets, for which there is a glaring need.

5.   Expand and modernise capital equipment and computing facilities (hardware equipment as well as software packages). Utilise these to exploit the new profitable opportunities in the money market and the production of the new financial services and try to reap the economies of scale which are particularly important in retail banking.

6.   Organise the provision of banking services on a customer rather than on a job basis. This will speed up procedures and cut down bureaucracy and red tape.

4   A WORD OF CAUTION

Introducing such far-reaching changes within a rather short period of time, that is by 1993, is an ambitious task, not only because of the break with a rigid behavioural pattern for all the parties involved, but also because of two additional constraining factors: first, a rather steep drop in the private propensity to save in the last few years, combined with a slow-growing national income, has substantially reduced the flow of real savings mobilised by the financial system; second, an explosive increase in the public sector borrowing requirement severely restricted private users' access to the current flow of financial savings.

Under these circumstances to propose such a swift and comprehensive liberalisation of the Greek commercial banking system might perhaps appear futile, particularly as the central bank may not be prepared to bear the cost or to take the necessary offsetting monetary actions. Finally it should be recalled that any action aimed at eliminating distortions in one sector of the economy only – the banking sector in this instance – may not lead to a more efficient configuration if distortions in other sectors, such as the labour market, remain intact, as the second best principle keeps reminding us. Knowing that there exist serious rigidities that could impede modernisation because of the labour market regulations and the antagonism of the labour unions highlights the problems. To conclude, therefore, it is clear that the chances of the readjustment of the Greek banking system being successful and efficient will be greatly strengthened if it is undertaken as part of a more general policy effort aimed at the stabilisation and restructuring of the Greek economy.

References

Bank of Greece (1989) *Annual Report of the Governor for the Year 1988*.

Brocci, W. (1989) 'Reform of the Interbank Market', Banco di Roma, *Review of Economic Conditions in Italy*, no. 1, January–April.

Filios, V. (1988) 'An Estimate of the Capital Adequacy of Banks and the EEC', *Bulletin of the Union of Greek Banks*, vol. 20, no. 4 (in Greek).

Lomax, D. (1987) 'Risk Asset Ratios – A New Departure in Supervisory Policy', *National Westminster Bank Quarterly Review*, August.

Masera, R. (1989) 'Monetary and Financial Markets in Europe: Regulation and Market Forces', Banco di Roma, *Review of Economic Conditions in Italy*, no. 1, January–April.

National Bank of Greece (1989) *Annual Report of the Governor for the Year 1988*.

Zavos, G. (1989) *The Banking Policy of EEC in view of 1992*, Union of Greek Banks.

Part III

Balance of Payments and External Economic Relations

9 Exchange Rate Policy Dilemmas in the Presence of Macroeconomic Imbalance

F 31 O/41

Greece

Maria Constantopoulos

ATHENS UNIVERSITY OF ECONOMICS AND BUSINESS

1 INTRODUCTION

In recent years the drachma has been crawling downwards at a pace insufficient to counterbalance the rise in domestic costs, especially labour costs. This was because of the government's decision to keep the rate of inflation down despite excess demand caused by the large public-sector deficit. Profit rates in the sectors producing exportables and import substitutes were squeezed, discouraging production and leading to balance of payments deficits. My purpose in this paper is to show that the exchange-rate policy followed facilitated macroeconomic imbalances and particularly overspending in real terms by the government. Furthermore it had two negative consequences:

1. It punished the productive, traded goods sector of the economy at a time when it needed all the help it could get.
2. It shifted the burden of adjustment on to the level of foreign exchange reserves and led to a dead-end out of which only a substantial devaluation with consequent inflation can drive the economy.

I shall use a diagrammatic apparatus which I have developed earlier (Constantopoulos, 1984). Its virtue lies in bridging the gap between general equilibrium models dealing with real aspects, and macroeconomic models dealing with monetary aspects, always assuming full employment of resources. The latter assumption is compatible with a 'natural' rate of unemployment.

1.1   Introduction to the Proposed Model

I usually start my International Trade Theory classes by outlining the differences between equilibrium conditions in an open and a closed economy. Two such differences are prominent. A closed economy is in equilibrium when (i) all markets are cleared: that is, domestic demand equals domestic supply; and (ii) total expenditure equals total income. In a closed economy the second condition is redundant since it is implied by the first. If we choose to keep it separate for methodological reasons, then the first condition need be met in n-1 markets only.

The major characteristic of an open economy is that markets do not clear domestically. In an open economy's markets we observe surpluses (exports) and deficits (imports). Violation of the condition that domestic demand equals domestic supply is the major characteristic of an open economy. The second condition may or may not be satisfied. It can be shown that satisfaction of the second condition implies equilibrium in the balance of payments.[1] Most of pure trade theory, however, is developed under the assumption that the balance of payments is in equilibrium and this is one important reason why some of its conclusions seem so unrealistic to students and policy makers.

My purpose in this paper is to examine the effects of a relaxation of the second assumption on absolute and relative prices and on the structure of production of the open economy. I shall use a model in which there are non-traded along with traded goods, because some phenomena are not satisfactorily explained within a model where there are no non-traded goods. One of them is the role of the exchange rate in influencing the price structure, a role totally absent when all goods are traded and the economy is a price taker in world markets. Thus I shall use a model with three goods: the exported good, X, the imported good, M, and the non-traded good, D. We shall, however, assume that only two goods are produced – the exported and the non-traded good – and only two goods are consumed – the imported and the non-traded good. This way, despite the fact that we have three goods, we deal with only two at a time. Those who doubt whether this model is more realistic than the standard two-good trade model may think of the domestic good as a composite good, made up of non-traded goods, import substitutes and exportables in fixed proportions.[2]

The proposed model has been used several times by Professor R. Jones (1979) in the analysis of the transfer problem. I shall develop an original geometric technique, which will illustrate the merits of the model and the particular role of the exchange rate in it.

2   CONSUMPTION POSSIBILITIES WHEN EXPENDITURE EQUALS INCOME

The production side of this model conforms to the neoclassical two-by-two workhorse: there are two factors of production, capital, K, and labour, L, which are indispensable for the production of two goods, the exposed, X, and the domestic (non-traded) good D. Factors of production can be substituted for each other along smooth isoquants, while one of the two goods is more labour-intensive at all factor price ratios. Production functions exhibit constant returns to scale, while price flexibility guarantees full employment of factors of production. Perfect competition in factor and commodity markets ensures equality of prices and marginal costs.

In the NW quadrant of Figure 9.1, called the production quadrant, we draw the resulting production transformation curve, measuring along the vertical axis the quantity of the domestic good and along the horizontal axis the quantity of the exported good. The SW quadrant is only used to transfer with the help of the 45° line the quantities of the exported good from the horizontal to the vertical negative semi-axis.

The SE quadrant, called the trade quadrant, is used to transform the country's exports into imports in world markets. When the country has no monopoly power in world markets it faces a linear foreign offer curve, as OR^* in Figure 9.1. The slope of OR^* equals the ratio p_M^*/p_X^*; that is the ratio

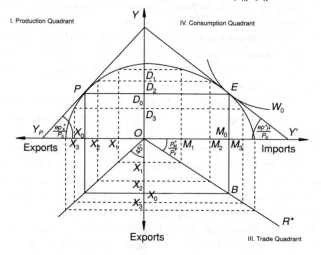

Figure 9.1   Construction of the consumption possibilities curve with fixed terms of trade, and derivation of production and consumption equilibrium

of the international price of the imported good to the price of the exported good – the terms of trade.[3] The lower this slope, the better for the country.

The NE quadrant, called the consumption quadrant, is the most important quadrant for judging welfare changes since, as is usually assumed, the country's welfare depends on its consumption. For each quantity of the domestic good, say D_1, the highest quantity of the imported good the economy can consume is given by transforming its exported good X_1 into M_1 via world markets. The combination (D_1, M_1) belongs to the consumption possibilities schedule of the economy.

The construction of this schedule is very easy. It can be verified that it differs from the production possibilities schedule only in having different units on the horizontal axis; each unit on the horizontal axis of the consumption quadrant equals p_M^*/p_X^* units of that corresponding to the production quadrant. The slope of the consumption possibilities curve equals that of the production transformation curve, multiplied by the rate of transformation of exports into imports:

$$\frac{\partial D}{\partial M} = \frac{\partial D}{\partial X} \cdot \frac{\partial X}{\partial M} = \frac{\partial D}{\partial X} \cdot \frac{p_M^*}{p_X^*} \tag{1}$$

As the terms of trade worsen, the lower end point of the consumption possibilities curve moves towards the origin, and *vice versa*.

By drawing in the consumption quadrant the country's social welfare indifference map, we find equilibrium at point E, where the indifference curve W_0 touches the consumption possibilities curve. The production bundle shown at P contains D_0 of the non-traded and X_0 of the export good. The latter quantity is exchanged in world markets for M_0 of imports, so that the consumption bundle at E contains D_0 and M_0.

All markets are in equilibrium: demand and supply for D equal each other; the supply of exports, p_X^*X, is just sufficient to provide the foreign exchange necessary to pay for the required value of imports, p_M^*M, so that the foreign exchange market is also in equilibrium. Consequently total demand equals total supply at the ruling prices, as witnessed by the fact that the expenditure constraint YY' in the consumption quadrant and the producers' income constraint in the production quadrant, YY_P' start at the same point on the vertical axis and are tangent to the corresponding curves at points E and P situated on the same horizontal level. Furthermore the difference in the slope of the two constraints just equals the terms of trade.

As can be seen in both the production and consumption quadrants, when the international prices are fixed, the slope of the income or of the expenditure constraint expressing the relative price of traded goods reflects the price of foreign currency in terms of the domestic good. Under these conditions the exchange rate determines the relative price of the traded good.

Let me point out an unorthodox characteristic of this approach, namely that consumption equilibrium with trade is always on the consumption possibilities curve. The usual trade triangle, OBM_0, can be found in the trade quadrant.

3 CONSUMPTION POSSIBILITIES WHEN EXPENDITURE EXCEEDS GDP

The virtues of the present approach are brought out when we analyse the case of a country spending more or less than its GDP. A country may spend more than its GDP if it receives payments for factors located abroad, gifts from abroad, loans, aid, or if it runs down its foreign assets. It may spend less than its GDP if purchasing power flows in the opposite direction – it remits factor payments to other countries, it aids them, lends funds to them or invests directly abroad. Since the decisions of the agents in the economy imply certain changes in the country's foreign assets, they may conflict with the plans of the central bank concerning the optimal level of these assets – when there are such plans. For the time being, however, we shall leave the central bank out of the analysis and return to it in the next section.

Assume now that the country receives a transfer of T^* units of foreign exchange. In Figure 9.2, this pushes the foreign offer curve to the position BR_T^*. OB equals T^*/p_M^* and indicates the quantity of imports that can now be bought thanks to the transfer without exporting any goods in exchange. The horizontal shift of BR^* by T^*/p_M^* causes an equal and *parallel* shift of the $C-T$ curve which now moves from its original position $C_P T_P$ to $C_E T_E$.

The agents in this economy do not observe $C_E T_E$, but the expenditure constraint $Y_E Y_E'$. The expenditure constraint's upper end point is found by dividing national expenditure into the domestic price of the non-traded good D, E/p_D. Its lower end point is found by dividing national expenditure into the domestic price of the imported good, E/p_M. The domestic price of the imported good equals its world price, p_M^*, multiplied by the exchange rate, e: it is ep_M^*. The slope of the expenditure constraint is ep_M^*/p_D and measures the opportunity cost of consuming the imported good.

Normally total expenditure equals total income (that is, GDP plus net factor payments from abroad) plus gifts and loans from abroad, and any means of payment (money) created within the period or dishoarded by individuals. A transfer of T^* units of foreign exchange will result in a

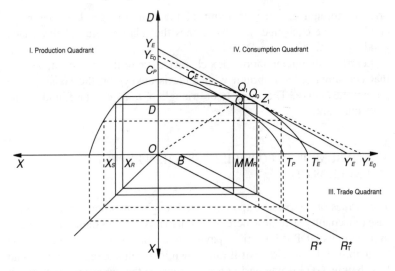

Figure 9.2   Effects of a transfer in the exchange rate when it is free to float

parallel shift of both the expenditure constraint and the C–T curve, which will increase aggregate demand. Provided both goods consumed (the non-traded and the imported good) are normal, excess demand will appear in the market for the non-traded good, while excess supply will appear in the market for the traded good.

Let us for the sake of simplicity assume that welfare indifference curves are homothetic. Equilibrium on $Y_E Y_E'$ is desired at point Q_1, while at these prices and the ruling exchange rate supply stays at Z_1. A transfer of purchasing power will produce an excess demand for D and excess supply for M. This means that the quantity of exports, X_R, required to provide the foreign exchange necessary to buy the desired level of imports, M_R – once an amount equal to T^*/p_M has been paid through the transfer – is lower than the quantity forthcoming at the initial level of prices and foreign exchange, X_S. In the foreign exchange market an excess supply will appear which can be absorbed if the exchange rate is allowed to fall, reducing the domestic price of the imported good, and pushing the left-hand end of the expenditure constraint outwards. At the same time, the rise in the price of the domestic good will force the vertical end point downward until $Y_E Y_E'$ touches $C_E T_E$ at Q_0. It is obvious that equilibrium along $C_E T_E$ cannot be achieved by movements of p_D alone, or by movements of the exchange rate,

e, alone, since the expenditure constraint must tilt; that is, its end points must move in opposite directions. The fall in the exchange rate (appreciation) draws the horizontal end point outwards, while the rise in p_D (domestic inflation) draws the vertical end point downwards.

Suppose now that the exchange rate is fixed. The horizontal end point of $Y_E Y_E'$ cannot move, unless total expenditure changes. The price of the non-traded good rises since this market must be cleared by all means. As the vertical end point of the expenditure constraint moves downwards, as shown in Figure 9.3, the constraint cuts the $C_E T_E$ curve. This means that the country spends less than it could have spent if all markets were cleared; the balance of payments will be in surplus. In detail, the rise in p_D draws Y_E downwards to Y_E^1; consumption equilibrium is at Q_1 while production equilibrium is on the same horizontal level at P_1, implying a trade surplus equal to p_M multiplied by $Q_1 P_1$ in foreign currency. In the next period, assuming that the transfer is repeated, the expenditure constraint moves to $Y_P^1 Y_P^{1'}$, since higher prices for the domestic good filter through to private incomes. For the reasons outlined above, P_1 cannot be an equilibrium point. Demand equilibrium is at E'', implying again excess demand for the non-traded good and excess supply for the traded good. The rise in p_D will draw Y_P^1 downward, restoring equilibrium in the domestic market and leaving a smaller payments surplus. The same process is repeated until we arrive at Q_0 – not shown in Figure 9.3 – the equilibrium that could have been immediately achieved, had the exchange rate been fully flexible.

The conclusion that we draw is that, if the exchange rate is flexible, immediate achievement of equilibrium is possible. On the contrary, if the exchange rate is fixed, a series of surpluses (or deficits in the case of a devaluation) will appear before equilibrium is achieved. The difference between the two equilibria is the following:

1. With instant equilibrium the means of payment in the economy will not rise in quantity since the transfer will be spent on imports, but the appreciation of the currency increases the purchasing power of the domestic means of payment relative to the means of payment abroad.
2. With equilibrium achieved after the gradual process described above, the exchange rate is constant, but the means of payment circulating in the economy have risen by the sum of surpluses realised during the process of adjustment. Thus the purchasing power of the means of payment circulating in the economy relative to those circulating abroad has risen again but through an increase in their quantity.

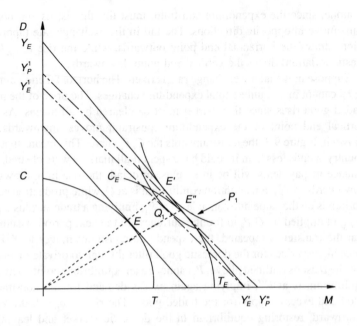

Figure 9.3 Effects of a transfer of purchasing power when the exchange rate is fixed

4 CONSUMPTION POSSIBILITIES WHEN THE CENTRAL BANK SETS GOALS FOR THE LEVEL OF FOREIGN EXCHANGE RESERVES

Flexibility of the exchange rate was shown to be necessary for the achievement of instant equilibrium when the equality of expenditure to income is disturbed. It is also necessary if the central bank wishes to impose its will concerning the level of foreign assets in the economy. The level of the rate of interest at home and abroad relative to the level of domestic and foreign prices determines the world's willingness to transfer temporarily purchasing power to our country (loans). Given loans and other autonomous purchasing power transfers, the plans of the central bank concerning the level – hence changes in – foreign exchange reserves determine the horizontal distance between $C_P T_P$ and the expenditure possibilities curve ($C_E T_E$). Let us call the expenditure possibilities curve compatible with central bank plans ($C_B T_B$).

The expenditure constraint corresponding to the spending plans of the agents in the economy need not be tangential to $C_B T_B$. Equilibrium, however, can only occur at a point of tangency. This means that foreign exchange reserves will exceed or fall short of their planned level, pushing the $C_B T_B$ curve to the position where it will touch the $Y_E Y_E'$ line. On the contrary, if the bank holds on to its plans, the movement of the exchange rate will force $Y_E Y_E'$ to shift and touch the $C_B T_B$ curve.

Assume, for instance, that owing to money creation or private dissaving the expenditure constraint moves to $Y_E Y_E'$ in Figure 9.4, with no matching increase in foreign exchange receipts. Any equilibrium out of $C_B T_B$ will imply a reduction in the country's foreign assets (for instance, foreign exchange reserves). If the exchange rate is fixed, the price of the traded good is fixed and the rise in p_D alone will not be able to absorb excess demand for the traded good. Consumption equilibrium will be at Q_1 while production equilibrium will be at P_1. A deficit of $P_1 Q_1 p_M^*$ will appear in the balance of payments. In the next period, assuming that the original disturbance disappears, the expenditure constraint will be $Y_P^1 Y_P^{1'}$. Demand equilibrium on it is at E'', implying excess supply of the non-traded good. The fall in p_D will produce a new smaller deficit and, after a number of periods, in which the balance of payments will register diminishing deficits, we will be back on $C_B T_B$ at E. When the exchange rate is flexible, instant return to

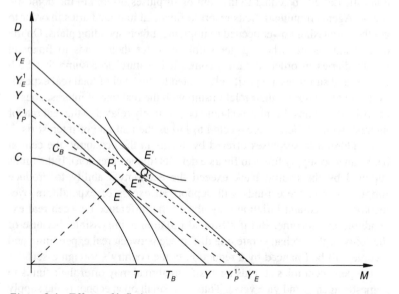

Figure 9.4   Effects of inflationary money creation when the exchange rate is fixed

E is possible, since the domestic currency will depreciate sufficiently to bring Y_E down to Y, allowing the central bank to achieve its target level of foreign exchange reserves.

Of course the central bank can manipulate the money supply and thus determine the position of the expenditure constraint – and the level of the rate of interest, which is not shown in this diagram. In a sense, then, the question is whether an increase in expenditure exceeding the corresponding rise in income originating in some sector of the economy will be allowed to lead to a total excess of aggregate expenditure over income in the economy as a whole or whether it will be matched by corresponding reductions of aggregate expenditure relative to income in other sectors. The reduction in aggregate expenditure can be produced by a reduction in the money supply or by a devaluation. The first has a deflationary effect on the price level whereas the second has an inflationary effect.

5   THE RECENT EXPERIENCE WITH MONETARY AND EXCHANGE RATE POLICY IN GREECE

In every economy there are agents who run deficits while others exhibit surpluses of income over expenditure. Equilibrium demands that the sum of domestic deficits be equal to the sum of surpluses offered to the domestic sector. Agents running deficits resort to financial intermediaries in order to get the purchasing power needed to implement their spending plans. On the other hand, agents who register surpluses offer their funds to financial intermediaries in order to earn income. It is natural to assume that both deficits and surpluses are positively related to the level of total real expenditure. On the contrary, their relationship with the real rate of interest goes in opposite directions. Surpluses should be positively related to the real rate of interest, while deficits are expected to fall as the real rate of interest rises.

In addition to surpluses offered by agents in the economy, the central bank can also supply funds to finance deficits (money creation). If the funds supplied by the central bank exceed the economy's ability to produce further income, these funds will support an excess of expenditure over income. Consequent inflation may absorb the difference between real expenditure and income. But if all-round inflation is impossible, because of the fixity of the exchange rate, the difference between real expenditure and income will be financed by a reduction in the country's foreign assets.

In open economies surplus agents from abroad may offer their funds to domestic agents, and vice versa. Thus, in a small open economy the supply of funds to agents running deficits is fairly elastic at real interest rates around their international levels, allowance being made for expected currency devaluation. This means that the ability of the central bank to change the real rate of interest is limited in a small open economy where capital is free to flow in and out of the country.

In Greece, the public sector as a whole started to run a deficit by the end of the past decade, that is 1979. In addition to this, the country's growth rate fell dramatically (1.1 per cent on average over the decade), while the public-sector deficit rose at high rates and now exceeds 20 per cent of the country's GDP. In order to finance such a high public-sector deficit, the private sector was discouraged from running deficits and many firms were forced to give up their plans for essential improvements and capital replacement. The rate of growth of gross capital formation in the country was zero during the decade of the 1980s. Given the low growth rate of the economy during the 1980s and the stagnation in the country's productive capacity, it was unwise to resort to (borrowed) funds from abroad in order to cover the deficit of the public sector. Since the government proved unable to raise taxes in order to cover its desired levels of expenditure, the exchange rate needed to be allowed to depreciate sufficiently to deflate total expenditure.

Since 1986 the depreciation of the drachma has been insufficient to cover the difference between the domestic and the world inflation rate. This policy has led to a situation where the drachma is today over-valued by almost 20 per cent relative to its 1987 level. Depreciation was not permitted by the authorities for fear of its inflationary impact, thus ignoring the fact that it is exactly because of its inflationary effects that depreciation can check the excess of real expenditure over income. Exchange-rate policy was designed to keep the inflation rate down while monetary policy did not manage to prevent the application of a fiscal policy leading to huge public-sector deficits. The real rate of interest was held down thanks to the limited ability of domestic capital to flow legally out of the country.

The fight against inflation represents a misuse of exchange-rate policy. The exchange rate represents the relative price of foreign currencies in terms of the domestic currency and in economies with non-traded goods it represents the relative price of traded in terms of non-traded goods. The relative appreciation of the domestic currency necessary to keep the rate of inflation down distorted prices against the sector producing traded goods, thus discouraging the production of and investment in the export and the import competing sectors. Furthermore this policy was applied at a very inopportune moment for the Greek economy.

Greece became a full member of the European Community (EC) in 1981. In principle this new status should make no difference to the country's trade in goods and services with the outside world. The country was an associate member of the EC for almost 20 years and the status of association was supposed to lead to the free movement of goods and services to and from the EC and to the establishment of a common tariff regarding trade flows with third countries. In principle the country's new status should make a difference only in matters of the free movement of the factors of production and in matters of application of common policies. Yet the country's accession to the EC significantly influenced trade flows. This was so because, up to 1981, the reduction in tariffs was counter-balanced by taxes and other devices – for instance, the arbitrary determination of the dutiable value of imports by customs officials. Becoming a full member of the EC meant an immediate discontinuation of such policies, so that goods and services started moving freely to and from the country.

Greece is a small economy. It is a fact that countries' size and their openness (measured by the ratio of imports to their GDP or by some other similar measure) are very closely related. The reason is that small economies cannot produce efficiently a large variety of goods. In other words, the bundle of goods produced in large economies is more varied than the bundle of goods produced in small economies. When a small economy enters a large market it is submerged by goods of great variety. Consumers can immediately buy the variety of goods which satisfy their tastes, but producers are in a more difficult position. Faced with a reduced domestic demand they have to search for markets in which the goods they now produce or the goods they might be able to produce can be sold. It is then fair to say that producers of traded goods bear the brunt of the small country's entry into a large market. It would therefore be reasonable for governments to assist the traded goods sector, especially the sector producing import substitutes, until the world markets to which its products can be channelled are found.

It was certainly easy to predict that Greece's accession to the EC would be followed by a period of *malaise* for the traded goods sector. Yet government policy was designed to undermine rather than help export and import-competing industries. This was so because the socialist government, which came to power in 1981, was more concerned with the distribution of income that with its creation (production). For instance, only a year after membership significant increases in minimum wages – close to 50 per cent – ruined a number of small and medium-sized labour-intensive firms. Selective support of domestic firms was not allowed by the competition rules of the EC and the system of export subsidies had to be dismantled gradually within a five-year period. In this situation the only way the government could help the traded goods sector was by adopting an exchange-rate policy

Table 9.1   The evolution of the relative price of traded goods (Z) in Greece during the last decade

Year	Exchange rate index	Exchange rate % change	Domestic price index	Domestic price % change	Foreign price index	Foreign price % change	Change in Z
1980	100.0	–	100.0	–	100.0	–	–
1981	103.9	3.9	107.0	7.0	103.5	3.5	0.4
1982	115.7	11.4	129.5	21.0	111.6	7.8	–1.8
1983	144.8	27.9	156.1	20.5	117.9	5.6	13.0
1984	172.6	19.2	184.4	18.1	124.0	5.2	6.3
1985	208.9	21.0	219.9	19.3	129.6	4.5	6.2
1986	250.8	20.1	270.6	23.1	132.3	2.1	–0.9
1987	271.5	8.3	315.0	16.4	135.9	2.7	–5.4
1988	290.4	7.0	357.6	13.5	140.0	3.0	–3.5
1989	310.0	6.7	418.0	17.0	145.0	3.6	–6.4

which allowed some percentage points of lead time in the prices of traded goods over those of non-traded goods. As one can observe in Table 9.1, this policy was used only temporarily, and was barely sufficient to counterbalance the elimination of export subsidies. Since 1986, exchange-rate policy has punished the traded goods sector, at a time when help was badly needed.

Notes

1.   Let us use the symbols S_i, D_i and p_i to denote the supply of, demand for and the price of good i. The equality of the value of aggregate production (GDP) in equation (1) implies equality of the values of exports and imports in equation (2):

$$\Sigma_i p_i S_i = \Sigma_i p_i D_i \qquad (1)$$
$$\Sigma_i p_i (S_i - D_i) = 0. \qquad (2)$$

2.   Fixed proportions are assumed in order to avoid the aggregation problems arising from changes in the composition of good D, in response to changes in the prices of its components.

3.   Starred variables denote world values; p_i is the price of the subscripted good: M for imports, X for exports and D for the non-traded good.

References

Blejer, M. and Leiderman, L. (1981) 'A monetary approach to the crawling peg system: Theory and evidence', *Journal of Political Economy*, vol. 89, pp. 132–51.

Constantopoulos, M. J. (1984) 'On the determinants of floating exchange rates in the presence of non-traded goods', in Prodromides, K. and Tzoannos, J. (eds), *ASOEE Scientific Annals* (Athens: Papazissis).

Dornbusch, R. (1973) 'Devaluation, money and non-traded goods', *American Economic Review*, vol. 63, pp. 871–83.

Dornbusch, R. (1976) 'The theory of flexible exchange rate regimes and macroeconomic policy', *Scandinavian Journal of Economics,* vol. 78, pp. 255–75.

Dornbusch, R. (1978) 'Monetary policy under exchange rate flexibility', in *Managed exchange-rate flexibility: the recent experience*, Federal Reserve Bank of Boston Conference Series, no. 20.

Frenkel, J. A. (ed.) (1983) *Exchange Rates and International Macroeconomics* (Chicago: University of Chicago Press).

Jones, R. W. (1979) *International trade: Essays in Theory* (Amsterdam: North Holland) chs. 9, 10 and 11.

Jones, R. W. and Kenen, P. B. (1985) *Handbook of International Economics* (New York: North Holland).

Kimbrough, K. P. (1980) 'Real aspects of the monetary approach to the exchange rate', unpublished PhD dissertation, University of Chicago.

10 The Effects of Devaluation on Gross Domestic Product in Greece

E 3 1

Stylianos A. Sarantides
UNIVERSITY OF PIRAEUS

1 INTRODUCTION

Most developing countries have faced the twin problems of a high domestic rate of inflation and a deficit in the balance of payments. The causes of these problems have often been attributed to fiscal deficits, resulting in excessive monetary expansion, and diminishing international competitiveness of the economy. Stabilisation programmes are put into action to cope with these problems. The effects of such programmes are simultaneously exerted on domestic output, the balance of payments, inflation and other economic variables. In Greece, the rate of inflation is very high in comparison with other EC countries. The raw materials and food price boom in 1973 and the two oil shocks contributed to domestic inflation from 1973 on. Other factors have also played a role during the last eight years, such as budget deficits, wage increases and inflationary expectations. The annual average rate of inflation as measured by the consumer price index was 15.2 per cent during the period 1971–81 (compared to 2.1 per cent during 1961–70) and 20.4 per cent during 1982–6. During the years 1986–8 inflation was running at 17.6 per cent after the implementation of the Greek government's stabilisation programme launched in October 1985. The rate of growth of gross domestic product (GDP) was 4.6 per cent during 1970–81 and 1.6 per cent during 1982–6. The current account deficit was US\$ 344 million in 1971, US\$ 2421 million in 1981, US\$ 1772 million in 1986 and US\$ 1010 million in 1988. The alleged improvement in the balance on current account from 1981 onwards is attributed to transfers from the EC. EC transfers jumped from US\$ 148 million in 1981 to US\$ 1392 million in 1986 and US\$ 1935 million in 1988. The most problematic part of the Greek balance of payments is the trade balance. The trade balance deficit stood at US\$ 1092 million in 1970 and jumped to

127

US$ 6696 million in 1981; it was US$ 5686 million in 1986 and US$ 7618 million in 1988. The commodity trade gap is the major organic problem of the Greek external accounts, since exports of commodities finance no more than 44 per cent of imports payments.

The balance of payments is probably the most noteworthy constraint to growth in most developed and developing countries and the savings and labour constraints most likely exist both in underdeveloped and developing countries. The improvement of the Greek balance of payments shifts the primary interest from it, at least in the short and medium term, to other problems of the economy, such as domestic inflation and sluggish domestic output.

2 DEVALUATION AS AN INSTRUMENT OF ECONOMIC POLICY

Devaluation is one of the main components of orthodox stabilisation programmes and foreign exchange policy simultaneously affects a set of economic magnitudes. A formal analysis of the devaluation effects could consist of analysing the demand- and supply-side effects. Our primary interest is not to investigate the devaluation effects on the balance of payments, but to investigate the overall effect on domestic output.

In *Keynesian* models of an open economy, devaluation leads to increased aggregate demand, income and exports, and an increase in prices. The *monetarist* aspect sustains that changes in exchange rates affect real variables in the short run only, leaving them unaffected in the long run. *Structuralists* argue that a monetary measure, such as devaluation, cannot eliminate problems due to structural deficiencies of the economy.

Seeds of doubt have been spread since 1950 over the theoretical aspects of devaluation, and empirical models constructed during the last ten years have questioned the effectiveness of devaluations. Meade (1951) accepted the possibility of contractionary effects of devaluation where the Marshall-Lerner condition is not satisfied. Hirschman (1949) maintained that devaluation may result in negative effects if imports and exports are not in balance, in which case the Marshall-Lerner condition does not hold and needs modification. Diaz-Alejandro (1965) maintained that devaluation can have a negative effect on aggregate demand and output because of different propensities to save between high-income and low-income groups. Cooper (1971) concluded that devaluation tends initially to depress economic activity, contrary to what had normally been expected. Krugman and Taylor (1978) in a Keynesian model showed that devaluation may result in a decrease in national income if: (i) imports initially exceed exports; (ii) there is a difference in the propensities to consume between profit-incomes and labour-incomes; and (iii) tax revenues increase after devaluation because of export taxes.

The present paper investigates empirically the effect of devaluations on economic activity (gross domestic product) in Greece during the period 1970–86, taking account of other economic variables, such as money supply, fiscal deficits and terms of trade, and challenges the traditional view of expansionary effects of devaluations.

3 CAN DEVALUATION HAVE CONTRACTIONARY EFFECTS ON ECONOMIC ACTIVITY?

There are several theoretical reasons why a devaluation can generate a decline in real product. We can investigate this by analysing the likely effects of a devaluation on both aggregate demand and aggregate supply.

In general, devaluation results in an increase of the general price level in the devaluing country. Initially there is an increase in the prices of imported inputs (in domestic currency) which gradually spills over to the prices of goods and services in the domestic market. If wages are fully indexed, adjusting fully to the increased cost of living after devaluation, and the money supply is kept constant, then real money balances will fall and in turn so will aggregate demand. This result may alleviate the current balance of payments situation, but it will lead to decreased economic activity, given that the expenditure-reducing effect offsets the expenditure-switching effect. After all, devaluations in developing countries have failed to bring the necessary change in relative prices – that is, the ratio of the prices of domestically produced goods and services to the prices of imported ones – because of inappropriate values of certain critical parameters. Even if the money supply is increased, the resulting increased demand might be channelled to imports and not to domestic production. This is because of the existing rigidities in the economy, very low elasticities of substitution between imported and domestic inputs and low price elasticities of intermediate and final goods imports. Moreover the redistribution of incomes following devaluation may have a negative effect on aggregate demand.

On the other hand, by raising the prices of imported inputs and nominal wages, devaluation raises the cost of production. This cost effect results in an upward shift in the aggregate supply curve and consequently a decrease in economic activity. If this cost effect is strong enough, it outweighs an existing positive effect of demand and stagflation may result. Any effect of devaluation, positive, negative or neutral, on real output is theoretically possible, but more crucial than anything else is the downward rigidity of wages and the values of structural and behavioural parameters of the economy. Foreign exchange rate policy is not a panacea and it should be implemented in an appropriate framework of economic policies and conditions.

Reviewing the recent empirical analysis one cannot come to a definite conclusion regarding the effects of devaluations on real output. Gylfason and Schmid (1983) have constructed a simple macroeconomic model to show the effects of devaluation on real income through the demand side (via exports, imports and domestic expenditure) and the supply side (via the cost of imported inputs). The authors, by imputing plausible values, taken from different studies, to corresponding structural parameters of the model for a group of ten countries, conclude that the demand effects dominate the cost effects in most cases, thus supporting the traditional view that devaluation has a positive effect in the short to medium term. In a fairly general macroeconomic model which incorporates the link between devaluation, foreign interest payments and the current account, Gylfason and Risager (1984) attempt to assess the empirical importance of this link for a group of highly indebted industrial and developing countries. Using available statistical estimates of the structural parameters of the model, taken from other studies, they come to the conclusion that 'high external debt and interest payments tend to reduce the short to medium run effect of devaluation on national income, especially in the less developed countries (LDCs), but make little difference to its generally positive effect on the current account'. Gylfason and Radetzki (1985), presenting the results of the simulation of a macro model for a group of developing countries, conclude that devaluation leads to a decline in real output, especially when wages are indexed. Connolly (1983), regressing the change in real growth rates on the change in the nominal exchange rate for a group of 22 countries, found some support for the hypothesis of the expansionary effects of a devaluation. Edwards (1986), using data for 12 developing countries in a reduced form model which incorporates the role of monetary and fiscal policies and changes in the terms of trade, came to the conclusion that 'devaluations generate a small contractionary effect in the first year. In the second year, however, this effect is completely reversed. In the long run devaluations are neutral.'

4 THE MODEL

The aim of this paper is to determine the effects of exchange rate policy on the Greek economy and to find out if exchange rate policy (together with fiscal and monetary policies, and terms-of-trade changes) has had a contractionary, expansionary or a neutral effect on real GDP. Until the beginning of 1975 the exchange rate of the drachma against the US dollar was that determined on 9 April 1953. After that date and up to 1979 the rate of the drachma against the US dollar and the other hard currencies was devalued slowly through the method of 'sliding down'. After 1980 the devaluation of the drachma was speeded up through the same method, and through two *de jure* devaluations in January 1983 and October 1985. During the period 1973/4 to 1986 the inflation rate was high, impeding the economy's international competitiveness. The implemented fiscal policy, especially after 1981, contributed to high fiscal deficits and high external debt and the monetary policy adopted was in the main accommodating the public sector.

This situation, coupled with high increases in wages and a slowing down of productivity, was the framework within which exchange rate policy has been called to play its role. Under such conditions our reduced form single equation model for the Greek case incorporates not only exchange rate changes, but also fiscal, monetary and terms of trade variables in explaining the behaviour of real domestic product. The model is as follows:

$$logy_t = ß_0 + {_y}T_t + ß_1 log(GE/Y)_t + ß_2 \Delta logM_t + ß_3 logRE_t + ß_4 logtt_t + \varepsilon_t \qquad (1)$$

where

y	=	*GDP*, at constant 1970 prices
T	=	time. It incorporates the so called 'residual factor'.
(GE/Y)	=	the ratio of government expenditure to nominal national income (GNI)
$\Delta logM$	=	the actual rate of growth of money (M1)
RE	=	the real exchange rate (drachmas against US\$), defined as the product of nominal exchange rate and the ratio of the wholesale price index of the USA to the consumer price index of Greece; that is, $RE = E. \dfrac{WSP}{CP}$

where

> E = nominal exchange rate;
> *WSP* = wholesale prices;
> *CP* = consumer prices.

RE is used as a proxy for the relative prices of tradables to non-tradables. We used the rate of the drachma to US dollar because a significant part of external transactions is carried out in dollars and psychologically the Greek public refers to the dollar to assess the external value of the drachma.

> tt = the terms of trade, defined as the ratio of the unit value of exports to the unit value of imports (in domestic currency).
> ε = an error term.

From the estimation of equation (1) one would expect *a priori* $\beta_1 > 0$ and $\beta_2 > 0$. Coefficient β_3 shows the effect of real devaluation on GDP. If devaluations have an expansionary effect, then $\beta_3 > 0$; if $\beta_3 < 0$, then we have a contractionary effect. Because equation (1) is of a reduced form, coefficient β_3 shows the *net effect* of devaluations on GDP. The sign of coefficient β_4 cannot be determined *a priori*.

In the estimation lagged variables were also introduced to show short- and long-run effects, which is very important especially for the real exchange rate variable, since this is the primary interest of this paper.

5   THE FINDINGS OF THE ESTIMATION

From a set of estimated equations which are variations of (1), with or without lags, we have chosen four, as shown in Table 10.1. As shown in this table the fiscal variable (*GE/Y*) has a positive effect on GDP which is statistically significant especially in equations (1.3) and (1.4), where the variable is lagged by one year. The effect of the monetary variable ($\Delta logM_t$) is strong and statistically significant.

In order to see if the rational expectations method is appropriate for the Greek economy, we introduced a money surprise term ($\Delta logM - \Delta logM^*$). The equation used to generate the expected rate of money growth (M^*) is as follows:

$$\Delta logM_t = \alpha_0 + \alpha_1 \Delta logM_{t-1} + \alpha_2 \Delta logM_{t-2} + \alpha_3 logBD_t + u_t \qquad (2)$$

where *BD* is the budget deficit. This variable was included because in many countries money creation is a source of deficit financing. As can be seen from Table 10.1 the coefficient of unexpected changes in money growth (lagged or not) is negative, though statistically significant, which leads to the conclusion that the method of rational expectations is somewhat inappropriate for the Greek economy. On the contrary, Edwards (1986, p. 505) found a positive coefficient in his model for 12 developing countries. As far as the effect of terms of trade on the real output is concerned, it is rather ambiguous and insignificant.

The main interest of this paper focuses on the effect of exchange rate changes on real output. This effect is negative either in the short or in the medium run, as shown in equations (1.1), (1.2) and (1.3). This result confirms the 'contractionary effect hypothesis' both during the period of devaluation and during the next two periods. We also came to the same conclusion when nominal exchange rates were introduced. A likely intercorrelation between the determining variables could not be resolved since the correlation coefficients matrix did not show any serious correlation between them.

The results mentioned above support the structuralist aspect that structural deficiencies in the economy do not allow exchange rate policy to act efficiently. Devaluations were not allowed to shift aggregate demand and supply in such a way that an increase in real output might result.

6   SOME REMARKS

The empirical results of our analysis show that, with other things given, exchange rate policy, as it was exercised, had a negative effect on real GDP. The 'sliding down' of the drachma and *de jure* devaluations could not switch demand from imported goods to those domestically produced. Wage indexation, inflationary expectations, a high dependence of economic activity on imported inputs (Sarantides, 1970), declining productivity and abstention from innovative investments were some of the main features of the period since the first oil crisis and especially since 1980, which rendered the exchange rate policy ineffective. Moreover the exchange rate policy was not implemented within an appropriate framework of fiscal and monetary policies.

Alogoskoufis (1989, pp. 37–38) in a study of macroeconomic policy and the external constraints in a dependent economy like Greece, suggests that

Table 10.1   Results of estimated equations of behaviour of GDP, 1970–86

| | Equation number | | | |
	(1.1)	*(1.2)*	*(1.3)*	*(1.4)*
Constant	14.20	14.22	15.17	13.46
T	0.0290	0.0316	0.0182	0.0419
	(5.53)	(10.97)	(4.18)	(6.66)
$log(GE/Y)_t$	0.178	0.1167	–	–
	(1.16)	(1.24)		
$log(GE/Y)_{t-1}$	–	–	0.5707	0.3121
			(3.70)	(2.16)
$\Delta logM_t$	0.6092	0.9983	–	–
	(2.98)	(7.08)		
$[\Delta logM_t - \Delta logM^*_t]$	–	–0.0250	–	–
		(–6.26)		
$[\Delta logM_{t-1} - \Delta logM^*_{t-1}]$	–	–	–0.0221	–0.0120
			(–4.45)	(–2.47)
$logRE_t$	–0.0706	–0.2378	–	–
	(–0.65)	(–4.49)		
$logRE_{t-1}$	–0.3759	–0.1953	–0.6367	–
	(–1.80)	(–1.98)	(–5.64)	
$logRE_{t-2}$	–	–	–0.2732	–
			(–1.81)	
$logE_{t-1}$	–	–	–	–0.3743
				(–4.43)
$logE_{t-2}$	–	–	–	0.1592
				(1.55)
$logtt_t$	–0.0368	–0.0949	–	–
	(–0.26)	(–1.31)		
$logtt_{(t-1)}$	–	–	0.2031	0.0459
			(1.72)	(0.36)
R^2	0.976	0.993	0.982	0.987
SEE	0.02296	0.00949	0.01441	0.01706
D–W	1.90	2.12	2.93	1.74
N	17	17	17	17

Notes:
1. Numbers in parentheses are the *t*-statistic.
2. SEE is the standard error of equation.
3. R^2 is the adjusted coefficient of determination.
4. D–W is the Durbin–Watson statistic.
5. N is the number of observations.

the effects of exchange rate policy depend crucially on the degree of indexation of nominal wages. With full indexation, exchange rate policy cannot affect competitiveness, and has no real effects even in the very short run ... Had there been no downward inflexibility of nominal wages and had there been mechanisms in place for a successful implementation of an incomes policy, there would have been no need for an active exchange rate policy.

And given the downward inflexibility, Alogoskoufis suggests a combination of exchange policy and incomes policy to tackle a large temporary shock which necessitates a fall in the real exchange rate. Dean and Koromzay (1987, p. 24) in an OECD study of current account imbalances and adjustment mechanisms suggest that 'whether or not exchange rate changes can be effective in promoting adjustment in the medium term depends crucially on the way economic policies respond'.

The estimated simple model has given the net result of devaluations on GDP without discerning favourable or unfavourable effects and consequently the matter is open to further investigation by more analytical models. However it has the advantage of taking into account the behaviour of other variables, like fiscal and monetary policies and external and residual disturbances.

7   EXCHANGE-RATE POLICY IN VIEW OF 1992 AND 2000

With the end of 1992 in view, the role of foreign exchange policy should be changed drastically. At the beginning of 1993 an internal market will be established comprising an area without internal frontiers in which the free movement of goods, persons, services and capital is ensured in accordance with the provisions of the Treaty of Rome, as envisaged by the Single European Act (SEA) and the White Paper. One of the provisions of the SEA is the economic and monetary cooperation within the framework of the European Monetary System (EMS).

The EMS, which was put into operation in March 1979, establishes fixed, though adjustable, exchange rates between the member-state currencies. Gyrating exchange rates have undesirable consequences for a country's economic stability, which could perhaps impair the process of economic and monetary cooperation between EC member countries. Pegging exchange rates at agreed levels or accepting fluctuations within very narrow margins demands a closer cooperation of monetary policies in member countries, more or less the same interest rates in all countries and inflation rates close to one another. Differences in inflation rates within the

EC countries should be faced by austere monetary and fiscal policies and not by competitive depreciations. Fixed exchange rates make it difficult for member countries to depreciate to compensate for the effects of wage increases beyond productivity on competitiveness.

The Greek drachma has been participating in the 'basket' of European currencies, the European currency unit (ECU), since 1984. This means that Greece, participating in the EMS, should take all the necessary measures of economic policy to reduce the balance of payments deficit and consequently to take part in the mechanism of the formation of bilateral exchange rate parities at least in the near future. The prospects of complete participation of Greece in the economic and monetary union render it very difficult, if not impossible, to devalue or let the drachma slide down continuously. Problems in the balance of payments should be solved by appropriate correction and adjustment to domestic economic policies.

The policy implications of Greece's participation in the economic and monetary union agree with the conclusions of this paper. Devaluation or sliding down of the Greek drachma cannot solve structural problems. After 1992 Greece will be compelled to cope with problems, such as balance of payments deficits and inflation, by appropriate domestic economic policies and not by exchange-rate depreciations. Balance of payments deficits were the result of excess aggregate demand, which in turn was fuelled by the large budget deficits of the 1980s, excess monetary supply, which is more or less a symptom of large deficits and wage increases greater than productivity increases. Aggregate supply should be strengthened by structural measures, mainly technological innovation, so that Greek production may become internationally competitive.

References

Alogoskoufis, G. S. (1989) 'Macroeconomics policy and the external constraint in the dependent economy', *Discussion Paper 89/3*, Birkbeck College, London.

Connolly, M. (1983) 'Exchange rates, real economic activity and the balance of payments: Evidence from the 1960's', in Claassen, E. and Salin, P. (eds), *Recent Issues in the Theory of the Flexible Exchange Rates* (Amsterdam: North Holland).

Cooper, R. N. (1971) 'Currency devaluation in developing countries', *Essays in International Finance*, no. 86, Princeton University.

Dean, A. and Koromzay, V. (1987) 'Current-account imbalances and adjustment mechanisms', *Economic Studies*, no. 8 (Paris: OECD) Spring.

Diaz-Alejandro, C. (1965) *Exchange Rate Devaluation in a Semi-Industrialised Economy: The Experience of Argentina 1955–61* (Cambridge, Mass.: MIT Press).

Edwards, S. (1986) 'Are devaluations contractionary?', *Review of Economics and Statistics*, vol. 68, August, pp. 501–8.

Gylfason, T. and Radetzki, M. (1985) 'Does devaluation make sense in the least developed countries?', *Seminar paper no. 314* (Institute for International Economics Studies, University of Stockholm).

Gylfason, T. and Risager, D. (1984) 'Does devaluation improve the current account?', *European Economic Review*, vol. 25, June, pp. 37–64.

Gylfason, T. and Schmid, M. (1983) 'Does devaluation cause stagflation?', *Canadian Journal of Economics*, vol. 16, November, pp. 506–21.

Hanson, J. A. (1983) 'Contractionary devaluation, substitution in production and consumption, and the role of the labor market', *Journal of International Economics*, vol. 14, pp. 179–89.

Hirschman, A. O. (1949) 'Devaluation and the trade balance: A note', *Review of Economics and Statistics*, vol. 31, pp. 50–3.

Krugman, P. and Taylor, L. (1978) 'Contractionary effects of devaluation', *Journal of International Economics*, vol. 8, pp. 445–56.

Meade, J. (1951) *The Theory of International Economic Policy, vol. 1 The Balance of Payments* (London: Macmillan).

OECD (1984) 'Macroeconomic policies and exchange rates', *Economic Studies* (Paris: OECD).

Sarantides, S. A. (1970) 'Estimation of the economic activity dependence on imported inputs in Greece', *Spoudai*, vol. 20, no. 5 (in Greek).

11 The Economic Union of the European Community and the Greek Economy: The External Sector

E. Pournarakis

ATHENS UNIVERSITY OF ECONOMICS AND BUSINESS

1 INTRODUCTION

The European Council at its meeting of June 1989 endorsed the Delors Report for the creation of an economic and monetary union within the European Community (EC). The Report calls upon all the member countries to commit themselves to a timetable that will permit a step-by-step evolutionary process leading to 'irrevocably fixed exchange rates' between members' currencies and ultimately to a single currency and a common monetary policy. This, of course, is by far the most challenging project and is seen as an extension of the internal market programme.

This paper looks into the problems likely to arise in the external sector of the Greek economy in its preparation to face this new challenge. The emphasis is placed on the necessary economic policy measures in the short and long run in view of the ongoing developments and the structural idiosyncrasies of the economy. After this introduction, section 2 reviews recent developments in the external sector while Section 3 looks ahead, both to the immediate and the more distant future, in terms of economic policy.

In the last decade the Greek economy has suffered persistent imbalances of large magnitude both internally and externally. Table 11.1 highlights those imbalances most closely related to the external disequilibrium of the economy. The picture conveyed by these data is basically one of long-lasting stagflation domestically with persistent deficits in the current account balance. Large and continuously increasing budget deficits throughout the decade, partially financed by the central bank, were accompanied by moderate but steady increases in the real money supply. Undoubtedly this combina-

Table 11.1 Greece: selected economic indicators, 1980–8 (annual percentage change unless otherwise specified)

	1980	1981	1982	1983	1984	1985	1986	1987	1988
Real GDP	2.1	0.2	0.6	0.4	2.9	3.4	1.3	–0.4	3.5
Consumer prices	24.9	24.5	21.0	20.2	18.5	19.3	23.0	16.4	13.5
Money supply (M$_3$)	18.4	23.3	22.1	13.7	29.4	26.8	19.0	24.8	22.8
Long-term interest rates (annual yield on public bonds)	–	–	–	–	18.5	15.8	15.8	18.5	19.0
Effective exchange rates	–13.3	–6.0	–8.9	–16.9	–11.5	–17.9	–22.0	–11.0	–7.2
Balance on current account (billions US dollars)	–2.2	–2.4	–1.9	–1.9	–2.1	–3.3	–1.8	–1.2	–1.0
Budget deficit (per cent of GDP)	–8.0	–12.7	–9.3	–9.8	–10.2	–13.9	–11.4	–14.3	–15.6

Sources: Bank of Greece, Monthly Bulletin, Annual Report (various issues); EC, European Economy (various issues).

tion of a heavily indebted government sector, high inflation rates and a basically accommodating monetary policy was, to a large extent, responsible for the negative changes in the effective exchange rates throughout the 1980s. At the same time, to the extent that exchange rate changes fed into the prices of tradable goods and consequently into the domestic sector of the economy, inflation was reinforced, creating a vicious circle phenomenon.

2   LESSONS FROM THE TWO DEPRECIATIONS

2.1   The Early 1980s

As regards the external disequilibrium, the Greek experience of the early 1980s (that is, 1982–5) confirms the vicious circle theory. Indeed the first discrete depreciation of 1983 as well as the gradual changes in the effective exchange rates did not enhance the competitiveness of the economy. The reduction in costs via the relative decrease of real wages, expected at that time, did not come about. Instead, with the practice of wage indexation, there was a quick response of money wages to price increases, so that this interaction led to a resurgence of inflation. In addition, inflationary expectations reinforced the existing inflationary trends, causing an increase in the cost of exports which more than outweighed the favourable effects of devaluation on competitiveness. As shown in Table 11.2, unit labour costs increased by an average annual percentage of 20.1 for the period 1982–6, while the current account deficit in 1985 was close to twice as high as in 1982.

Table 11.2 shows the remarkable parallel movement in import prices and price deflators. It is well known that Greece is the EC economy most vulnerable to international inflation on account of the large share of imported raw materials in the cost of domestic supply. Unit labour costs increased faster than in any other EC country in the last five years. Furthermore the liquidity ratios of the Greek economy in the same period were among the highest. Finally Greece during this period experienced the largest negative changes in its nominal effective exchange rates within the EC. These four factors: (i) unit labour costs, (ii) higher import prices, (iii) liquidity, and (iv) changes in effective exchange rates accounted for the fact that the Greek economy's price deflator was consistently three times higher than the EC average.

Table 11.2   Greece: selected inflation indicators (annual percentage change)

	1982–6	1987	1988	
Wholesale price index (total)	18.0	11.4	9.8	
Wholesale price index for imported products	20.6	12.3	9.3	
	1986	*1987*	*1988*	*1989*[*]
Price deflator imports of goods and services (excluding intra-EC imports)	8.4 (−10.7)	2.4 (−1.0)	8.1 (2.1)	12.4 (4.5)
Unit labour costs	12.2 (4.2)	14.7 (3.7)	14.5 (3.4)	11.9 (3.3)
Liquidity ratio (M3/GDP)	1.7 (1.8)	5.7 (3.8)	6.4 (2.3)	4.4 (1.3)

Notes:
* Forecast by EC *European Economy Supplement A* (April 1989).
  Figures in parenthesis refer to average for the 12 EC members.

Sources: As Table 11.1.

2.2   The Devaluation of 1985

The devaluation of the drachma in October 1985 is in striking contrast to that of 1982 as far as results are concerned. Of course it is not without importance that this time the devaluation was accompanied by tight macroeconomic and incomes policies. The improvements in the balance of payments which started in 1986 may be attributed primarily to a decrease in aggregate demand and real wages. The relief in the current account deficit was primarily the result of increases in the invisible trade surplus. In the two years that followed devaluation the current account deficit was reduced to the lowest level of the decade. In addition high real interest rates helped create non-debt private capital inflows and provided relief to the previously heavy foreign borrowing, which led to a comfortable foreign reserve position.

The experience of the 1985 devaluation, notwithstanding coincidental favourable developments in the capital account of the balance of payments, provides convincing proof that prudent macroeconomic policy is a *sine qua non* for the success of discrete parity adjustments in a small and very open economy with the structural idiosyncrasies of Greece. Most of the credit for improvement in the balance of payments is due to the monetary policy which, among other things, had to overcome the obstacle of 'crowding out' and the heavy borrowing requirement of the public sector. However it must have been a pleasant surprise to the Bank of Greece to see how much could be accomplished in the external sector simply by raising real interest rates to levels comparable to those of other countries. It would seem that, even when the repatriation of capital decreased considerably, capital mobility due to interest change sensitivity was quite high. In addition high interest rates were decisive in weakening inflationary expectations. In the final analysis, this latter factor of lower inflationary expectations was a catalytic one for this partial turn-around in the Greek balance of payments.

3   WHAT LIES AHEAD: ECONOMIC POLICY POSSIBILITIES IN THE SHORT RUN

Perhaps the most important lesson to emerge from the experience of recent developments in the external sector of the economy was the realisation that, in a small open economy with a large and steadily widening trade deficit and with a similar situation in the public sector, there *are* things that can be done to improve the balance of payments situation. No doubt the root of the balance of payments problem lies with the limited competitiveness of Greek goods due to high production costs. The structural weaknesses of the balance of trade, however, reflect serious misallocations of a broader nature in the economy as a whole. These structural inadequacies are strictly long-run issues that must be corrected with a plan for the reorientation of production trends in the economy. In the meantime there is an urgent need for short-run measures to cope with the problems of the external sector. Let us turn to these priorities.

3.1   Top Priorities

When the economic problems of a country are as numerous and serious as the ones currently facing the Greek economy, it makes no sense to seek magic policy formulae to cope with all of them at once. It would seem, therefore, that, in view of 1992, economic stability should be the primary concern, to be pursued even at the expense of growth. Reducing large imbalances and high inflation rates must be the primary targets of economic policy in the short run.

The central bank of Greece is called upon to deal *quickly* and effectively with the compound problem of inflation and the deficit in the balance of payments. In the external sector, as discussed above, capital inflows *can* bring about the needed relief in the balance of payments deficit in the next few years. With all interest rates determined by market forces and monetary aggregates appropriately managed, monetary policy could be effective in (a) controlling liquidity, (b) pursuing a consistent policy of disinflation and (c) bringing about improvements in the balance of payments. This, of course, would require a high borrowing requirement and a continuously increasing average interest rate for the debt. The public sector economic policy makers would simply have to abstain from intervening to reduce interest rates for debt servicing purposes and to impose on banks quotas for subscription to short-term treasury bills in order to implement 'crowding-out' activities.[1]

Following the recent endorsement by the European Council of the Delors Report for the creation of an economic and monetary union, Greece is expected to speed up the adjustment process to meet this challenge. Monetary policy must be considered in this perspective when setting targets and using the appropriate tools for implementation.

The evolutionary process leading to monetary unification in the EC makes it mandatory for Greece to follow a flexible interest rate policy in accordance with the conditions prevailing in domestic and international financial markets. The current domestic inflationary trend and the emerging fear of a resurgence of inflation abroad suggest a need for a restrictive monetary policy and high real interest rates. Furthermore, consistent with the recently inaugurated process of the deregulation of the financial system, one would expect a complete dismantling of regulations on portfolio management by credit institutions. This would entail, among other things, that the public sector resort to the open market to satisfy its borrowing needs through sales of long-term bonds.

The need is obvious for cooperation between the fiscal and monetary authorities. The two issues needing immediate attention from both sides are the monetary financing of the budget and the broadening of the tax base. The main responsibility for this lies with the fiscal authorities. The need for fiscal restraint is obvious. More important, the role of the public sector does not end with the negative adjustment of its total demand. There is a crying need for improvement on the supply side. Obviously there is room for productivity improvement and lower unit costs in public production. In the competitive environment of the EC there is no room for the sheltering of inefficient firms, whether public or private. Better resource management is obviously a major source of improvement in the short run. This in itself ought substantially to ease the existing constraints.

Putting the Greek household in order and doing away with unnecessary waste is, I would think, the most urgent short-run objective. Inevitably, with the market mechanism providing guidance, the fiscal and monetary authorities can afford to be selective during this interim period. What it is hoped would come out of these short-run policy measures of managerial improvement and fiscal restraint is a much-needed weakening of inflationary expectations. This in turn will provide the basis for greater flexibility in the hands of monetary authorities.

3.2   Joining the Exchange Rate Mechanism of the European Monetary System

One has to assume that participation in the exchange rate mechanism (ERM) of the European Monetary System (EMS) is more a matter of time and less of choice. For the EC countries who are members of the EMS the two basic prerequisites of a monetary union, that is (i) convertibility of currencies and (ii) complete freedom of capital movements in fully integrated markets, will definitely be met with the creation of the single market. In some EC economies these conditions for monetary union already exist. The third condition and by far the most essential is permanently fixed exchange rates, which when achieved will deprive the central banks of EC members of their independent monetary policies.

'Irrevocably fixed exchange rates', as the final stage of economic union, is beyond the scope of the Greek monetary authorities at this stage. Of more immediate concern is the issue of whether in the prevailing economic situation the Greek economy could adopt the present EC system of fixed but adjustable parities. As we saw earlier, between 1985 and 1988 there was considerable improvement in reducing imbalances in the external sector and inflationary expectations internally. Current developments abroad and domestically, however, do not justify unqualified optimism for this trend to continue. There is a real risk of rekindling inflation and of disrupting the external equilibrium. Thus, following the moderate decrease in budget deficits in 1986 and 1987 as part of the overall contractionary economic policy, the public sector borrowing requirement (PSBR) is back on an increasing trend.

The fiscal problems of Greece are related to inflation and, eventually, to the choice of exchange rate regime in more than one way. Table 11.3 shows the inadequacy of the Greek fiscal structure as regards public receipts, compared to other EC economies. Greece and Portugal are the only two countries whose governments generate substantial revenue through money creation. Low tax revenues in Greece, where tax coefficients are already high, reflect the structure of an economy with a large agricultural sector and extensive self-employment that suffers from a narrow tax base and tax evasion.

This fiscal asymmetry in the EC imposes an extra burden on monetary policy in the selection of exchange rate targets and in being able to stay with them. If the trend towards a gradual decrease in the monetary financing of the budget is reversed as a result of a resurgence of inflation together with high capital mobility, this would impose a severe constraint on the central bank's exchange rate policy.

In spite of these difficulties, the monetary authorities are expected to pursue an economic policy which would shorten the time needed for Greece to become a member of the EMS. Our discussion suggests that one cannot expect substantial improvement in the performance of the Greek economy in the foreseeable future, as this would require major structural improvements, which are long-run matters. In the meantime the increasing uncertainty caused by the present status of the exchange-rate policy militates against the creation of the necessary climate of confidence in the viable sectors of production. A total review of the situation by the monetary authorities might lead to the conclusion that the privilege of 'beggar-thy-

Table 11.3   Public receipts and monetary financing of the budget
(percentage of GDP)

Countries	Public receipts		Monetary financing	
	1974–89	*1988*	*1976–87*	*1984–7*
Greece	29.0	35.7	3.0	2.1
Portugal	–	35.5	5.3	4.5
Spain	27.3	37.4	1.5	−0.5
Rest of EC	39.1	43.5	0.1	−0.5

Source: EC, *European Economy* (May/June 1989).

neighbour' of the present parity system is valued too highly at a time when the rest of the EC is advancing steadily towards monetary unification.

Now the decision for Greece to enter the ERM in the near future would raise the relevant question of the need for a devaluation of the drachma. As shown earlier, the recent history of devaluation in pursuit of stronger competitiveness of domestic products might suggest that this prescription is not suitable for the Greek economy. However, within the context of the change in the exchange rate regime, one cannot afford to be so dogmatic. It is possible that the need might arise for a corrective devaluation for preventive purposes when the time comes for Greece to join the EMS. In this sense it would serve no purpose to take an irrevocably negative position on this issue.

4   THE LONG-TERM OUTLOOK

For the industrial countries of the EC, further integration of the commodity markets and the creation of the single market is viewed as a natural evolution that will not irreparably upset existing equilibria. Instead the major concern lies with the planned shift to irrevocably fixed exchange rates to achieve monetary unification. To begin with, these countries are required to shift from a system which, in its present form, has performed quite well, at least in bringing about inflation convergence. Furthermore, under the present system of fixed but adjustable parities, the possibility of exchange-rate realignment during periods of unforeseen developments is seen by some countries as a means to even out obvious imbalances. While one could view parity realignment as a tool of a potentially aggressive monetary policy by individual member countries at the expense of the Community's interest, this last point is offered as one of the arguments for permanently fixed exchange rates, since such 'beggar-thy-neighbour' policies will be eliminated.

But, whereas permanently fixed exchange rates in a way safeguard economic cooperation according to the rules of the game, the question still remains as to whether fixed exchange rates on an EC-wide basis are viable. The system has managed to survive instability shocks from inside and outside the EC area thanks to the availability of exchange controls. Several times in the past, central banks in the EC were forced to activate the exchange control valve in order to overcome speculative attacks against their currencies.

Obviously, to the extent that macroeconomic asymmetries exist in the EC, one can justify a hesitatant or outright negative position on the issue of monetary unification. In this sense the third phase of economic union, that is, irrevocably fixed exchange rates, is far from being firmly agreed.

4.1 The Financial Shock

If the industrial countries of the EC view 1992 as the shock of financial integration, then countries like Greece are candidates for a double shock. The internal market project is an equally big challenge for an economy facing the kind of problems discussed earlier.

If cross-country asymmetries within the EC constitute a legitimate reason for many EC countries to resist financial unification in the foreseeable future, our discussion about the state of the Greek economy suggests that Greece could not possibly keep pace with the others on this issue. For Greece monetary union is strictly a distant and future issue. In the first place, in an economy as vulnerable to vicious circles as that of Greece, there is only limited room for the immediate liberalisation of capital movements. Inevitably the central bank has to proceed with care. As mentioned earlier, following complete deregulation of the financial system, integration within the EMS should be the next target. An arrangement similar to the one in Italy would allow Greece to retain the privilege of parity adjustment, while the rest of the EC economies (with the possible exception of Portugal) will have entered *de facto*, or experimentally, into the permanently fixed exchange stage. This period should coincide with substantial structural changes in the Greek economy if the country is to take advantage of the EMS. The convergence of the economy to EC standards should lead to full monetary union in due course.

4.2 The Product Market

Now we come to the important question of the economic policy to be pursued in the product sector of the economy over this long interim period. As mentioned earlier, the state of the current account and the trade balance in particular mirror the conditions prevailing in the internal sector. It has become clear at this point that achieving and safeguarding external equilibrium requires lower production costs.

Economic predictions about the distant future or, even worse, the suggestion of long-term economic policy measures by economists are often unwelcome. In the case of the Greek economy the job is, I think, a relatively easy one. Simple logic suggests that a long history of poor performance by an economy which obviously has the potential to do better implies a long sequence of bad judgements by policy makers. If there is merit in the advice not to make the same mistake twice, one can see that, in the case of the Greek economy, this is a good starting-point for policy recommendations.

In the last 30 years economic policy in Greece has been preoccupied with industrialisation. During this period we have basically seen three different strategies for industrial production: (i) the strategy of import substitution prevailed throughout the 1960s; (ii) in the 1970s export-led growth seemed to be the main concern, accompanied by remarkable monetary accommodation; (iii) the 1980s were characterised by more selectivity. Today Greece is still looking for viable export industries. It would seem that the time has come for Greece to review the orientation of the economy in an EC context rather than insist on industrialisation at any cost.

It is indeed a violation of the basic principle of economic integration for the Greek economy to enter a powerful economic block and insist on promoting sectors which have no comparative advantage, at least in the forseeable future. Furthermore this industrialisation syndrome entails a high alternative cost, to the extent that it crowds out other, more efficient lines of production.

One does not need to go into a detailed analysis of statistical data to show that the target of industrialisation was misconceived and that any legislation aimed at preferential treatment of industrial units ought to be highly selective. The most promising areas within industry in the context of Greece's integration within the EC are well known. For the most part they are related to the sectors in which Greece possesses advantages over the other EC members; that is, primary and tertiary activities. The highly aggregated data in Tables 11.4 and 11.5 tell the story very eloquently. Greece's trade deficit arises from her trade with EC member countries. Therefore the battle for lower costs must be waged within the EC. Subsequently the signals for the correct resource allocation should be given by the EC market. *That* market should help to correct the mistakes of misallocation, and be used as the guide to plan for preferential treatment in production. In all probability, if this were done, we would find that agriculture was destined to play a role of vital importance for several years, while, in the more distant future, services will become important.

Reorientation of resource allocation with the help of the market should therefore be the key to long-term policy making. The availability of good management and updated technologies should ensure that the much needed productivity increase eventually takes place.

Of course these changes will not come about in a short period of time. It is in this sense that the monetary authorities cannot afford to be in a hurry

Table 11.4   Greece: trade balance (billion ECUs)

	1982–6	1987	1988	1989[1]
Trade balance (total)	–6.2	–5.4	–5.8	–6.8
Trade balance with EC	–2.8	–3.2	–3.5	–4.0

Note:
1. Forecast by EC, *European Economy Supplement A* (May/June 1989).
Source: EC, *European Economy* (various issues).

Table 11.5   Greece: sectoral contribution to changes
in real GDP (per cent)

Sector	1984	1985	1986	1987	1988	Total
Primary	0.9	0.3	0.1	–0.6	0.8	1.5
Secondary	0.4	1.1	0.1	–0.4	1.5	2.7
of which:						
manufacturing	0.3	0.7	0.0	–0.4	1.0	0.7
Services	1.6	2.0	1.1	0.6	1.2	6.5
GDP	2.9	3.4	1.3	–0.4	3.5	10.7

Source: Bank of Greece, *Annual Report* (1989).

to adopt financial market integration practices. It is also in this sense that cooperation between fiscal and monetary authorities is necessary throughout this long transition period.

5   COORDINATION OF FISCAL AND MONETARY POLICY

To summarise the argument for coordination of monetary and fiscal policy in tackling the compound problem of inflation, deficits and unemployment: first, let us agree that in the external sector of the economy it is the concept of *basic balance* derived by subtracting net borrowing from the official balance that is most relevant in the present context. With the capital account of the balance of payments playing such an important role and given the present situation facing the Greek economy, it makes sense for monetary policy to carry the main burden for the achievement of external equilibrium, while the internal sector should rely more heavily on fiscal policy in a broad sense. Interest rates and flexible exchange rates must be the main tools of stability. Gradual disinflation should be the goal. Ironically, flexible parities are needed to help undo what they are obviously partially responsible for causing; that is, inflation. Although fixed exchange rates would bring about a much needed discipline, flexibility cannot be abandoned abruptly if the economy is to come out of its low equilibrium trap internally. Even if it is desirable, by EC standards the Greek economy cannot afford to disinflate too fast in response to the call for convergence by Brussels. A combination of relatively high real interest rates and hopefully fixed, but potentially adjustable exhange rates, could secure a relatively steady capital inflow, in an adjustment effort to improve the external sector and control inflation.

Fiscal policy will be expected to supplement monetary policy on the supply side. In addition to phasing out monetary financing of the budget, there is a clear need to widen the tax-rate pyramid and to chop off its top in order to encourage private savings. Fiscal expansion, designed to keep the desirable level of demand, as well as income policies, needs to be handled consistently, *vis-à-vis* the implementation of the adjustment process. *Consistency* in making intertemporal choices is of key importance. It will bring about the much needed *credibility* in economic policy. Among other things, credibility will help with the crucial issue of labour market rigidities and wage restraint, so that fixed-term contracts can be introduced, while fiscal incentives to reduce labour costs could bring about more flexibility in the labour market and eventually allow the use of productivity criteria to determine wage levels.

Notes

1. In the European Community obligations on banks to invest in government paper exist also in Portugal, Ireland and Spain. As a percentage of total bank resources compulsory investment in these countries ranges between 5 per cent in Portugal and 15 per cent in Ireland. Greek banks have to hold 38 per cent of their deposits for investment in government paper and bonds issued by public enterprises.

2. Financing of the public sector by the central bank is also important for Spain, Italy and Belgium. Central bank credit for Spain and Italy can reach 12 per cent and 14 per cent respectively of these countries' total government outlays. For Greece this percentage is 10 per cent. In Belgium is was 7 per cent in 1988, but the annual ceiling is in absolute values.

3. Outstanding loans from the central bank of Greece to the general government are substantial, although, when expressed as a percentage of GDP, the level has declined (from 12.5 per cent in 1985 to 8 per cent in 1988). However provisional data for 1989 as well as current developments show the likelihood of a reversal of this trend.

12 The Integration of Greece into the European Economy

Loukas Tsoukalis
UNIVERSITY OF ATHENS

F02

Greece, EC

1 HISTORICAL BACKGROUND

There have been three important turning-points in Greece's external economic relations in the postwar period. The first was in 1953, with the 100 per cent devaluation of the drachma against the dollar and the first serious steps towards trade liberalisation. The second followed in 1961, when Greece became the first country to sign an Association Agreement with the six founder members of the European Community (EC). This agreement envisaged the establishment of a customs union for industrial products. Despite the limited reciprocity as regards tariff liberalisation, especially in the early stages of the agreement, and the delays resulting from the imposition of military rule in Greece from 1967 to 1974, the association with the EC led to the further opening up of the Greek economy, while also contributing to the reorientation of Greece's external economic relations towards western Europe. The third turning-point came with the country's accession to the EC in 1981, which can be seen as the next logical step in the gradual process of integration into the western European economy.

For a period of almost twenty years, until 1973, the Greek economy enjoyed high rates of economic growth, second only to Japan inside the OECD, together with price stability. This long period of unprecedented growth produced a radical transformation of the Greek economy, while also sharpening its dualistic character. In contrast to the country's earlier history, the balance of payments, especially during the latter half of this period, did not act as a major constraint to economic growth. The large and persistent trade deficits (the export coverage of imports was invariably far below 50 per cent) were paid for through surpluses on the invisibles account (tourism, migrant remittances and shipping) as well as capital inflows.

The Association Agreement with the EC offered the possibility of export-led growth for some of the most dynamic industrial sectors, while the process of dismantling domestic protection, in its non-tariff form in particular, was rather slow (Tsoukalis, 1981, pp. 17–49). External protection in Greece was rarely employed as part of an overall industrialisation strategy until then; instead, it was usually the result of an incoherent response by the political authorities to domestic pressure groups.

The first oil shock of 1973, followed by a recession in the world economy, brought about a significant change in the international economic environment, which in turn created the need for domestic economic adjustment. However this adverse change coincided with the fall of the military dictatorship, and democratic consolidation in Greece took precedence, naturally, perhaps, over economic adjustment. In fact a very similar situation existed at the time in both Spain and Portugal, and the political reactions, at least in the first years, were also similar. While other western European countries introduced measures of economic adjustment, in southern Europe government activity grew rapidly, and so did wages and salaries. This led to a wage–price spiral and a deterioration in international competitiveness.

The resistance to economic adjustment proved to be much more stubborn in Greece. The second oil shock coincided with the intensification of the domestic political struggle on the eve of the 1981 elections which brought the Socialists to power. The new government put the emphasis on rapid structural adjustment and internal redistribution, with the state expected to act as the main driving force of economic development. But, in the pursuit of its economic policies, the new government took little notice of the external constraints imposed on a small and open economy and the gross inefficiency of the Greek public sector.

While the rest of western Europe quickly shifted into deflationary gear, which caused unemployment to rise to unprecedented levels, Greece continued with expansionary policies, but the attempt to bring about adjustment through growth failed. Rapidly widening public sector deficits and high rates of inflation were combined with depressingly low rates of growth and investment. The balance of payments constraint forced the government to adopt a stabilisation programme at the end of 1985, following a devaluation of the drachma. But political considerations soon put an end to economic stabilisation. The same story was repeated in the late 1980s, when public-sector deficits and inflation rates reached new peaks. Thus the divergence of Greek macroeconomic policies from those pursued in the rest of the EC became even more pronounced.

Although statistics are not very reliable, unemployment in Greece appears to have remained consistently below the EC average, thus offering the only bright spot on an otherwise dark economic horizon. But this has been achieved through the continuous expansion of the public sector, characterised by excessive over-manning and the operation of political patronage, and the artificial survival of many debt-ridden firms which have been kept alive through state subsidies. This policy is hardly sustainable in the long term, as public-sector deficits have reached record levels (exceeding 20 per cent of GDP in 1989).

Import penetration of the Greek market by EC suppliers has grown rapidly, especially in the more traditional sectors which in the past enjoyed high rates of protection, especially of the non-tariff kind. There has been both a trade creation and a trade diversion effect. On the other hand, Greek exporters proved unable to secure higher export shares of European markets. The inevitable result was the steady worsening of the trade deficit and a depressing effect on domestic industrial production. The liberalisation of the economy also seems to have contributed to the gradual shift of Greek entrepreneurs back to traditional sectors such as food, beverages, textiles and clothing, thus further strengthening the inter-industry division of labour between Greece and the rest of the Community (Giannitsis, 1988). Greece's main competitors in the manufacturing sector are the third world newly industrialising countries (NICs), which operate on very low wage costs: a factor which will continue to act as a major constraint on the further expansion of Greek exports.

2   ADJUSTMENT OF THE GREEK ECONOMY TO THE EC

The structural weaknesses of the Greek economy have, undoubtedly, been an important factor behind the difficulties of adjusting to strong European competition. Low levels of development and technology, the small size of firms, poor infrastructure and a long history of external protection have created serious handicaps for Greek industrialists. This also explains the continued reference to infant industry arguments and the appeals for greater flexibility in the application of EC rules made by some Greek economists (Giannitsis, 1988). Such arguments were repeatedly used in the past by the socialist government as a justification for the lengthening of the transitional period following Greece's accession, and the granting of derogations from EC rules, although these were almost invariably used as a means of postponing adjustment.

Structural weaknesses are only one part of the explanation for Greece's difficulties in adjusting to the new European and international environment. The struggle for international competitiveness was strongly undermined by continuous macroeconomic mismanagement which helped to shift resources away from investment and exports and also led to the progressive overvaluation of the drachma. For years the exchange rate has been used, together with monetary policy, as the main instrument in the fight against inflation, while fiscal policy was allowed to continue on its own independent and irresponsible course. Economics are intimately linked to politics: a highly polarised society and a predominantly inward-looking political class have acted as important constraints on economic adjustment.

As expected, accession to the EC has been accompanied by a significant transfer of resources through Community funds, improved access to sources of lending at attractive rates of interest and a deterioration in the trade balance. Annual transfers now exceed 4 per cent of GDP, a non-negligible amount of money which makes Greece, together with Ireland, one of the biggest beneficiaries of the EC budget. However the bulk of EC money, and especially the transfers arising from price intervention in the agricultural sector, went into consumption rather than investment; furthermore there is evidence of considerable wastage of resources through the Regional Fund and the Social Fund and the Integrated Mediterranean Programmes.

Capital inflows into Greece, especially in the form of foreign direct investment, seem hardly to have been influenced by accession to the EC, and until now Greece has been relatively little affected, with the exception of the food and beverages sector, by the wave of transnational mergers and acquisitions which are part of the current restructuring of European industry. Greece has remained on the margin of these developments, unlike the more recent members of the Community, namely Spain and Portugal. This is doubtless related to the negative economic climate which has prevailed in Greece for some years.

Short-term capital movements, and the balance of payments in general, have reflected the ebb and flow of public confidence in the Greek economy and its currency. Low confidence, usually also associated with devaluation expectations, has been quickly translated into a deterioration of both the current and the capital accounts through leads and lags and the illegal export of capital (administrative controls being largely ineffective in an open economy with a big invisible account). Such developments were behind the rapid deterioration of the balance of payments situation in both 1985 and 1989.

3 THE FUTURE WITHIN THE EC

The current acceleration in the process of European economic integration is bound to lead to a more competitive economic environment, through the elimination of many of the remaining barriers in intra-EC trade and also through a certain degree of deregulation which is an integral part of the 1992 target. However the greater emphasis on competition and the market, as the main driving forces of economic growth, will be complemented by the strengthening of EC redistributive mechanisms and the gradual transfer of powers to the Community level in the macroeconomic field, particularly as regards monetary policy. Developments in the latter area will depend on the speed with which the EC moves towards the establishment of an economic and monetary union.

Greece will benefit from an even bigger transfer of resources, which is expected to reach 6–7 per cent of GDP on a net annual basis by the end of 1992. This should help to alleviate the balance of payments constraint and boost investment activity, mainly in terms of public infrastructure. The establishment of the internal market should contribute towards the creation of a stable framework governing economic exchange, thus eliminating the uncertainty from which private agents in Greece have suffered for so long. It should also accelerate the process of liberalisation and deregulation in an economy where government intervention has usually been irrational, at least in economic terms, and self-contradictory.

The rigidity of domestic structures and the refusal for so long to accept the constraints imposed by a small and open economy have created a serious handicap for Greece in the highly competitive European environment. The country is faced once again with a major stabilisation effort aimed at correcting both domestic and external financial imbalances. Domestic consumption needs to be brought down to a level compatible with the external balance and a high rate of economic growth in the future, which in turn means the transfer of resources towards exports and investment. The achievement of macroeconomic stability will require a drastic reduction in budget deficits. This promises to be a painful exercise because of the high cost of servicing the accumulated debt. The recent experience of Ireland could be indicative in this respect (Dornbusch, 1989).

4   ACTIONS FOR ECONOMIC ADJUSTMENT

The curtailment of public expenditure, which should be part of a more general process of rationalisation and modernisation of the public sector, needs to be accompanied by a greater exposure of state-owned enterprises to market forces, including privatisation in sectors where there are no natural monopolies. In some cases this will necessitate an appeal to foreign capital. It should also lead to the privatisation of numerous lame-ducks and the closure of others which have for years been dependent on public money. An increase in unemployment, at least in the short and medium term, may be the inevitable consequence of such action.

The gradual loss of international competitiveness may point to a need for further devaluation of the drachma in real terms, either as a one-shot affair or through an acceleration of the downward floating of the currency. The high degree of openness of the economy and the dependence on imported raw materials, together with the system of indexation of wages and salaries, means that there is a serious risk that devaluation will be quickly translated into higher inflation rates, thus eliminating the positive effects on the competitiveness of domestic firms. The success of a devaluation, therefore, would be dependent on the pursuit of restrictive policies and a further dilution of the indexation system: a policy instrument that needs to be used sparingly in an open economy.

Transparency and consistency in terms of the basic rules of the economic game, together with macroeconomic stability, manifested primarily through a marked reduction in inflation rates, are preconditions for the much needed change in the economic climate. In order to strengthen the credibility of the new macroeconomic stance of the Greek government, a reduction in domestic inflation should be accompanied, at a relatively early stage, by the decision to join the exchange rate mechanism of the EMS, perhaps opting for the wider margins of fluctuation adopted by the peseta, and by accelerating the process of capital liberalisation to which Greece is committed through the EC Directive of June 1988. The creation of flexible labour markets, with a strong emphasis on a high level of training and education, should also be a major priority.

I shall resist the temptation of trying to identify areas of comparative advantage for Greece in the context of the European single market. The rapid changes on the international economic scene and the negative experience of Greece in the past militate against a very active role for the state in this respect. This conclusion is based less on a firm belief in the absolute efficiency of markets and more on the acknowledged inefficiency and inflexibility of the Greek state. The creation of a favourable environment should in itself constitute a significant contribution to economic growth and development.

The process of economic liberalisation in Eastern Europe, and the Balkan countries in particular, should provide Greece with a valuable economic 'hinterland' and new prospects for trade and cooperation. The advantages may, however, be partly outweighed by increased competition for foreign investment and budgetary transfers from the EC.

References

Dornbusch, R. (1989) 'Credibility, debt and unemployment: Ireland's failed stabilisation', *Economic Policy*, April.

Giannitsis, T. (1988) *I Entaxi stin Evropaiki Koinotita kai Epiptoseis sti Viomichania kai sto Exoteriko Emborio* [Accession to the European Community and Effects on Industry and External Trade] (Athens: Institute for Mediterranean Studies).

Tsoukalis, L. (1981) *The European Community and its Mediterranean Enlargement* (London: Allen & Unwin).

Part IV

Structural Issues and Industrial Policy

13 Inflexibility and Adjustment of the Greek Economy under Liberalisation

Alexander H. Sarris
UNIVERSITY OF ATHENS

1 INTRODUCTION

The purpose of this paper is to discuss the short- and medium-term prospects for Greek economic growth in the light of the liberalisation of current and capital accounts due to take place in the context of the Single European Act, as part of the completion of the EC internal market by 1992. The discussion will first delineate the structural features of the Greek economy that affect current short-term macroeconomic adjustments, and then consider the prospects for developments after 1992.

There are four crucial structural features of the Greek economy that have conditioned macroeconomic developments in the past: the structure of production, the behaviour of the state, the nature of the labour markets, and the structure of the financial system. The interaction of these four areas will determine future patterns of growth in Greece.

2 STRUCTURAL CHARACTERISTICS AND RIGIDITIES OF THE GREEK ECONOMY

2.1 Industry

As regards the structure of production, the Greek economy can be described as semi-industrialised, with the bulk of both production and exports concentrated in the primary and light manufacturing sectors. Capital-intensive, technologically advanced industries constitute a relatively small part of manufacturing activity, and a minute part of exports. Services account for slightly over 50 per cent of GDP, with public or publicly controlled services holding the dominant share.

In terms of industrial structure, the Greek economy is characterised by strong duality. In both the manufacturing and service sectors, a few large (by Greek standards) firms account for most of the production of exported or import-competing goods. These firms, which have been protected against import competition, have commanded a disproportionate share of loan funds from the official banking system, and with the help of generous interest rates and other investment and trade subsidies, have expanded their capacity to levels far beyond those warranted by the size of the markets for their products. Consequently they are characterised by low capacity utilisation (on average less than 60 per cent), excessive indebtedness and persistent losses. By contrast there exists a dynamic small-scale industrial sector, which has evolved largely outside the influence of the state-sponsored system of incentives, which can be considered competitive. The average size of firms in this sector is very small (about five employees) and their products do not have a wide market. In recent years this sector has been profitable and has expanded, while the large-scale 'formal' sector has contracted.

2.2 The Public Sector

The behaviour of the public sector has been one of the key determinants of Greek economic development and there is a danger that it could impede smooth adjustment in the future. Expenditure by the public sector currently accounts for 50 per cent of gross national product (GNP), a 21 per cent increase on 1958. Public investment as a share of total public expenditure has dropped from 24 per cent in the early 1960s to about 11 per cent currently, while transfer payments (including interest on domestic public debt) have risen from 28 per cent of total public expenditure in the 1960s to 48 per cent currently. Expenditure of goods and services, of which two-thirds are for wages and salaries, has declined from 48 per cent of total public expenditure in the early 1960s to about 40 per cent currently.

On the revenue side, more than half of tax receipts are from indirect taxes, and the tax base for direct taxes is very small, because large segments of the population escape taxation officially (such as, farmers) or unofficially through tax evasion. The need for sufficient funds to maintain the level of public expenditure has brought about only minor reforms aimed at expanding the tax base, but has substantially increased the tax burden in real terms on salaried employees. The Greek salaried worker has one of the highest average tax rates in the world, with marginal tax rates in excess of 50 per cent at relatively low levels of income.

The public sector deficit, while small in the pre-1981 years (less than 4 per cent of GNP on average), jumped to 12 per cent in the 1981 election year and since then has continued at between 10 and 17 per cent of GNP, with election-induced increases in 1985 and 1989. A very large portion of public expenditure (60–70 per cent) is inelastic, which implies substantial rigidity in the total spending pattern of the economy. The policy of various governments to use the public sector as a counter-cyclical employment generator has swollen the ranks of civil servants, as well as people employed by public enterprises. The simultaneous policy of keeping salary differentials between skilled and unskilled employees small has lowered public-sector productivity and helped to maintain the deficits. The massive internal deficits have spilled over into the external sector, which suffered not only from a rising demand for imports, but also from autonomous declines in emigrant and shipping remittances. These two deficits have been financed by domestic and external borrowing, which increased the public debt from about 47 per cent of GDP in 1981 to nearly 100 per cent of GDP currently. The interest on this debt is a significant inelastic component of total spending.

2.3 The Labour Market

Turning to the structure of the labour market, again there is strong duality. On the one hand, there are the wage and salary earners employed by the public sector and most medium and large public and private enterprises, who constitute only 50 per cent of total employment. The rest are mostly owner–operators. More than 95 per cent of agricultural employment, and more than 30 per cent of manufacturing, construction and tertiary employment, is non-salaried. Many of these workers pay little or no direct taxes. Within the formal salaried category, the majority of wage agreements are governed by bargaining between unions and employers, usually led by wage settlements agreed between the public-sector unions and the state. However there is a significant unorganised segment of wage employment, mostly in small-scale firms, where wages are more market-determined. Another characteristic of the Greek labour markets is multiple job holdings. Many formal sector employees have sources of income from the unincorporated sector. It is this pattern of income that has maintained demand and material living standards at levels higher than is justified by the low level of formal sector wages.

Significant labour market rigidity arises from this pattern of income. On the one hand, most formal sector wages are set by bargaining at levels that do not correspond to labour market supply and demand. Employment in this sector is reasonably secure, with limits and other restrictions imposed on lay-offs. On the other hand, the small-scale and unincorporated sectors are much more flexible in terms of levels, as well as in rewards, of employment. This implies that intersectoral labour reallocation is easier in the small-scale industrial and service sectors and, therefore, adjustment costs are lower there. This in turn implies that industrial restructuring, given the right incentives, will be easier in sectors where small-scale industries can flourish.

2.4 The Financial System

The Greek financial system is dominated by state-controlled banks and especially by the two largest (the National Bank and the Commercial Bank), which control about 85 per cent of total commercial bank assets. Given the undeveloped state of the equities market, a large portion of domestic private savings has been channelled into bank deposits, despite occasional negative real interests rates. Private deposits account for about half the increase in new funds. On the asset side, a large share of commercial bank assets is reserved for financing the deficits of the public sector. Currently 38 per cent of bank deposits are channelled into treasury bills, 7.5 per cent to compulsory deposits with the Bank of Greece, and 10.5 per cent are reserved for compulsory financing of public enterprises and entities, giving a total of 56 per cent of deposits. Furthermore the state attempts to control the flow of the remaining loanable funds by designating the proportion that has to be loaned to certain sectors. A substantial portion of the public sector borrowing requirement (PSBR) is financed directly by the sale of securities to the public (this share rose from 4 per cent in 1986 to 40 per cent in 1988). Of the total new credits to the economy in 1985, 71 per cent went to the public sector (compared to a forecast of 62 per cent). In 1986 the actual figure was 72 per cent, compared to a forecast figure of 65 per cent. In 1987 the forecast was 71 per cent (no figures available for the percentage realised).

The consequence of the increased financing demands of the public sector has been a decline in the share of commercial bank assets available for loans and advances to the private sector, from 62 per cent in 1970 to 36 per cent in 1986. The result of this crowding-out of the private sector has been the development of a parallel market for funds, especially those for working capital where official allocations are small. Interest rates in this parallel market are substantially higher than those in the official market (a differential of 10 per cent is not uncommon). Furthermore the widespread use of post-dated cheques in commercial transactions (albeit forbidden) in effect augments the money supply.

A rising share of the total demand for new credit has been financed by foreign sources, of which official borrowing is the largest. In 1985, foreign inflows (mainly debt) financed 34 per cent of the growth in total liabilities, although they were forecast to finance only 26 per cent. In 1986 the realised share was 35 per cent compared to a forecast 24 per cent. In 1987 the forecast was for 23 per cent.

The picture that emerges is one where the public sector through its massive deficits has squeezed the private sector for funds. In the absence of any further possibility of foreign private borrowing, as well as the issuing of domestic stock, it must be concluded that financing is one of the most severe constraints on Greek private enterprises. In fact a disproportionately high share of new investment in Greece (compared to other developed countries) is financed from retained earnings, and this highlights the significant role of profitability and the lesser role of interest rates in determining private investment.

3 RECENT PATTERNS OF ADJUSTMENT

Since accession to the EC, Greece has experienced a marked opening of the current account. Import protection has declined and all types of related – production and input – subsidies have also declined. The result has been an initial cheapening and a subsequent surge of imports. The simultaneous decline in emigrant remittances and income from shipping, and the stagnation of export earnings further widened the current account deficit. At the same time, domestic demand in the early post-accession years was maintained through increased public-sector deficits and generous public-wage rises along with the introduction of laws that rigidified private employment by controlling lay-offs. Adjustment to the external sector was achieved through increased official foreign borrowing, balanced on the internal side by increased domestic borrowing. The squeeze on private savings available for investment led to very low, and in some years negative, private real investment growth.

The stabilisation programme of 1985–6 tried to reverse policies by controlling aggregate demand mainly through lower real wage growth and curtailment of public spending. However, although the public deficit declined as a share of GNP, it did not fall below 10 per cent. The external deficit declined as aggregate demand slowed, but was not eliminated. Recourse by the state to the public for financing of the deficit, through direct sales of treasury bills, drained the supply of funds to firms at the same time as available loan funds from the banking system were declining. The result was a further squeeze on private firms and continued stagnation of investment. The government tried to pursue a high real interest rate policy to attract private and foreign savings. The liberalisation of the capital account that allowed repatriation of new foreign capital, coupled with a policy of rapid devaluation and high real interest rates, was successful in augmenting foreign capital inflows, especially short-term portfolio ones.

A significant development that was prompted both by the liberalisation of capital flows as well as the financial squeeze on private firms has been the substantial increase in foreign, and especially EC, company purchases of Greek private firms. This is a process that can be considered as resulting from the opening of the capital account, and the weak financial structure of most Greek firms. Corporations that have access to foreign financing have a significant advantage over Greek firms.

Turning to medium-term adjustment under the prospect of further current- and capital-account opening, the following observations can be made. First the capital account opening could make the financial structure of firms worse if domestic savers are allowed to purchase foreign assets directly. This will diminish the small supply of domestic savings available for private financing, especially if the public sector borrowing requirement is kept at a high level. However this effect could be counter-balanced by the possibility of Greek firms (especially the larger ones) borrowing directly in foreign exchange from European banks.

Traditionally the portfolio structure of Greek households has not included foreign assets and domestic equities because of capital controls and lack of domestic capital markets. If these two restrictions were eased one might reasonably expect a reallocation of private-saver portfolios, away from traditional assets such as real estate and other non-productive durables, into marketable equities. The larger Greek corporations might be able to take advantage of this by issuing new stock. However it is not these large firms that have been starved of funds in Greece, but rather the smaller ones. If the supply of funds available to them through the informal parallel market diminishes, they might be further squeezed, with adverse consequences on profits and growth. Some of them might follow the trend of the larger firms and be sold to European interests.

The buy-outs of several Greek firms by EC corporations will tend to increase their capital intensity through the adoption of advanced imported technology and hence could increase unemployment. This might not happen with smaller firms, because of the financial bottleneck. However, overall this development might weaken the labour market, especially for those without specific skills.

A cure for the unemployment problem in Greece has traditionally been public-sector employment. The capacity to continue such a policy, however, has been severely restricted by the massive public-sector deficits and the squeeze on loanable funds that this has created. If this tendency to absorb the unemployed in the public payroll were to continue or increase it would severely restrict the growth potential of the private sector, for two reasons. First the drain on private savings would mean a continued squeeze on funds available to private firms for investment and working capital. Second, the maintenance of public current expenditures at a high level would deprive public investment of funding. This would depress private-sector productivity and hence would have an adverse impact on private sector profitability.

Further opening of the current account will increase competition for Greek tradables, especially manufactures, and will decrease the demand for import substitutes. Given the inflexibilities in the labour market, unemployment in the import competing sector might not easily be absorbed in other sectors or in the public sector. This will tend to lower the overall growth rate, as aggregate demand and hence GDP slow down.

Growth comes from investment, and there are three possible sources for it. Public investment has been a major contributor to maintenance of construction activity and aggregate demand in the post-accession years, but its share of public expenditure is small and has stagnated. Indeed, sizeable funds available from the EC through the Integrated Mediterranean Programmes (IMP) could not be absorbed because of the inability to provide local counterpart funds, and this bottleneck is unlikely to be eased in the near future, given government emphasis on current consumption.

Investment by large private companies will depend on profitability and availability of funds. The latter constraint will be eased after 1992, as mentioned above, through access to international financing. Profitability, however, which generates internal savings, is expected to suffer from increased competition in the international market. In the European firms of the 'north', research and development (R&D) and general cost cutting through economies of scale and other restructuring are the keys to maintaining a post-1992 competitive edge. In Greece, most large firms produce low-technology products, and the main components of cost are labour and material inputs. Very little R&D is taking place. Since Greek firms are too small to achieve the economies of scale necessary to market traditional products on an international scale, and since competition for many of these products from newly industrialising and other developing countries will be keen, the medium-term profitability prospects are low unless labour costs are squeezed further, an uncertain prospect at best. One possibility would be to encourage product concentration in 'niche markets', but this entails intense R&D as well as international marketing strategies, fields in which the larger Greek firms have not so far excelled. This leads to the conclusion that there is little room for optimism about the potential for new investment in the larger Greek firms.

Finally the investment prospects for the smaller and more agile firms will depend on the expansion of markets for their largely non-traded products and profitability. With the expected decline in the medium term of aggregate domestic demand, and the squeeze on formal loanable funds, these prospects appear bleak.

The overall conclusion from this brief analysis is that aggregate investment prospects in Greece for the medium term do not appear too promising. This could lead to a decline in gross domestic product (GDP) from the level that would prevail without the 1992 policies, and substantial pressure in the domestic labour market, with an increased inability of the public sector to absorb the slack and maintain aggregate demand.

4 CONCLUSION

The inevitable reality that must be faced by Greek policy makers is that structural adjustment in the medium run will entail a painful reduction in both the overall size of the public sector and the pattern of public expenditure, with an increased share of money required for investment. Furthermore there is need for substantial tax reform directed at the expansion of the direct tax base, together with a lowering of the average direct tax rate. If the costs of private firms are to be maintained at low levels using current technology, significant real-wage reductions must be expected, in conjunction with increased unemployment of those with lower skills.

Industrial restructuring primarily towards human capital-intensive industries will entail a need for a much greater differentiation in the labour market, so that those with higher skills receive substantially greater rewards relative to the unskilled, in order to provide incentives for them not to migrate to the Europe of the 'north'. This differentiation is already occurring in the private sector, which is starting to appreciate the utility of skilled human capital, but it has not yet taken place in the public sector. If this type of restructuring does not occur, the result will be a further gradual weakening of the productivity of the public sector, as skilled employees quit to find more lucrative private-sector jobs. This would intensify the public-sector vicious cycle of continued low productivity and high deficits. This process has already started in the banking and the large-scale manufacturing sectors, where private firms, both domestic and foreign, are luring away highly skilled employees from publicly controlled corporations.

The conclusion from the above discussion is that the constraints most likely to impede medium-run adjustment and growth in Greece are related to the rigid structure and behaviour of the public sector. Both the labour market and the private enterprise sector have shown signs of adapting to the changing environment, but the speed and nature of adjustment will be heavily conditioned by the restructured behaviour of the public sector. Major state restructuring entails sacrifices and political costs, and the key to enhanced medium-term growth will be political stability and a firm determination to succeed in improving the functioning of state institutions to meet the needs of the coming decade.

14 Structural and Technological Imperatives in the Light of Development Prospects for the Greek Economy

Nikos Vernardakis

UNIVERSITY OF PATRAS

1 INTRODUCTION

The growing importance of technological change in world production and employment is one of the salient characteristics of the last four decades. In fact technological change at present is not only perceived as a progressively important determinant of growth but also as an increasingly potent weapon in the stiffening international competition.

Rising international competition mostly met through and in conjunction with technological change – especially since the recessionary 1970s – has led to the emergence of a new international division of production and employment and to what has been termed 'deindustrialisation'.

For the champions of technological change – the most developed economies – deindustrialisation seems a natural development since this new phase of development, that is, the transition to the tertiary sector, is the result of their successful achievement of high rates of productivity in the secondary sector, long after having achieved spectacular rises in productivity in the primary sector.

For the laggards in technological change – the less developed economies – the problem is vastly different and much more threatening. The less successful among them – including Greece, which long ago stopped the catching up process – have failed to achieve high rates of productivity in the secondary sector and never managed to achieve the successful transition from the primary to the secondary sector. For these economies, the dilemma of whether to deindustrialise or not is not a real one, since the choice is dictated by external imperatives. As international production becomes more and more concentrated in the most efficient *loci* of production, not only do the laggards face the displacement of their labour by capital – which is the main issue for the champions of technological change – but their inefficient production is also under threat of shrinking. Besides, as simple users of technology, they cannot count on the employment-generation potential of the innovative sectors as do the champions.

The choice left to the laggards of technological change is not therefore whether to deindustrialise or not, but whether to plan for deindustrialisation or be dragged in that direction. In this sense, planning for deindustrialisation amounts to stretching the duration of the transition period, thus allowing additional time for the tertiary sector to attempt to become better equipped for the tasks ahead.

For Greece, to be dragged towards deindustrialisation, a process already started in the late 1970s in terms of the share of manufacturing in total GDP,[1] implies a heavy burden upon the tertiary sector in terms of employment creation. For the flow of surplus labour from the secondary sector will, for quite some time, be supplemented by a flow of surplus labour originating in the primary sector, which still constitutes a substantial source of employment,[2] especially if one takes into account EC future plans for the primary sector.

In other words, the tertiary sector is called upon to achieve a staggering performance, otherwise Greece will face substantial unemployment in the not too distant future. This is all the more difficult considering that the tertiary sector with its low level of skills is geared towards activities of low value-added, with a less than promising future in terms of demand.

Surveying the prospects for services on an international basis we realise that the most promising category is the one for services provided to producers (Dalton and Boyd, 1984). These are highly specialised activities provided mainly to the secondary sector and more specifically to the most innovative and dynamic sectors within the secondary sector (Momigliano and Sinisalco, 1982). Countries possessing the relevant sectors have already benefited by employing a substantial proportion of their labour force in such activities and may expect to benefit further in the future. For the USA, it was estimated that, by 1990, 12.6 per cent of the labour force would be employed in such knowledge-based activities and that by the year 2000 this percentage would have risen substantially (US Bureau of Labor Statistics, 1983).

If Greece is not to miss the opportunity of moving into such services and exploit these rich sources of future employment, she will have to preserve at least some of her industrial sectors, presumably the most dynamic and competitive ones, and be in a position to offer such services. Additionally, if she is not to witness a further erosion of her overall position in the new international division of production and employment, she must address the urgent need to improve competitiveness throughout the economy.

2   THE NEED FOR AN INDUSTRIAL STRATEGY AND POLICY

Most countries have realised that the process of encouraging specific sectors to develop is a process close to their vital interests and certainly not one that could be brought about through market forces (Jones, 1981). Accordingly most countries, developed and developing, have already acted and some of them have even announced their policy intentions (Rothwell and Zegveld, 1981). Countries which are among the leaders in technological change and rely on well-functioning large economies have tended to put more emphasis on policies aimed at encouraging the desired activities through policies on technology – research and development – aimed at further strengthening their technological lead through innovation in those activities (OECD, 1986a). This in no way means that these countries do not additionally act through direct industrial policy intervention, as witnessed by Japan's frequent MITI interventions (Allen, 1981; Feigenbaum and McCorduck, 1984). The same is true for the USA, as witnessed by that country's stance on a number of vital issues such as fifth-generation computers (the formation of the consortium of Microelectronics and Computer Technology Corporation), semiconductors (formation of the Sematech consortium) and the more recent initiatives on the formation of a consortium on high-definition television, to name just a few.

For those countries not so fortunate as to be among the technological high elite, the priorities are reversed. They too use both avenues, but they seem to rely more on direct industrial policy intervention, rather than on technological policy. However, in contrast to the leaders, they are more likely to realise the potential benefits of diffusion as compared to innovation, although in both groups of countries diffusion gets insufficient attention (OECD, 1987).

Greece urgently needs to design and implement a technological and industrial strategy. This of course entails a new or modernised role for the administration: a supportive, consultative, co-ordinating role for both the public and the private sector. As to the strategy and policy, it will have to be differentiated according to the level of technological sophistication involved in each instance. For the low- and medium-technology sectors, where technological change is slow and technology easily accessible, Greece should proceed with an imitative strategy. In the high-technology sectors, where technological change is very rapid and the technology is not easily accessible, she should take an 'opportunistic' path; that is, exploit the 'niche' opportunities left unexploited by the champions of technological change, involving small volumes of production but with a high value-added.

Additionally emphasis should be placed on sectors characterised by their tendency to use new production processes rather than on sectors with a tendency towards new products, while diffusion should bear a much higher priority than innovation. Finally the sectors to be singled out for encouragement, or helped to develop, should be those emanating from the basic concepts of dynamic comparative advantage (Vernardakis, 1988b.)

Greece's task, if she is to hold her own in the future, is obviously very difficult to achieve, for it will require both self-discipline and determination besides the building-up of a consensus on priorities. Her task will be rendered even more daunting as the degrees of freedom of action at her disposal are becoming progressively circumscribed as a result of the implications of her accession to the EC. For the process required, which we have described, is not one that can be brought about through market forces but one that needs direction. Yet precisely the opposite is envisaged through the formation of the European single market (ESM) of 1992. While the EC attempts to impose a unique policy on its members on a multitude of issues ranging from VAT to capital movements, to monetary unification and even to taxation on deposits, the determination of activities to emerge in the future is to be left to market forces.

Besides the fact that the formation of the ESM will cut across the effort to restructure and redirect Greece's productive capability by essentially cutting short a readjustment process that could have evolved under more normal time constraints, Greece will be adversely affected on two specific important issues: the size of competing units and the EC attitude towards the rest of the world.

Competition through market forces favours large units, especially those which in the ESM are export-oriented. Countries which do possess such units will definitely benefit while countries like Greece stand to lose, as her own units, which are very small, will be displaced by the much larger foreign ones. The search for critical mass has already started within the EC – including Greece – with horizontal mergers vastly outnumbering vertical ones (Jacquemin, Buigues and Ilzkovitz, 1988). And this process is likely to be reinforced in the future by technological change, which for the first time ever encourages horizontal mergers. As programmable automated production allows the rapid shift from the production of one product to that of another, the importance of marketing and distribution is enhanced – hence also the importance of size – relative to production.

In the light of the above considerations and developments, and given the limited time until the completion of the ESM, it would be naïve to attempt an across-the-board change in the structure of production in Greece with the plethora of miniscule production units.[3] Besides their very small size, these units lack specialisation, are ill-equipped and highly inefficient. What could be attempted in such a short timeframe would be to apply development incentives liberally to a relatively small number of carefully selected firms that fall within the desired sectors, are dynamic and enjoy good management practices and future prospects. It should also be possible to introduce a focused policy to encourage the larger-size firms – the sort of policy long ago adopted by other developing countries, but discredited in Greece. Such a policy was adopted, for instance, by South Korea and Taiwan and to a lesser extent by Hong Kong and Singapore. According to *Fortune* (1989), in 1988, South Korea had 11 firms among the 500 largest international corporations. A policy that encouraged size would of course have to be reflected in the development law 1262/82 as well as in merger and acquisition legislation.

With respect to Europe's attitude *vis-à-vis* the rest of the world, Greece stands to lose if 'fortress Europe' is the outcome and, despite pronouncements to the contrary, developments seem to confirm that trend. The EC's balance of payments surplus with the USA and Japan is diminishing rapidly but the original surplus countries, such as the Federal Republic of Germany, still exhibit surpluses, except that now they are accounted for by the lesser members of the Community, such as Greece. This trend is also reflected in a parallel development: in terms of comparative advantage, the EC as a whole, as well as her strongest economies, is losing ground in the high technology category and becoming progressively specialised in medium and low technology activities (OECD, 1986b). Interpreting these facts, one can only conclude that the EC's strongest economies are reluctant to engage in the real fields of international competition – that is, high technology fields – and instead prefer to opt for a larger share of the promised ESM pie, but in activities more akin to medium and low technology. Obviously this limits the ambitions for development of the lesser member countries, besides having adverse effects on consumer welfare.

The same is true of reciprocity, where the EC intends to make a stand *vis-à-vis* the rest of the world and bargain over four specific sectors, thus delineating European future growth plans. Greece will be adversely affected by such plans, especially in textiles, one of her largest sectors and second export revenue earner.

Because a unique policy on division of production and employment seems so abhorrent to most of the stronger member economies, there is no way for a lesser member country such as Greece to counter these developments except to argue on political grounds for an open Europe and to make her voice heard on the issue of reciprocity.

3   THE NEED TO IMPROVE OVERALL PRODUCTIVITY AND TO ACQUIRE THE ABILITY TO PROVIDE KNOWLEDGE-BASED NEW SERVICES

Until the mid-1970s Greece exhibited rates of productivity increase roughly double those achieved on average by the 12 EC member states. However the virtual stagnation of private investment in manufacturing ever since the first half of that decade implied progressively lower rates of further growth in productivity, which indeed fell to levels significantly lower than the EC average after the late 1970s (Deleau, 1987). Correspondingly, income rates of growth have decelerated substantially, rendering the EC intention of cohesion and convergence a wish rather than a reality, despite the Integrated Mediterranean Programmes and other forms of support.

With productivity increases diminishing significantly since the late 1970s, competitiveness was sought through exchange-rate policies resulting in the virtual stability of income throughout the 1980s. Greece in 1980, the last year before her accession to the EC, had a *per capita* income at current prices, corrected for purchasing power, which represented 58.4 per cent of the EC average. It is estimated that it dropped to 53.6 per cent in 1988, and Greece is still ranked last among all member countries.[4] There is little doubt that Greece's accession to the Community was from this point of view something short of a success; it is worth noting that, since accession exports have stagnated, though import penetration by member countries rose from 13.3 per cent in 1980 to at least 23.8 per cent in 1987, and was of course accompanied by considerable trade diversion, as imports from EC member states displaced imports originating in non-member countries.[5]

The need for an across-the-board productivity rise as both a short- and a long-term goal is equally evident. It is common knowledge that the application of new technologies and more specifically of information technology and telecommunications (ITT) at present constitutes one of the most significant, if not the most significant, factor in economic growth (Goddard *et al.*, 1987). The higher the penetration rate of ITT in an economy, the more the economy will be in a position to benefit not only from advances in these sectors *per se*, but also through their applications throughout the rest of economic activities. Unfortunately Greece has a very low rate of ITT penetration, in fact, the lowest of all EC members, and several times lower than her GDP *per capita* level would justify (Vernardakis, 1988a). In addition, however, ITT penetration is a function of the sophistication level of the whole production process; that is, production proper, management, planning, marketing and distribution, as well as all other aspects spanning economic life. In a word, penetration depends on society's overall receptivity to technological change. In contrast to the northern European countries, in southern Europe, including Greece, the problem is not so much one of supply but of deficient demand for ITT services, despite the fact that infrastructure is indeed a limiting factor, for the moment at least (Gillespie *et al.*, 1985).

Improving the level of receptivity implies a long, drawn-out process, which could be achieved either through incentives or education – in the broader sense – or both. The development law 1262/82 should reflect the importance and uniqueness of the high-technology sectors in terms of needs. ITT applications to production, management, planning, distribution and procurement need to be encouraged. Education at all levels should attempt the giant transformation needed to reorient itself to meet the needs of a modern society and contemporary production methods. The implication is that the upgrading and constant re-education of educational staff are just as important, if not more so, than application to the overall productive human capital. It should be noted here that, unlike most applications of information technologies, deficient telecommunications infrastructure is not, for most intents and purposes, a serious limiting factor in education.

Given Greece's low level of technological achievement, expectations as to the role of innovation are rather limited. On the contrary, the role of diffusion of already available technology becomes of primary importance. The creation of regional data banks and information centres is essential and facilities of information technologies should be supplemented by the use of existing capacity in local universities or training centres.

In contrast to the case of the advanced economies, industry in Greece constitutes one of the sectors with the lowest ITT penetration and lags far behind commerce and banking. The encouragement of links between universities and industry should be pursued and current policies discouraging such links should be eliminated. Free consultancy services should be considered, subsidised until the need for such services is recognised.

With respect to Greece's myriad very small firms, special programmes should be made available through the creation of technological parks, the formation of links with these parks and technological centres, increased information and contacts with complementary firms and the provision of help and advice on the absorption of technology.

Last but most important, in the domain of standardisation policy, which is rapidly evolving into Europe's main defence on information technology and telecommunications, Greece needs to become involved as fast as possible in conformance testing services in the domain of open systems interfaces. However, Greece's participation should not be limited to the lower layers, since that would deny her opportunities in the area of new development (Vernardakis and Cullen, 1989). Conformance testing is simultaneously a high-technology service, an educational process for producers and an activity leading to innovation, but above all it constitutes possibly the fastest mechanism available with respect to high-technology diffusion.

To put it simply, Greece should make an attempt to provide the preconditions for a higher level of receptivity to technological change. Unless the level of penetration of information technology and telecommunications reaches a critical level, the overall impact on the Greek economy will remain negligible.

4 CONCLUDING REMARKS

We have attempted in this paper to address the short- to medium-term issues facing Greece, most of which are relevant to the formation of the ESM, as well as longer-term issues covering the next decade and beyond. In the case of some of our suggestions, such as the measures we propose for overcoming the small size of production units, their introduction may be anticipated in the not too distant future. Others, such as the measures proposed for the rise in receptivity of technological change in Greek society, will take longer to implement. Short- and long-term issues, however, have one thing in common: the urgency with which their respective measures should be applied; a start needs to be made at once. Time is indeed running out.

Notes

1. The highest share of GDP ever achieved by manufacturing was 21.8 per cent in 1979 (Report of the Governor of the Bank of Greece, several issues).
2. The primary sector still employs about 29 per cent of the labour force, though it is acknowledged that part-time employment is substantial in that sector.
3. According to the Statistical Service of Greece, the still unpublished estimates

show that 98.2 per cent of all firms in 1984 employed less than 50 employees and the average number of persons employed per producing unit was 4.5 in that year. (Average for the whole of manufacturing.)
4. 'Some Macroeconomic Considerations on Chances and Conditions for the Catching-up Process of the Poorer Countries of the Community', II/275/88-EN, Commission of the European Communities, Statistical Annex, Table 1.
5. Data kindly provided by the Internal Economy Section of the Economic Research Division of the Bank of Greece.

References

Allen, G. C. (1981) 'Industrial Policy and Innovation in Japan', in Carter, C. (ed.), *Industrial Policy and Innovation*, NIESR, Joint Studies in Public Policy, 3 (London: Heinemann) ch. 6.

Dalton, D. and Boyd, J. (1984) 'Growth Trends in the Service Sector', *US Industrial Output* (Washington DC: US Dept. of Commerce).

Deleau, M. (1987) 'Industrial Investment in Greece: Analysis and Recommendations', unpublished, Ministry of National Economy, Athens.

Feigenbaum, E. A. and McCorduck, P. (1984) *The Fifth Generation, Artificial Intelligence and Japan's Computer Challenge to the World* (London: Pan Books).

Fortune, 31 July 1989.

Gillespie, A. *et al.* (1985) *The Effects of New Information Technology on the Less Favoured Regions of the Community*, Regional Policy Series no. 23 (Brussels: Commission of the European Communities).

Goddard, J. *et al.* (1987) *Research and Technological Development in the Less Favoured Regions of the Community*, STRIDE (Brussels: Commission of the European Communities).

Jacquemin, A., Buigues, P. and Ilzkovitz, F. (1988) *Horizontal Mergers and Competition Policy in the European Community*, II/322/88-EN (Brussels: Commission of the European Communities).

Jones, D. T. (1981) 'Catching up with Our Competitors: The Role of Industrial Policy', in Carter, C. (ed.), *Industrial Policy and Innovation*, NIESR, Joint Studies in Public Policy, 3 (London: Heinemann) ch. 7.

Momigliano, F. and Sinisalco, D. (1982) 'The Growth of Service Employment: A Reappraisal', *Quarterly Review*, Banco Nazionale del Lavoro, September.

OECD (1986a) *Industrial Policies, Development and Outlook in O.E.C.D. Countries* (Paris: OECD).

OECD (1986b) *Science and Technology Indicators no. 2, R&D Invention and Competitiveness* (Paris: OECD).

OECD (1987) *Science and Technology Policy Outlook, Technology Diffusion* (Paris: OECD).

Rothwell, R. and Zegveld, W. (1981) *Industrial Innovation and Public Policy, Preparing for the 1980s and 1990s* (London: Frances Pinter).

US Bureau of Labor Statistics (1983) *Monthly Labor Review*, vol. 106, no. 11, November.

Vernardakis, N. (1988a) 'The Economic Context in Greece and Portugal', in *Oppor-*

tunities for Applications of Information Technologies and Telecommunications in Rural Areas for the Commission of European Communities, DG XIII (Cambridge: Analysis), November.

Vernardakis, N. (1988b) *The Train of Development and Greece in the Fifth Kondratiev Cycle* (in Greek) (Athens: Papazisis). Translated into English by the Commission of the European Communities, DOC. XIII/132/88.

Vernardakis, N. and Cullen, A. (1989) *Study on the Establishment of Conformance Testing Laboratories in Greece in the Areas of Information Technology and Telecommunications*, CEC DG XIII (Athens: Zenon) January.

15 Structural Characteristics of the Greek Economy, with Particular Reference to the Small and Medium-size Enterprises Sector

Joseph Hassid

UNIVERSITY OF PIRAEUS

1 THE MACROECONOMIC ENVIRONMENT AND STRUCTURAL CONSIDERATIONS

1.1 General Remarks

To understand the present state of the Greek economy, one might begin by considering a number of its structural characteristics and performance indicators. Whenever possible these factors should be compared to those prevailing in other European Community (EC) countries. If this analysis were supplemented by a review of the institutional factors affecting the operation of enterprises, the resulting observations ought to provide a satisfactory basis for assessing the economy's overall performance, as well as its main problem areas.

It is important to emphasise that the long-term growth of the Greek economy has followed a particularly erratic path. Compared to the fast growth rates experienced in the 1970s, which exceeded those of other EC member countries by 1 to 3 percentage units, the average annual growth rate of the Greek economy since 1980 has fallen below the Community average. Generally speaking, industry has been the sector most adversely affected during the 1980s, while the service sector has continued to grow (although at a slower rate than before).[1]

These developments were obviously linked in a cause–effect relationship with the gradual emergence of serious competitiveness problems. The seriousness of such problems was made more acute by the fact that national discretion over economic policy formulation was substantially reduced by Greece's commitment to harmonisation of EC legislation. Consequently export subsidies, import restrictions or privileged access of domestic products to public procurement (to mention only a few of the policy measures employed in the past) are or are about to be abandoned as compensatory measures for losses in real competitiveness.

The substantial socioeconomic cost of continuing to subsidise uncompetitive activities or producers (such as the artificially low cost of bank financing which affects banks' profitability) and artificially restricting competition in the market place to allow room for the marginal producer provides additional arguments in favour of policies aimed at encouraging and assisting firms to upgrade their internal organisation and their real capacity to compete. At the same time it is realised that such assistance is conditional on the firms' positive response, which also determines the size of the resulting benefit.

These observations are consistent with the intensive discussion on the need to design and implement sectoral industrial policies which could attract EC support to supplement domestic resources. This obviously emphasises the need for identifying comparative advantages and opportunities in the various sectors and market segments and for adopting policies specifically addressed to the 'less-privileged' (but potentially dynamic) groups of producers. In this context, the case of small and medium-size enterprises (SMEs) is attracting particular attention, since the small size of Greek companies is generally regarded (rightly or wrongly) as a factor negatively affecting the overall competitiveness of Greek industry.

To complete the series of general observations on the present state of the Greek economy, Table 15.1 below presents a number of selected structure and performance indicators, together with corresponding figures for the other EC member countries.[2] It is interesting to note the following:

1. The importance of the non-agricultural sector in the Greek economy, which in terms of employment, is the lowest of all EC countries. The percentage of total employment in industry and the service sector, at 27.3 per cent and 43.8 per cent respectively, is also the lowest among EC member-countries.

2. Lack of investment activity is particularly pronounced, as indicated by the negative rate of gross fixed capital formation over the last five years. Belgium and Portugal are the only other member countries with higher negative rates.

3. Costs and particularly labour costs (wages) have in recent years been

Table 15.1 EC, comparative statistics, 1985

EC member countries	Industrial employment*	Service employment*	Per capita GDP (US$)	Gross fixed capital formation 5-year per cent change	Wages, 5-year per cent change	CPI, 5-year per cent change	Exports as per cent of GDP	Imports as per cent of GDP
Greece	27.3	43.8	6 296	-2.8	25.1	20.4	17.2	34.6
Belgium	29.7	67.4	12 150	-4.0	4.4	5.7	86.8	86.7
Denmark	28.1	65.2	13 311	2.1	6.2	6.3	36.6	39.4
France	32.0	60.4	12 643	-0.1	8.7	7.4	23.4	25.2
Germany	41.0	53.5	13 265	-1.3	3.7	2.6	38.8	30.3
Ireland	28.9	55.1	7 795	-1.9	12.0	9.0	69.4	63.8
Italy	33.6	55.2	10 093	0.3	12.6	11.3	27.2	27.9
Luxembourg	33.4	62.4	14 385	-2.8	–	5.3	–	–
Netherlands	28.1	67.0	11 710	-1.0	3.3	2.9	64.5	60.3
Portugal	35.3	41.5	5 021	-4.5	19.2	21.5	34.7	45.6
Spain	31.8	50.6	8 279	-1.4	15.0	11.1	16.5	21.3
UK	32.4	65.0	11 068	2.1	9.1	5.5	23.8	28.1

Notes:

* Per cent of total civilian employment.

1. Total employment is defined as total civilian employment.
2. CPI: consumer price index.

Source: OECD, *Economic Indicators* (various issues).

increasing considerably faster in Greece than in the rest of the EC. The rate of wage increases in the last five years has been more than double that of all other EC countries, with the exception of Portugal and Spain, where corresponding rates were nevertheless lower by 6 and 10 percentage points respectively.

4. Prices followed a similar trend, with the Greek consumer price index increasing at an annual rate of around 20 per cent (almost double the rate in the rest of the EC, again with the exception of Portugal, where the rate was slightly faster).

5. Finally Greece seems to be among the least extrovert economies in the EC, since GDP shares accounted for by either exports or imports are among the lowest.

Whatever the underlying explanations – which are not further explored in this paper – the above comments, together with the fact that Greece has the second lowest *per capita* GDP in the EC (at current prices and current purchasing power parities) show the seriousness of the competitiveness problems to be faced, and the need for introducing policy measures along the lines discussed.

1.2 Small and Medium-size Firms

The small size of Greek companies is a fundamental structural characteristic of Greek industry. Very small family establishments employing on average only two persons are estimated to account for about one-third of total employment in the manufacturing and handicraft sectors. Moreover Greek companies employing less than 20 persons accounted for 24 per cent of the total annual turnover of industry in 1980, while, according to Eurostat statistics, companies of this size in Germany, France and the United Kingdom accounted for only 7.2, 8.1 and 8.8 per cent respectively in 1983.

At the other end of the scale, large companies – defined in the EC as those employing more than 500 persons – make a much smaller contribution to the economy of Greece than that of similar firms in other European countries. Thus undertakings with more than 500 persons represent barely 0.1 per cent of the total number of Greek firms (establishments), while in terms of total employment their corresponding share was 12.2 per cent of total employment in industry. Using this EC definition of size, Table 15.2 shows comparable figures for the relative importance of SMEs in selected EC member countries. In Greece, the SME share of both the number of firms and total employment, in manufacturing industry and the service sector, is larger than in most other EC countries.

Table 15.2   Proportion of employment in small and medium-size firms

Country	Year	Manufacturing		Services	
		% of units	% of employment	% of units	% of employment
Greece[a]	1978	100	88	100	92
Greece[a]	1984	100	88	100	100
Belgium[b]	1981	99	62	100	80
Denmark[b/e]	1981	99	85	n.a.	n.a.
France[b]	1981	74	99	91	100
Ireland[a]	1982	99	83	100	90
Italy[a]	1981	100	84	100	90
Luxembourg[b]	1978	97	51	99[e]	86[e]
Netherlands[a]	1983	99	80	100	80[e]
UK[a]	1980	98	49	100	50
West Germany[a]	1982	98	49	n.a.	n.a.

Notes:
[a]   percentage of establishments.
[b]   percentage of enterprises (an enterprise may have more than one establishment).
[e]   estimated.

Source: Economist Intelligence Unit, *The European Climate for Small Business* (1983). Greek figures January 1984 are taken from the Census of Industry (1978 and 1984).

At the same time, however, it is worth noting that differences in the relative importance of SMEs are far more pronounced in terms of employment than in terms of the number of firms. This implies that the 'size problem' of Greek firms would be better defined as 'absence of an adequate number of large companies, rather than the existence of an excessive number of small ones'.

The share of small establishments, defined as those employing less than 100 persons, in total employment is particularly marked in the clothing, wood, furniture, leather and even non-electrical engineering industries. Furthermore, while the average share of employment in total manufacturing has remained at approximately the same level (68 per cent in 1978, 70 per cent in 1984), the SMEs have increased in importance in several industries. On the other hand, commercial establishments employing less than 100 persons further increased their dominance, rising from 93 per cent in 1978 to 94 per cent in 1984 of total employment in the wholesale and retail trade sector.

Table 15.3   Distribution of manufacturing companies by value of total assets

a. Number of companies

Total assets (drachma million)	1980	1981	1982	1983	1984	1985
Under 50	1 317	1 331	1 165	1 007	864	754
50 to 99	552	591	646	681	678	680
100 to 249	478	559	652	713	775	841
250 to 499	230	261	313	330	331	363
500 to 999	139	167	193	199	213	227
1 000 to 2 499	101	104	129	141	161	192
2 500 and over	43	61	78	86	91	109
Total	2 860	3 074	3 176	3 157	3 113	3 166

b. Percentage distribution

Total assets (drachma million)	1980	1981	1982	1983	1984	1985
Under 50	46.1	43.3	36.7	31.9	27.8	23.8
50 to 99	19.3	19.2	20.3	21.6	21.8	21.5
100 to 249	16.7	18.2	20.5	22.6	24.9	26.5
250 to 499	8.0	8.5	9.8	10.4	10.6	11.5
500 to 999	4.9	5.4	6.1	6.3	6.8	7.2
1 000 to 2 499	3.5	3.4	4.1	4.5	5.2	6.1
2 500 and over	1.5	2.0	2.5	2.7	2.9	3.4
Total	100.0	100.0	100.0	100.0	100.0	100.0

Source: Federation of Greek Industries, *Annual Reports* (1981–6).

An alternative approach to size structure is to consider the distribution of the number of companies according to the volume of their assets, as presented in Table 15.3. The average ratio of public companies' equity to total assets in the 1980–5 period has been gradually declining, from approximately 24 per cent in 1980 to less than 15 per cent in 1985.[3] Closely associated with the small size of firm, is the *type of ownership*, which can be indirectly assessed from the entrepreneurs' and own family members' participation (without explicitly receiving a salary) in the firm's labour force. High participation rates are, by definition, expected in very small handicraft firms (those employing, for example, one to four persons), where the phenomenon of exclusively family-run businesses is widespread. In larger establishments, entrepreneur participation gradually declines. For manufacturing establishments employing more than 20 persons, this participation is estimated at approximately 1 per cent, exhibiting a slow rate of decrease over time (1.1 per cent in 1977).[4] Table 15.4 provides information on the relative importance of 'very small' manufacturing establishments, which could be taken as an indication of the extent of the family-run share of manufacturing activity. Furthermore this could be interpreted as reflecting only the minimum level of owner-family control exercised over Greek manufacturing industry, as delegation of managerial authority to non-family members of the labour force is rather limited, even in larger firms.

Any discussion of the type of ownership and control of firms must take account of the legal form of the company, particularly as Greek law only requires certain legal entities, namely *sociétés anonymes* (SA) and limited liability companies (Ltd), to publish their annual accounts or balance sheets in the press and the government gazette. In recent years the number of firms doing so has been increasing steadily, reflecting the growth in size of firm and upgrading of the legal status of the company. This is illustrated in Table 15.5.

Among commercial SMEs, the predominance of owner-run establishments is even more pronounced. In 1978, owners and non-paid members of the owners' family accounted for 68 per cent on average of total employment in the commercial sectors.[5] In the same sector, the importance of 'very small' establishments in the total number of establishments increased from 84 per cent in 1978 to 87 per cent in 1984, while in terms of employment their share was 45 and 50 per cent respectively.

Table 15.4   'Very small' establishments' participation in manufacturing industry

	1978	*1984*
Number of establishments employing 1–4 persons	109 291	124 049
% of total number of establishments	84.7	85.7
Employment in 'very-small' establishments	192 895	218 507
% of total manufacturing employment	28.7	31.3

Note: 'Very small establishments' defined as those employing less than 5 persons.

Source: National Statistical Service of Greece, *Industrial Census* (1978 and 1984).

Table 15.5   Number of public companies
(SA and Ltd manufacturing companies)

Year	SA		Ltd		Total public companies		per cent growth
	No.	Per cent	No.	Per cent	No.	Per cent	
1970	755	74.8	254	25.3	1 009	100.0	–
1975	1 267	73.4	460	26.6	1 727	100.0	+71
1980	2 108	73.7	752	26.3	2 860	100.0	+66
1985	2 632	83.1	534	16.9	3 166	100.0	+11

Source: Federation of Greek Industries, Annual Reports.

2   STRUCTURE, PERFORMANCE AND POLICY IMPLICATIONS

To the extent that structure (expressed in this case by size of firm) determines – or at least influences – performance, the obvious question is
whether the relatively small firms are performing less well compared
to their larger counterparts. While clearly the conventional 'structure–
conduct–performance relationship' needs to be examined with some caution in the case of Greece, particularly in view of various external influences
on performance, such as price controls, protection against imported competition and discriminatory treatment of large firms by the banking system,
nevertheless the available information on relative performance of manufacturing firms by sector and sizes is still of interest. This information,
which refers to the year 1981 but is still considered to retain its indicative
value, is contained in Table 15.6.

The sectoral rates of return on total assets suggest that, if the smallest
size class (firms employing less than 10 persons) is excluded, the category
performing best by size is that which could be defined as containing the
'small and medium-sized' firms, that is those employing more than 10 and
less than 500 persons. This finding should, however, be interpreted with
caution. First, it only refers to firms which are obliged by law to publish
their financial results annually. Second, it could be argued that, rather than
indicating superior performance by SMEs, the results should be interpreted
as reflecting the abnormally weak competitiveness of the 'very large'
manufacturing firms, mostly concentrated in low-demand sectors and bur-
dened by financial expense, owing to their high dependence on bank loans.
The third objection to a straightforward interpretation of the figures in

Table 15.6 Sectoral rates of return on total assets by size of firm

Sector	Size of firm (employment)					Average
	0–9	10–49	50–99	100–499	500+	
	Percentage return on total assets					
Food	-1.6	1.2	1.9	1.6	3.4	2.2
Beverages	:	7.7	7.2	-0.8	2.4	1.7
Tobacco	n.a.	:	n.a.	-1.3	3.8	2.6
Textiles	-0.8	1.6	0.7	3.5	2.2	2.5
Clothing & footwear	6.7	4.5	3.4	4.3	:	4.0
Wood & cork	:	3.8	3.3	7.2	3.8	4.4
Furniture	0.5	-1.6	-0.8	5.3	:	1.3
Paper & products	4.4	4.3	3.6	-6.3	-9.0	-6.6
Printing & publishing	14.7	4.5	5.9	-3.2	:	2.1
Leather	2.9	2.3	-3.4	3.9	n.a.	0.4
Plastics and rubber	-3.5	1.1	2.1	2.6	3.7	2.8
Chemicals	4.0	0.1	2.9	6.7	1.0	3.9
Oil products	:	0.5	7.0	23.6	1.5	3.1
Non-metallic minerals	5.1	2.9	2.8	4.5	4.9	4.5
Metallurgy	n.a.	:	2.5	7.2	5.2	5.5
Metal products	2.0	3.0	3.5	4.4	-1.1	1.6
Mechanical engineering	-2.3	-2.1	-1.0	1.3	:	-0.1
Electrical engineering	5.9	-1.1	1.9	0.3	-1.5	-0.2
Transport equipment	-1.3	0.2	2.0	-3.8	-0.7	-1.3
Total		1.8	2.3	3.0	1.7	2.2

Note:

: insufficient number of firms

Source: ICAP Directory (1982).

Table 15.6 is that owners of small firms usually fail to account fully for those costs associated with their own personal work (or that of their family) within the firm. This casts some doubt on the validity of the argument in favour of Greek SMEs, although their crucial importance in almost all economic areas is beyond question. Nevertheless it is considered of paramount importance that, in the context of an appropriately designed policy for the SMEs, every effort should be made to provide such firms with sufficient support and guidance to allow them to overcome their inherent inability to exploit the technical and managerial economies of scale available, at least in principle, to larger firms. This is dealt with in the next section.

2.1 Proposed Principles for SME Policy

It is proposed that the design and implementation of such a policy should be based on the following principles and actions:

1. Economies of scale and more efficient market development need not necessarily imply that firms should become larger. Combining certain functions (market research, raw materials purchasing and so on) and cooperation among firms (such as common quality control laboratories, mutual specialisation, joint selling) should be sufficient to improve results and profitability.
2. Institutional change will be necessary to encourage such initiatives. New and modern legislation to promote institutional change is needed to deal with such practices as subcontracting, cooperative action, management buy-outs, cooperation with foreign firms and joint ventures of all types.
3. A review of the long-held view that certain 'traditional' industries, such as food, textiles or clothing, have exhausted their development potential, and that it is the 'hi-tech' activities which should in future absorb most of our policy making and the resources associated with the implementation of policy. One specific area for revision would be the replacement of calls for the 'production of high-technology products' by the systematic encouragement of the implementation of high technology in all types of production, whether of traditional goods or not.
4. Contrary to the recent expansion of the state's intrusion into every area of activity where the welfare of the inefficient producers and workers was under pressure from market forces, local or imported, the newly-designed policy should be based exclusively on providing support to the potentially competitive firms – small or otherwise. The process of

completing the EC internal market integration – in which Greece is inadvertently a partner – obviously requires the strict application of market criteria to policy making, irrespective of social or political repercussions. For what to some people appear to be short-term benefits now, could lead to far higher costs in the not so distant future!

Notes

1. In agriculture, there was no significant change in trend.
2. The statistics in Table 15.1 refer to 1985, the latest year for which reliable comparative figures could be established at the time this paper was prepared.
3. Equity capital equals share capital plus reserves (retained profits).
4. Above-average participation rates are recorded in the traditional sectors of clothing, footwear, wood, furniture and leather.
5. The percentages were 36.3 per cent for wholesale trade and substantially higher (78.3 per cent) for retail trade establishments.

16 Shipping and Tourism in the Context of the Greek Economy

John Tzoannos

ATHENS UNIVERSITY OF ECONOMICS AND BUSINESS

1 INTRODUCTION

Both shipping and tourism are export-oriented sectors of great importance to the Greek economy as illustrated *inter alia* by their contribution to its foreign exchange earnings. In 1988, foreign exchange earnings from shipping and tourism amounted respectively to US$ 1382 million and US$ 2396 million, representing 18 per cent and 31 per cent of the balance of trade deficit.

Before examining the structural issues facing these sectors in the context of the Greek economy it should be clarified that shipping consists of three distinctly separate branches of activity: (i) ocean-going cargo, (ii) cruising, and (iii) coastal passenger and cargo fleets. The first branch is by far the largest, the second is closely linked to the tourist industry and should be viewed primarily as such, while the last branch is a trunk industry serving the other sectors of the Greek economy.

2 THE GREEK MERCHANT FLEET

The composition of the Greek merchant fleet by main type of vessel at the beginning and towards the end of the 1980s is shown in Table 16.1. The same table presents the composition of the EC member states taken as a whole.

It is worth noting that the composition of these fleets changed drastically between 1980 and 1988, in parallel with a significant decrease in their total capacity measured in gross registered tonnes (GRT). The changes in the fleet composition reflect developments in new technology, such as the use of containers, as well as the profitability and prospects of specific areas of trade.

Table 16.1 Distribution of fleets by type of vessel, 1980 and 1988

| | Greece | | | | EC | | | |
| | 1980 | | 1988 | | 1980 | | 1988 | |
	Tonnage 000 GRT	%	Tonnage 000 GRT	%	Tonnage 000 GRT	%	Tonnage 000 GRT	%
Oil tankers	11 780	30.5	8 492	38.4	51 435	44.2	2i 253	36.3
Liquid gas carriers	33	0.09	62	0.28	1 893	1.6	909	1.6
Chemical tankers	8	0.02	5	0.02	455	0.4	614	1.0
Other tankers	23	0.06	22	0.10	120	0.1	65	0.1
Total tankers	11 844	30.6	8 581	39.3	53 903	46.3	22 841	39.0
Bulk oil carriers	2 741	7.1	982	4.5	7 609	6.5	2 820	4.8
Ore/bulk carriers	13 614	35.2	9 077	41.6	25 586	22.0	15 123	25.8
Total bulk carriers	16 355	42.3	10 059	46.1	33 195	28.5	17 943	30.6
General cargo	10 382	26.8	2 287	10.5	22 180	19.1	8 622	14.7
Container ships	38	0.1	200	0.9	4 550	4.0	5 989	10.3
Ferries, passenger & other types	68	0.2	684	3.1	2 570	2.1	3 148	5.4
Total general cargo & other types	10 488	27.1	3 171	14.5	29 300	25.2	17 759	30.4
Total all types	38 687	100.0	21 811	100.0	110 398	100.0	58 543	100.0

Source: Lloyds Register of Shipping statistical tables.

2.1 The Ocean-going Fleet

Most ships in the Greek ocean-going merchant fleet operate outside Greece as cross-traders serving the transportation needs of third countries, primarily of raw materials carried in bulk. The Greek economy can generate demand for transportation services that can support only an insignificant percentage of Greek tonnage (less than 3 per cent). Thus this branch of Greek shipping has been fully exposed to the forces of fierce international competition, since it possesses no captive markets. This exposure requires and results in a high degree of operational efficiency.

It is also worth noting that the formation of most of the vast capital stock tied up in the Greek ocean-going merchant fleet has taken place outside the national boundaries of the Greek economy. It is mainly the result of the maritime and trading activities over a long period of time by Greeks established in various international commercial and financial centres, such as the City of London and New York, utilising funds originating from capital markets outside Greece. This involvement of Greek shipping in international economic activity has endowed it with valuable know-how concerning the operation both of shipping and factors of production markets world-wide.

More than half (53 per cent) of the total capacity of the Greek-owned merchant fleet operates under the flags of other nations, usually open registry flags such as those of Liberia, Cyprus and Panama. Ocean-going vessels registered under the Greek flag are treated under Greek law as imported foreign capital, which gives its owner a constitutional guarantee of the right to re-export the principal, interest or profit abroad.

Moreover Laws no. 89/1967 and 378/1968 permit the establishment in Greece of foreign companies engaged in activities including shipping outside Greece while exempting their income derived abroad from Greek corporate taxation and providing for freedom in their foreign exchange transactions. Many Greek shipowners who are non-residents of Greece have made use of the above laws and established ship management subsidiaries in Piraeus. It is obvious that the legislation was intended to attract Greek shipping enterprises and capital established abroad to Greece.

It should also be noted that, irrespective of the place of establishment of the shipowning company, ships registered under the Greek flag are subject to an annual tax levy, in lieu of income tax, which is estimated on the basis of their size and age. On the other hand, Greek shipping does not benefit from any direct or indirect subsidies, which are very common in other maritime countries (Tzoannos, 1980).

The links between ocean-going shipping and the Greek economy are threefold: (i) recourse to the Greek labour market for seamen; (ii) establishment of ship management companies under the aforementioned regime; and (iii) registration under the Greek flag.

Most of the labour force on board Greek-flag vessels, both officers and lower deck crew, comes from the national labour market, but there is also extensive employment of mariners from developing countries in the Greek-owned fleet under foreign flags. The main feature of the labour market for Greek seamen is the inelasticity of its supply side with respect to earnings. This is attributed to the growth over the years of other sectors in the Greek economy, such as tourism, demographic factors affecting traditionally maritime regions in the country, and the prolonged shipping crisis of the 1980s, which discouraged young people from entering a seafaring career.

The changes in the supply curve of Greek seamen during the last shipping crisis can be seen in Table 16.2, which shows the number of Greek seafarers on board Greek-flag and Greek-controlled vessels under foreign flags at the time of the census carried out by the Ministry of Merchant Marine, together with the number of registered unemployed.

The links between Greek-owned ocean-going shipping with the Greek economy have been under severe pressure during the last shipping crisis, as reflected by the flagging out of the Greek flag, and the recourse to open-registry flags and non-domicile crews. Operations under the Greek flag incur much higher costs than those under open-registry flags or those faced by shipowners in newly industrialised countries, such as Taiwan or South Korea, which also enjoy the protection of national cargo reservation policies (Metaxas, 1985; Yannopoulos, 1988).

Table 16.2 Supply of Greek seamen

	1982	1988
Number serving on board Greek-flag vessels	36 738	26 103
Number serving on board Greek-controlled foreign-flag vessels	3 909	2 632
Registered unemployed	7 826	2 842
Total	48 473	31 577

Source: Ministry of Merchant Marine (various years).

This loss of competitiveness also applies to other traditionally maritime nations in the EC and the OECD. The basic difference in the case of Greece is that shipowners in the other countries are primarily involved with the liner trade, which is organised into conferences (forms of cartels) and through them creates quasi-captive markets, whilst the Greeks primarily operate tramp vessels.

2.2 Prospects for Greek Shipping in the EC

The prospects for Greek shipping in the context of the world market depend to a large extent on the outcome of the ongoing battle between liberalism and protectionism in international maritime trade. Needless to say, the interests of Greek shipping lie on the side of liberalism, since it is vital for it to have access to the international freight markets. In that respect, the adoption and implementation of the package of four maritime regulations by the EC in 1986 (regulations no. 4055/86, 4056/86, 4057/86 and 4058/86), representing the first stage of EC maritime policy, must be viewed as a positive development for Greek shipping (*Official Journal*, 1988).

The first regulation applies the principle of freedom to provide services to maritime transport between EC member states and between them and third countries. It abolishes restrictions on the provision of maritime services by persons established in a member state or by vessels flying the flag of a member state. The second regulation lays down detailed rules for the application of the competition rules of the Treaty of Rome to maritime transport (that is, against the abuse of the dominant position by liner conferences). The third regulation aims at fighting unfair pricing practices by third countries in maritime transport, and the fourth concerns co-ordinated action by member states to safeguard free access to cargoes in the ocean trades. The implications of EC maritime policy are fully examined by Bredimas-Savopoulo and Tzoannos (1990).

The Commission has recently presented its proposals for the second stage of EC maritime policy, which relate to the supply side of shipping services. The main feature of these proposals consists of the creation of a Community ship registry which will operate in parallel to the national registries of member states. The Commission sees this as a first step towards a long-term objective of a single Community register (EC Commission, 1989a).

The proposals provide *inter alia* that all officers and half of the rest of the crew on board vessels registered in the new register shall be nationals of a member state. The remaining half could be non-domiciled seamen employed at wages agreed with the trade unions of their home country. Through the latter provision the Commission is trying to find a solution at Community level to the problem of labour costs which some member states have dealt with through the use of off-shore registries (for example, the Isle of Man for the UK) or parallel national registries (Denmark, Germany). The proposals on a European registry also envisage some limited cargo being reserved in favour of its ships for the carriage of Community food aid cargoes to third countries. However, apart from that provision, there is no change in the liberal orientation of the existing external maritime policy of the Community. Another crucial provision concerns the abolition of national cabotage restrictions, that exist in five member states (France, Greece, Italy, Spain and Portugal), for ships with a capacity below 6000 GRT to be registered in the European registry.

In parallel, the Commission has produced a policy document which sets the framework for what is permissible with regard to state aids to shipping under the Treaty (EC Commission, 1989b). The Commission adopts a rather lenient approach, on the basis that there exists a need to maintain a strategic capacity for the Community merchant fleet in order to safeguard the employment of Community seamen and to modernise the fleet. Nevertheless the document states that, for state aids to shipping to be permissible, these must not be out of proportion to the aim of restoring competitiveness; they must be transparent and temporary, and should not specifically contribute to increasing capacity in sectors with manifest over-capacity. At the same time the Commission, in this policy document, is recommending to the governments of member states that they provide for the favourable tax treatment of shipping companies and of seamen with the objective of improving the cash-flow position of the former.

It is too early to judge the fate of the Commission's proposals concerning the creation of the new European registry and its provisions, since these are still at an early stage of discussion at Council level. A first assessment suggests that the Commission may be attempting to take on new powers, hitherto vested in national governments, without being able to take any practical measures to improve the competitiveness of the Community shipping industry. Since these measures unavoidably involve the national exchequers of member states, they are unlikely to have an easy ride.

Depending on the final form that the second stage of the EC maritime policy takes, there will be either a strengthening or a loosening of the link between Greek-controlled ocean-going shipping and the Greek economy, as well as that with the Community as a whole. A new tier of bureaucratic controls by the Commission in Brussels might be expected to have a negative impact. The proposal on the abolition of cabotage, if adopted, could have a serious direct impact upon the cruise and coastal passenger and cargo fleets, as discussed below.

2.3 Cruise Fleets and Coastal Operations

The Greek-controlled cruise fleet, both under the Greek and foreign flags, has a presence in all the major world cruising markets (such as the Mediterranean and Caribbean). These markets are experiencing steady growth in demand, matched by the entry of new modern tonnage, the trend being towards ever more luxurious 'floating hotels'. This trend in turn requires vast capital investment, as well as a supply of substantial numbers of highly trained personnel to provide hotel-type services.

The Greek-flag cruise fleet is obliged under Greek law to employ exclusively Greek personnel for all functions on board its vessels. This puts it at a competitive disadvantage, given that its major competitors employ specialist non-domiciled personnel from low-income third countries for the hotel-catering functions, which are labour-intensive. This to a large degree explains the resort by many Greek cruise operators to open-registry flags.

This cost disadvantage is to some extent counter-balanced by the prerogative of cabotage in Greek home waters. The Greek cruise fleet operating in home waters gets the majority of its customers from middle-income groups, which are normally influenced by the policies of organised tour operators in their home country. It is likely, therefore, that any future abolition of cabotage restrictions would (i) necessitate a change in the existing labour policy for the cruise industry to permit the employment of non-domiciled persons in the hotel-catering functions, and (ii) put pressure on Greek cruise ship operators to integrate their activities with those of the big international holiday groups offering complete holiday packages.

The operation of the Greek coastal passenger and cargo fleet is highly regulated by government, for example with respect to pricing, and carries various public-service obligations, for example to operate during off-peak seasons and to provide a service to remote islands.

If cabotage were to be abolished there would be a need for a fundamental revision of the internal transport policy of Greece. However abolition is unlikely to materialise in the foreseeable future, given the national defence considerations inherent in seaborne transport in the Aegean.

3   THE TOURIST INDUSTRY

The other sector under examination, the tourist industry in Greece, is currently in the midst of a crisis. The rate of increase for tourist arrivals from abroad is declining, while the number of nights spent in hotels, after a significant increase in the mid-1980s, has also decreased in absolute terms.

The number of tourist arrivals from abroad is estimated by the National Tourist Organisation of Greece to reach 8.42 million in 1989, representing an increase of 2.3 per cent over 1988. The rate of increase in 1988 compared to the previous year was 2.8 per cent, and in 1987 compared to 1986 it was 9.0 per cent. The number of nights spent by foreigners in Greek hotel establishments showed a 3.9 per cent decrease in 1988 compared to 1987. Figures for 1989 are not yet available.

During the last decade there has been a substantial increase in hotel capacity, as a result of investment in new rooms and beds. The new investment, however, has in the main consisted of smaller units catering for the mass tourism market of the lower- and middle-income groups. The change in the capacity of the hotel industry in Greece, measured by the number of rooms available and the average size of the establishments, can be seen in Table 16.3. The data are based on official figures published by the National Tourist Organisation of Greece. The increase in capacity depicted in this table does not include the substantial number of establishments operating without official approval. Their operation represents a major problem for the image of the Greek hotel industry, as it takes place without any official quality control. It also constitutes a source of unfair competition for the rest of the industry, which operates with government inspection and control.

At the same time as these developments have been taking place in Greece, new capacity catering for the same market has been created in other Mediterranean countries, increasing the competition for market share. The competitive climate in the mass tourism market has been further exacerbated by the introduction of new destinations in low labour-cost developing countries to the package holiday market.

It is essential, therefore, that the Greek tourist industry should move into other segments of the tourist market, without of course abandoning its existing markets. It must upgrade its services and sell a more complex and specialised product-mix. The new target market segments should include the high-income tourism groups, which are interested in cultural events, history, or incentive travel, in addition to the 'sun and sea' product.

Table 16.3 Total capacity and average size of hotel establishments in Greece

Type of establishment	Total number of beds			Average number of beds per establishment		
	1982	1987	per cent change	1982	1987	per cent change
Hotels	284 155	327 983	+15.4	80.2	75.6	–5.7
Bungalows	3 881	5 574	+14.4	129.4	132.7	+2.6
Motels	2 083	2 949	+41.6	94.7	105.3	+11.2
Furnished apartments	5 243	18 387	+250.7	41.9	30.8	–26.5
Hostels	10 852	15 435	+42.2	29.9	28.6	–4.3
Total, all types	306 214	370 328	+20.9	75.0	66.8	–10.9

Source: National Tourist Organisation of Greece.

This upgrading will necessitate extensive capital investment in new high-quality capacity or the upgrading of the existing capacity. In addition it requires a massive investment in improving the country's tourist infrastructure, such as the airports and other transport services. In parallel such an upgrading would also require the special training of personnel in the tourist industry, to ensure they will be capable of responding to the higher standards.

Furthermore, as discussed in *Hotels and Restaurants International* (1989), the future prospects of the hotel industry in Greece are going to be affected by the increasing trend towards the formation of big international and national hotel chains world-wide. These chains are sometimes part of big international holiday and leisure groups offering an integrated and full range of tourist services, whereas in Greece, this practice is very limited indeed. The hotel industry at present consists of numerous independent one-hotel companies which, while they enjoy the benefits of flexibility, are at a disadvantage in terms of economies of scale when marketing their hotel services and purchasing the various inputs required for the production of hotel services. In order to overcome these disadvantages, hotel operators in Greece will have to face the increasing pressures by rationalising their operations through mergers or other forms of consortia covering specific functions, such as the purchasing of raw materials or the marketing of their services.

Thus the organisation of the hotel industry in Greece into a large number of small independent operators makes the need to upgrade the level of service and to introduce specialised tourist products even more essential. In conclusion, it is likely that the Greek tourist industry and the hotel sector in particular will be forced to undergo major structural change during the coming decade, which will include mergers and the acquisition of hotel companies, if it is to offer a competitive and attractive product.

References

Bredimas-Savopoulou, A. and Tzoannos, J. (1990) *The Common Shipping Policy of the EC* (Amsterdam: North Holland).

Commission of the EC (1989a) 'The Future for the Community Shipping Industry: Measures to Improve the Operating Conditions of Community Shipping', COM(89) 266 final, Brussels, 3 August.

Commission of the EC (1989b) 'Financial and Fiscal Measures Concerning Shipping Operations with Ships Registered in the Community', SEC(89) 921 final, Brussels, 3 August.

Hotels and Restaurants International (1988) July and August.

Metaxas, B. N. (1985) *Flags of Convenience* (Aldershot: Gower).

Official Journal (1988) no. L378, 31 December (Brussels: Commission of the EC).

Tzoannos, J. (1980) *The Fiscal Regime for Shipowning Firms in the EEC* (Athens: Institute of Economic and Industrial Research).

Yannopoulos, G. N. (1988) 'The Economics of Flagging Out', *Journal of Transport Economics and Policy*, vol. 22, no. 2, May.